A Return to Cooking

ALSO BY ERIC RIPERT

Le Bernardin Cookbook: Four-Star Simplicity
(with Maguy Le Coze)

ALSO BY MICHAEL RUHLMAN

The Making of a Chef: Mastering Heat at the Culinary Institute

The Soul of a Chef: The Journey Toward Perfection

A Return to Cooking

ERIC RIPERT | MICHAEL RUHLMAN

PAINTINGS BY VALENTINO CORTAZAR

PHOTOGRAPHS BY SHIMON AND TAMMAR ROTHSTEIN

DESIGN BY LEVEL

ARTISAN | NEW YORK

Published by Artisan
A Division of Workman Publishing Company, Inc.
708 Broadway, New York, New York 10003-9555
www.artisanbooks.com

Library of Congress Cataloging-in-Publication Data
Ripert, Eric.
A return to cooking / by Eric Ripert and Michael Ruhlman.
p. cm.
Includes index.
ISBN 1-57965-187-9
1. Cookery. I. Ruhlman, Michael, 1963- II. Title.
TX652.R568 2002
641.5—DC21   2002074761

Printed in Italy
10 9 8 7 6 5 4 3 2 1
First Printing
Book Design by Level, Calistoga, CA

To the great architect of the universe and Mother Earth;
to my wife, Sandra, my family, my friends, my mentors; to "the Team";
to Maguy and my Le Bernardin "family," and to our supporters

— E.R.

AN HOMAGE It's a beautiful summer day, and we are seated beside a pool, rivulets running down the wineglasses. Lunch is croque-monsieur and salade Monique, followed by a plum tart.

Eric Ripert squints into the sun and makes an unusual statement: "This is why I'm here. I want to leave the chef that I am and let the cooking fill me again."

Strange. He has been a chef his whole adult life; work that has brought him renown, a lucrative business, and extraordinary esteem in his profession. He wants to leave this? Cooking doesn't fill him?

And then stranger: The most revealing dish he will create on this trip is a restaurant dish, a staple that he has been serving almost daily for years.

For this croque-monsieur, the classic grilled ham and cheese, I use smoked salmon instead of ham, and season it with lemon zest and chives. The cheese, as always, is Gruyère; the bread is buttered and grilled in a pan, though it could be pressed in a traditional croque-monsieur mold and held over a flame as my grandmother Émilienne did.

I've been serving it for four years at Le Bernardin, ever since she died. I would stay with her during summer vacation, and she would ask me what I wanted. I always answered the same, because the way she did it, it was like nothing else in the world.

Yes, it was grilled ham and cheese, but not the ugly sandwich you eat at the bar while you wait for the train. The way she did croque-monsieur—it was like a delicacy. It was a masterpiece of cooking. The bread was crunchy and moist, the cheese was creamy, the thinly sliced ham salty. And the mold, it is such a beautiful instrument. The night of the croque, it was a ritual. She would make me twenty-five if I asked.

The croque-monsieur refined for Le Bernardin is my homage to Émilienne Ripert. And I serve it at this home in Sag Harbor because she is here with us, her actual spirit. We have spirits who look after us. I don't know why it is Grandma Ripert who looks after me—there were other relatives I was closer to. But it is she who is with me, and so I must make the croque-monsieur, an homage.

Smoked Salmon Croque-Monsieur

SERVES 6

6 ounces Gruyère cheese

**Twelve ½-inch-thick slices pullman bread
(or good-quality white bread)**

¾ pound sliced smoked salmon

**1 tablespoon Lemon Confit (page 21),
cut into tiny dice**

1 tablespoon thinly sliced chives

**8 tablespoons (1 stick) unsalted butter,
softened**

PREP: 20 minutes — COOK: 5 minutes

Using a Japanese mandoline or a vegetable peeler, slice the Gruyère very thin.

Lay the bread slices out on a work surface. Place the Gruyère on 6 slices and the smoked salmon on the other 6 slices. Sprinkle the salmon with the lemon confit and chives. Close the sandwiches. Cut off the crusts, using a serrated knife. *(You can make the sandwiches up to this point 2 hours in advance. Cover with plastic wrap and refrigerate.)*

Spread the softened butter on both sides of the sandwiches. Heat two large nonstick sauté pans over medium-high heat. Add 3 sandwiches to each pan, Gruyère side down, and cook for 2 minutes. Turn them over and cook for 1 minute longer.

To serve, slice the sandwiches in half on the diagonal, then in half on the diagonal again (to make 4 triangles), and arrange the triangles on a plate.

A chef describes who he really is when he cooks. Ripert was launched out of obscurity and into national attention after the tragic death of Gilbert Le Coze in 1994. He went on to be ranked in the top tier of the country's chefs, and to prove himself to be perhaps the most talented chef of the post–baby-boom generation.

He got there by way of grilled ham and cheese. And so that begins a lunch, the neo–croque-monsieur. He will also make a salad that is equally powerful, simple, pure, and evocative, and, for dessert, a fruit tart.

I named Salade Monique after my mother, an amazing woman. My parents divorced early, and my father died when I was ten, so I'm lucky to have the mother I do. I cooked at her side when I was a boy. She's the one who said to me, "Be a chef, and you can be anything." She cared about food. She shopped every day at markets. I don't think she set foot in a grocery store—ever. She worked but would come home every day to make lunch. Often they were big rustic salads. It's only when I'm putting the ingredients together in a big bowl—an abundance of blanched and raw vegetables, apple, avocado, radishes, potato, haricot verts, corn, all from a roadside market—that I recognize where this salad comes from.

A chef's being is composed of three parts: his history, the experience cooking at home, and the experience in restaurant kitchens. Now that I understand which part of me this salad comes from, I don't even make a vinaigrette. My mother didn't have time to make a vinaigrette, so for Salade Monique it's important simply to pour olive oil and balsamic, judging by sight.

Every morning my mother got up early and made a fruit tart big as a pizza, and I would devour it. So we'll have a peach and plum tart for dessert, with store-bought puff pastry, because store-bought puff pastry is fine for the home. And this is what I think is a perfect summer lunch.

Eric's food is delicious sustenance, but here it has arrived entwined with usable lessons: When you cook, you do more than simply pay attention to the season and place, to ingredients that are close and fresh. When you cook—when you *really* cook—you pay attention to your past. When you cook, you welcome ghosts, and you honor them.

Opposite: Salade Monique, page 6. Above: Peach and Plum Tart, page 7.

Salade Monique pictured on page 4

Serves 6

½ pound small potatoes

¼ pound haricots verts, ends trimmed

¼ pound asparagus, tips only

1 ear corn, shucked

½ pound mesclun greens

¼ hothouse (seedless) cucumber,
   cut lengthwise in half and thinly sliced

12 grape tomatoes, halved

2 scallions, white part only, thinly sliced

2 radishes, thinly sliced

¼ green banana pepper,
   cut into tiny dice

½ avocado, thinly sliced

½ apple, cored and thinly sliced

Fine sea salt and freshly ground
   white pepper

2½ tablespoons balsamic vinegar

6 tablespoons extra virgin olive oil

PREP: 20 minutes — **COOK:** 25 minutes

Place the potatoes in a small pot of cold water, add 2 tablespoons salt, and bring to a boil, then lower the heat to a simmer. Cook until the potatoes are tender when pierced with a small knife, about 15 minutes. Drain and cool in the refrigerator. Once they are cool, peel the potatoes and thinly slice them.

Place three pots of water over high heat and bring to a boil. Add salt to each pot. Drop the haricot verts, asparagus, and ear of corn into the pots. Blanch until the vegetables are tender but still a bit crisp: about 3 minutes for the asparagus and corn and 4 minutes for the haricot verts. Plunge all the vegetables into an ice water bath to stop the cooking.

Cut the corn kernels off the cob.

Place the greens and all the vegetables and fruit in a large bowl and season with salt and pepper. Drizzle the balsamic and olive oil over and toss to coat. Divide the salad equally among six chilled plates. Serve immediately.

SERVES 6

4 peaches (about 1 pound), pitted, peeled, and cut into small dice
8 tablespoons (1 stick) unsalted butter
¼ cup sugar
1 sheet frozen puff pastry (7 to 8 ounces), thawed
5 plums, thinly sliced

PREP: 30 minutes — **COOK:** 1 hour and 25 minutes

Place the peaches in a medium pot over medium heat, add 4 tablespoons of the butter and 2 tablespoons of the sugar, and cook, stirring occasionally, until the peaches begin to break down and are the consistency of jam, about 1 hour. Transfer to a bowl and refrigerate to cool. *(This can be done early in the day.)*

To make the tarts, on a floured surface, roll out the puff pastry to a thickness of ¼ inch. Using a large cookie cutter or an inverted small plate and a knife, cut out six 5-inch circles. Place the pastry circles on a baking sheet lined with parchment paper and refrigerate until firm, about 30 minutes.

Preheat the oven to 400°F. Line a large baking sheet with parchment paper.

Using a fork, prick holes all over the puff pastry circles to prevent them from puffing during cooking. Spread peach puree over each circle. Arrange the plum slices in an overlapping circular pattern on each tart.

Melt the remaining 4 tablespoons butter and brush the plums with the butter. Sprinkle the remaining 2 tablespoons sugar over the tarts.

Place the tarts on the baking sheet. Bake for 25 minutes, or until the tops are caramelized. If necessary, turn on the broiler to achieve a beautiful golden brown on the top; be careful—they will brown very quickly.

Serve the tarts warm or at room temperature.

{ **summer** }

Sag Harbor—A Return to Cooking

"An experiment," he said. "Cooking in a group—the best kind of cooking. I'm bringing a friend, Valentino, an

amazing painter. Cooking is an art—Valentino will paint what we do. I want him to be free to explore his art. I want

to be free to explore mine. There are no boundaries, no expectations. You must tell the story . . . but you are free,

too. You can write poetry if you want! And I will cook. I want to explore cooking. I want to return to cooking."

Eric grinned so hard, I couldn't say no. Who would resist such an experiment?

Steamed Littlenecks with Parmesan-Cucumber Sauce, page 45

Black Pepper and Cognac Shrimp, page 64

HOW THE CHEF BECOMES A COOK

A cook and a chef are different entitities. "Chef" is a title. A chef can be good or bad or everything in between; he or she can be hotel chef, restaurant chef, TV chef, personal chef, corporate chef. "Chef" denotes a job. But when you are a cook, that is who you *are*. It's your spine and your soul. It suffuses all that you touch. When you see the soil bursting with young lettuce, with tomatoes, with light green vines of peas, all the molecules between your gaze and those vegetables are charged with the energy of cooking. The air sparkles.

Eric Ripert is a cook who also happens to be executive chef and a partner of Le Bernardin in New York City. His food—mostly seafood—is among the most refined in the city, and his restaurant regularly voted one of the best in the Zagat guide. He travels the world as a chef, doing charity dinners, consulting, and speaking.

But it is an irony of success that often the better you are, the further away you are taken from what you love, the source of your success. Eric senses this is happening to him, that he is losing himself as a cook. And so we're all in Sag Harbor, Long Island, where he's brought us to a house in the woods to cook, to return to the source of cooking. The idea, whimsical but never lightly considered,

had been born two years earlier out of a spontaneous combustion of culinary and artistic energy.

Eric had returned late from working at the restaurant one night to find his house guest, Valentino Cortazar, sketching. The two friends talked for hours.

Hungry, Eric began to make a salad. Valentino, intrigued by the shapes appearing on the counter, sketched Eric working with them. The French chef created an impromptu meal, and, simultaneously, the Colombian artist created several sketches of the cook at work. Eric was amazed by them. He loved Valentino's work, owned several pieces, but he had never seen Valentino depict *his* own material— food—and the results electrified him. As he cooked more, Valentino drew more. Each inspired the other, and by dawn, the chef and the artist had decided to create a book to explore the relation between cooking and art—not a conventional cookbook, but rather a book *about* cooking and spontaneous creation, a book about art and the creative mind and the process of transforming raw products into finished dishes, finished paintings, a big book, filled with canvases and stories and recipes.

THE CAST

Valentino, the artist, is the lead member of Eric's ensemble.

"Paint no matter what," he said to me, describing a decision he made as a young man, "good times and bad times, always, always. I always live in beautiful places so I always have something to paint." From the beginning he has pursued beauty. He has lived in Crete, in Spain, on the island of Ibiza in the Mediterranean, and now in the ancient Colombian seaport of Cartagena, not far from the coffee plantation where he grew up. He has made his way through life as a painter. "Maybe artists have an aura around them," he explains when I ask how he got by. "People have always been generous to me."

Tammar and Shimon Rothstein, the photographers, had been in business only five years when they left Israel for New York, arriving without so much as green cards. They worked hard, learned from their mistakes and, with a mixture of drive and naiveté, hung a shingle in Manhattan—and thrived.

Andrea Glick, a former Le Bernardin cook who moved up to become Eric's all-around assistant, would undertake the work of recipe writing and testing, no small endeavor in this cookbook experiment.

I started writing at age ten, and have written something almost every day in the ensuing twenty-seven years; age ten was also when, perhaps not coincidentally, I started to cook, and I've cooked compulsively ever since. This work would combine the two things I've been doing consistently for more than a quarter century.

And so Eric delivered us to a house on the rural southeastern edge of Long Island to let the cooking flood in again. We would cook at home as a group. Restaurant cooking is all well and good, he said, a grand entertainment, but in the home, small groups preparing food and eating it together—*there* is the soul of cooking.

Parsley, cilantro, chives, basil, mint, and lavender are available in the garden, but Eric chooses fennel, which has begun to bud, for the tagine. The day was clear and hot, but now the evening is cool, and lavender is still fragrant in the air. "Lavender is for the armoire, to keep the socks smelling nice," he says. "You don't put it in your *food.*"

In the kitchen, we begin turning the artichokes. Eric holds one at face level, vertical knife blade toward him, and rotates the artichoke counterclockwise, leaves falling like petals onto the board. He drops the heart into acidulated water, leaving the choke in. It has taken perhaps twenty seconds. The artichoke is perfectly cut, and beautiful.

I ask him if he's spent a lot of time turning artichokes.

"One day, at Robuchon, we did ten cases. But once you do them, you never forget." His hands, he says, retain the memory.

The artichokes are done long before the Moroccan stew and set aside to cool. A vinaigrette is fashioned out of the strained cooking liquid. The hearts are sliced and served with delicate greens. Eric slices the hearts thin and arranges them fastidiously—but he later realizes that this was the chef and the restaurant butting in and wishes he'd done it more simply.

Couscous is prepared in a smaller tagine simply by pouring boiling stock, flavored with harissa, over the uncooked pasta to rehydrate it. The harissa, a fiery North African paste of hot peppers and seasonings, gives the couscous an exciting kick.

Warm Artichoke Salad with Barigoule Vinaigrette

SERVES 6

1 lemon

10 large artichokes

½ cup extra virgin olive oil

3 shallots, thinly sliced

5 garlic cloves, thinly sliced

5 cups water

1 cup dry white wine

¼ teaspoon coriander seeds

Fine sea salt

1 tablespoon Dijon mustard

2 tablespoons aged sherry vinegar

Freshly ground white pepper

3 tablespoons canola oil

1½ cups baby arugula or watercress

PREP: 30 minutes — COOK: 25 minutes

When you begin to cook, you see what you have, and you ask yourself what you feel like making. We have lots of artichokes, which were plentiful where I grew up in the South of France. Sometimes they were so young and tender we ate them raw. I'm going to braise them with aromatic vegetables, and make a vinaigrette from the cooking liquid for an artichoke salad—a hearty vegetarian opener for a summer night. I believe barigoules often use too much wine and olive oil and you lose the flavor of the artichoke, so ours will be a water-based braising liquid.

Fill a large bowl with water. Cut the lemon in half and squeeze the juice into the water.

To prepare the artichokes for cooking (see Note below for alternative cooking instructions), cut off the stems. One at a time, using a small knife, starting at the base of each artichoke and holding the knife blade parallel to the leaves, remove the leaves. Trim off all of the green parts from the base of the artichoke (if you leave any green parts, they will turn brown during cooking). Leave the choke in the artichoke. As you finish each artichoke, place it in the bowl of lemon water.

Heat a large heavy-bottomed pot over medium-high heat. Add 3 tablespoons of the olive oil, then add the shallots and garlic and sweat until limp and translucent. Add the water, white wine, coriander seeds, and 1 tablespoon salt and bring to a boil. Lower the heat to a simmer, add the artichokes, and cook until a knife is easily inserted in the center, about 25 minutes. Turn off the heat and cool the artichokes in the cooking liquid.

When the artichokes are cooled, strain and reserve 2 tablespoons of the cooking liquid. Use a spoon to remove the chokes from the centers of the artichokes. Cut the artichokes into ⅛-inch slices. The shorter end slices are not big enough for this presentation; you can reserve them for an addition to a green salad.

Arrange the artichokes in an overlapping circular pattern on each of six plates. Cover with plastic wrap and refrigerate until you are ready to serve the salad.

For the vinaigrette, whisk together the mustard, the reserved 2 tablespoons cooking liquid, the sherry vinegar, a pinch of salt, and a pinch of pepper. Whisking constantly, very slowly drizzle in 3 tablespoons of the olive oil and the canola oil. Set aside.

Preheat the oven to 350°F.

To serve, warm the artichoke plates in the oven for 2 to 3 minutes. Brush the artichokes lightly with the remaining 2 tablespoons olive oil and season with salt and pepper. Toss the greens with enough vinaigrette to coat. Place about ¼ cup of the salad in the center of each plate.

NOTE: If you find it too difficult to prepare the artichokes the recommended way, you can cook the artichokes whole (cut off the tips of the leaves and the stems before cooking), then pull off the leaves after cooking and scoop out the chokes.

Chicken and Lamb Tagine with Mediterranean Spices

Serves 6

¼ cup extra virgin olive oil

One 3½- to 4-pound chicken,
  cut into 8 pieces

1½ pounds boneless lamb shoulder,
  cut into 1-inch cubes

Fine sea salt and freshly ground
  white pepper

About 1 teaspoon ground cumin

About 1 teaspoon turmeric

About 1 teaspoon curry powder

8 fresh fennel seeds (you can substitute
  ¼ teaspoon ground dried fennel seeds)

8 saffron threads

3 cilantro sprigs, leaves picked

1 medium onion, quartered and
  thinly sliced

½ fennel bulb, thinly sliced

1 head garlic, cloves separated, peeled,
  and thinly sliced

1 tablespoon finely chopped ginger

2 Lemon Confit quarters (page 21),
  cut into small dice

½ red bell pepper, cut into ½-inch dice

1 medium zucchini, cut into ½-inch dice

1 medium eggplant, cut into ½-inch dice

2 tomatoes, peeled, seeded, and
  cut into ½-inch dice

1 cup water

½ teaspoon harissa (found in Middle
  Eastern grocery stores)

2 cups chicken stock

3 tablespoons unsalted butter

2 cups couscous

PREP: 30 minutes — **COOK:** 1½ hours

I love this dish, the tagine. I love to eat it, to cook it, to play with it. Spices are the key. Too much, and it will taste terrible; too little, and it will have no character. But it isn't like seasoning with salt, which only has to dissolve. The powders I use—turmeric, cumin, and curry—take time to open up. Ingredients in this dish are added one by one, in layers, and each is seasoned and spiced individually so that the spices develop in layers and build. This is really cooking, because you are smelling it all the time, tasting as you go. The vegetables are releasing their liquid, the meat and bones are creating a stock. You become completely involved in the process, adding the onions and fennel, seasoning them, and then allowing them to cook. Then you add the summer squash, season, and cook, tasting the liquid, smelling the cooking aroma. You are fully involved with the tagine.

Place a tagine (or large heavy-bottomed casserole—at least 10 inches wide) over high heat and add the olive oil. Meanwhile, lay the chicken and lamb on a cutting board and season generously with salt and pepper. When the oil is hot, place the chicken pieces skin side down in the pot. Arrange the lamb around the chicken. Allow the oil to come to a boil, then lower the heat to medium (slow cooking will make the meat tender). Sprinkle a pinch each of the cumin, turmeric, and curry powder, 2 fennel seeds (or a pinch of ground fennel), and 2 saffron threads all around the chicken. Cook until the chicken is golden brown, about 15 minutes.

Check to make sure that the chicken is not sticking to the pan. Scatter the cilantro leaves over the chicken and lamb. Spread out the onion, fennel, and garlic on a cutting board and season generously with salt and pepper (this method ensures that all vegetables are properly seasoned). Add them to the pot, covering the chicken and lamb. Sprinkle a pinch each of cumin, turmeric, and curry, 2 fennel seeds (or a pinch of ground fennel), and 2 saffron threads all over the vegetables. Add the ginger and lemon confit, cover, and cook for 15 minutes, or until the vegetables are tender.

Spread the red pepper and zucchini on the cutting board and season with salt and pepper. Scatter them over the vegetables in the pot. Sprinkle a pinch each of the cumin, turmeric, and curry powder, 2 fennel seeds (or a pinch of ground fennel), and 2 saffron threads over all. Cover the pot and cook until the zucchini is tender, 15 to 20 minutes.

Spread the eggplant on the cutting board and season with salt and pepper. Add the eggplant to the pot, spreading it out so it covers all the ingredients. Sprinkle with a pinch each of the cumin, turmeric, and curry. Add the remaining 2 saffron threads and 2 fresh fennel seeds (or a pinch of ground fennel) to the pot, cover, and cook for 15 more minutes, or until the eggplant begins to melt into the casserole. Taste the broth to check the seasoning.

Combine the water and ¼ teaspoon of the harissa and whisk to blend. Add the liquid to the pot. Spread the tomatoes on the cutting board and season with salt and pepper. Scatter them over the stew, and check the broth for seasoning; if it seems a little spicy, add only a pinch each of cumin and curry. Continue cooking, covered, for another 15 minutes. If the liquid evaporates, add a little more water to the pot.

Meanwhile, bring the chicken stock, the remaining ¼ teaspoon harissa, and the butter to a boil in a small pot. Season with salt and pepper. Place the couscous in a bowl and pour the boiling stock over it. Cover with plastic wrap and let sit for 5 minutes, or until the liquid has been absorbed. Uncover and lightly toss with a fork.

To serve, place about ½ cup of couscous on each plate and top with a few cubes of lamb, a piece of chicken, and an assortment of vegetables. Spoon some cooking liquid over each plate.

The *tagine,* which refers to the funky Moroccan cooking vessel, is a rustic and powerfully flavored stew of meat and vegetables. I love rustic, one-pot meals, and I love robust seasoning. Everything is too high-tech today.

LEMON CONFIT pictured on page 22

---

3 cups kosher salt

6 lemons

SPECIAL EQUIPMENT

1-quart canning jar with tight-fitting lid

PREP: 15 minutes — **CURING:** At least 1 month, preferably 3 months or more

Place the canning jar and lid and in a pot of boiling water to sterilize them. Dry on a rack upside down.

Pour a layer of salt into the bottom of the jar. Cut 1 inch off one end of a lemon, then quarter the lemon, starting at the cut end, but leaving the uncut end intact. Open the lemon over a bowl and pour salt inside. Place the lemon in the bottom of the jar. Continue with the remaining lemons (use the remaining salt and the salt that falls into the bowl), packing them into the jar and covering each layer of lemons with salt. Seal the jar and refrigerate.

The lemons can be used after 1 month, but they are best after 3 months and will keep for up to a year.

To use the confit, cut the lemon quarters apart. Cut away all the flesh from the rind; discard the flesh. Use as directed in the individual recipe, or blanch briefly, dice or julienne, and add to salads, stews, or grain dishes.

LEMON CONFIT

As Eric works through his Moroccan stew, he reaches into a jar and pulls out a lemon that has cured there for more than three months in slushy salt. He rinses it, slices the fruit off the rind, and then dices the rind and adds it to the tagine. As he works, he explains that lemon confit is something he cannot cook without. He uses it as a seasoning and a condiment, and says it gives dishes a beguiling flavor you can't quite identify. Sprinkle it on vegetables. Use it in stuffings. If you cook a whole fish, put confit in the fish belly, or put it in the cavity of a chicken or between the meat and the skin. Lemon goes beautifully with fish, pork, chicken, and veal, particularly in the sauces that accompany them. You can add it to virtually any kind of stew to brighten the flavors. It can make a rich heavy meat stew sparkle. "I love it," Eric says, "because you get the full lemon flavor without the acidity."

Lemon confit is simple to make and will keep for a year or more in a dark cupboard. While three months curing time is optimal, in as little as a month, the salt will have worked its magic, pulling all the water out of the rind, transforming it into a flavorful ingredient that can be as versatile as a vinegar, salt, or spice.

When you're ready to use it, simply dig out a lemon, wash off the salt, and scrape away the flesh from the lemon rind. It's the rind you are after. If it is not going to be cooked in the dish it is to season—if it is to be sprinkled on a salad or on smoked salmon, for instance—then it should be blanched in water to remove the salt. Given its countless uses, lemon confit is a great addition to any pantry.

Sautéed Melon and Phyllo Crisps with Balsamic-Port Sauce

SERVES 6

12 tablespoons (1½ sticks) unsalted butter

4 sheets phyllo dough

¼ cup sugar

2 cups port

3 tablespoons balsamic vinegar

**1 cantaloupe, halved, seeded,
    and cut into 12 wedges**

**1 pint good-quality store-bought vanilla
    ice cream**

PREP: 15 minutes — COOK: 30 minutes

Preheat the oven to 400°F. Line a heavy baking sheet with parchment paper.

To make the phyllo crisps, melt 8 tablespoons of the butter. Place 1 sheet of phyllo dough on a cutting board; cover the rest of the phyllo dough while you are working so it doesn't dry out. Brush some melted butter over the phyllo sheet and sprinkle with 1 tablespoon of the sugar. Lay another sheet of phyllo on top, brush with butter, and sprinkle with sugar. Continue with the remaining sheets. Using a sharp cookie cutter or a paring knife, cut 12 leaf shapes, 5 inches long and 1½ inches wide, from the stacked phyllo.

Transfer the phyllo leaves to the parchment-lined baking sheet, cover with another piece of parchment paper, and place another baking sheet on top to ensure flat crisps. Bake for 20 minutes, or until the phyllo is golden brown and flaky. Place on a cooling rack.

Meanwhile, for the sauce, combine the port and balsamic vinegar in a small pan and bring to a boil over high heat. Lower the heat to medium and simmer until reduced to 1 cup, about 20 minutes. Reduce the heat to low and add 1 tablespoon of the butter, shaking the pan to incorporate the butter. The sauce should be shiny and clear. Set aside.

For the melon, heat a large nonstick skillet over medium-high heat. Add 1½ tablespoons of the butter and allow the butter to brown slightly. Add half of the melon slices and sauté— do not move the slices around too much, or they will not caramelize—until they are lightly browned on both sides. Turn them over in the pan juices, then transfer them to a plate and set aside, covered loosely with aluminum foil to keep warm. Add the remaining 1½ tablespoons butter to the pan and sauté the remaining melon slices.

To serve, stand 2 slices of melon on each plate. Cut a slit in the center of each one and insert a phyllo crisp. Place a scoop of vanilla ice cream on each plate, drizzle the sauce over the melon and ice cream, and serve immediately.

It's a sure thing—fresh summer melon sautéed in butter, sweet crispy phyllo, and a cream sauce. But there isn't any cream. Eric pauses. "What kind of sauce, then? A reduced port? Do we have any port?"

He looks in the refrigerator and sees a bottle of port, takes a swig from it, grins. "That one we drink," he says. He finds another, tastes it, and nods. He begins reducing, dips a spoon into it, adds a drop of balsamic vinegar to the spoon, tastes, and nods. "This will be a good dessert. I'll be proud of it!"

You're either born a saucier or not. Robuchon used to say that—usually to me when I didn't make my sauce well. I had to do the sauces twice a day, but sometimes I couldn't because I was *dans la merde*. He would taste and say, "This is from this morning." And I would say, "No, no, no, it's fresh." He would say, "You're lying," and walk away. I would taste and taste and taste and think, How did he know? But you taste and taste and taste and you begin to figure it out, begin to make those fine distinctions. Jean-Louis [Palladin] was the same way. I would use an old sauce, and he would say, "This is old; you did nothing to refresh it." I'd say, "No, no, no, it's fresh." Jean-Louis would take some of my sauce and do something to it, to refresh it. Today, when a cook gives me a sauce, I can tell you when it was made. An hour makes a big difference.

When you're making a sauce, you have to focus everything on it—everything. You can't talk to anyone or be distracted in any way for the two minutes you need to finish it, because there are so many variables that make a difference. Are you taking care not to let it stick to the sides of the pan? Because if you aren't, it will burn and the sauce will have a bitter note. Is it boiling too hard, cooking down too far? Is everything emulsifying just right? Is the seasoning perfect? Are the flavors balanced? Is it the perfect consistency? You never use a slurry—starch and water—to thicken a sauce; you use that when you've made a mistake, to hide the misery of what you did.

It takes ten years to master this work. Being the saucier is like having your doctorate.

Think of a sauce as you would tea or coffee: water that's infused with flavor, but flavor that is very unstable. Coffee that sits around on a heater for several hours, any coffee drinker knows, isn't the same as freshly brewed coffee. Do you keep your coffee or tea for two days in the refrigerator and reheat it? Sauces are similar in that they are continually changing, and you have to pay attention to them. They're best when finished, or refreshed, right before serving.

When you do any kind of sauce, you are trying to capture certain flavors: herbs, butter, or meat. Sauces made from meat stocks generally are the ones that can be "refreshed," ones for which you can begin with a base—leftover stock or sauce—and elevate it just before serving. If you are starting with a leftover sauce, you cannot simply reheat it; it must be refreshed, meaning you must treat it as a plain stock. To refresh the sauce, add sweated shallots, carrots, and any scraps of the meat you are using, some wine, some herbs, then adjust the consistency, season it, and enrich it with fat. The "refreshed" sauce will taste new.

But you have to be aware of how the sauce is evolving. Herbs and vegetables will release their flavor quickly, but that flavor will dissipate quickly as well. Hard or dried spices take more time to give their flavor, and that flavor tends to last longer.

Fish sauces you almost always have to do *à la minute* because they're delicate and therefore volatile. At Le Bernardin, we did a lobster consommé that was infused with ginger, kaffir leaves, lemongrass, and Thai spices. We would make it as close to service as possible, around five o'clock, but by seven o'clock the flavors had completely changed. So we solved this problem by making sachets—cheesecloth filled with our aromatics, an Asian tea bag— and dropping one each hour into a fresh pot of clarified lobster stock to infuse it.

Halibut with Grapes and Red Wine–Port Sauce, page 28

Eric has decided to go classical with the halibut—it's a delicate, beautiful fish, and he crisps one side in a sauté pan, then flips it gently and just kisses the other side with heat. Grapes have been peeled. The real pleasure in this dish, though, is in the sauce, a classical red wine reduction, and in its deep red color and mirror-like shine. Red wine is reduced with aromatics, then strained, added to reduced port, and heated almost to a simmer. It is then removed from the heat, and the butter is incorporated, not by whisking but by shaking the pan, which results in the glassy shine. It's a technique that requires experience: Eric "hops" the sauce, as if he were sautéing vegetables. He flips it and adds a little more butter, and as it thickens, it starts to make a "plop" sound. Eric is using both sound and sight to determine the quality of the sauce. "It's a feeling you have," he says. When he hears a distinct "plop, plop, plop" with each hop, he says, "That's the sound you want." No longer cloudy and opaque, the sauce has become shiny. He spoons it onto the plate, sets a piece of halibut on top. We can see the perfect reflection of the halibut in the sauce.

Halibut with Grapes and Red Wine–Port Sauce pictured on page 27

Serves 6

1¼ cups dry red wine

¼ cup red wine vinegar

1 garlic clove, peeled

½ carrot, peeled

¼ onion, thinly sliced

1 teaspoon fresh fennel seeds
   (you can substitute ¼ teaspoon
   dried fennel seeds)

½ teaspoon peppercorns

1 cup port

5 tablespoons unsalted butter

30 seedless red grapes, peeled and halved

Six 5-ounce thick halibut fillets

2 tablespoons canola oil

Fine sea salt and freshly ground
   white pepper

1 teaspoon chopped tarragon

½ teaspoon fresh lemon juice

SPECIAL EQUIPMENT

Kitchen twine

PREP: 25 minutes — **COOK:** 40 minutes

For the sauce, place the red wine, vinegar, garlic, carrot, onion, fennel seeds, and peppercorns in a medium pot over medium heat. Bring to a simmer and cook until the liquid is reduced by half, about 25 minutes.

Meanwhile, put the port in a separate pot and reduce by half, about 15 minutes.

Strain the red wine reduction and combine the two reductions in a medium saucepan. Set aside.

Melt 1 tablespoon of the butter in a small pot. Add the grapes and warm over low heat. Set aside in a warm place.

For the halibut, wrap a 7-inch piece of kitchen twine around each fillet, pulling it tightly so the fillet forms a circle, and knot to keep the shape. Place 1 tablespoon of the canola oil in each of two large nonstick sauté pans and heat over high heat. Season the halibut generously on both sides with salt and pepper. Add 3 of the halibut fillets to each pan and sear for 4 minutes, or until golden brown on the first side. Turn each fillet over and cook for another 4 minutes, or until a metal skewer inserted into the center of each fillet comes out warm.

Meanwhile, bring the sauce to a boil over high heat. Add the remaining 4 tablespoons butter and off the heat, shake the pan in a back-and-forth motion, as though you were popping corn, until the butter melts. Do not stir or whisk to incorporate the butter. The sauce will still be a bit cloudy at this point: continue to shake the pan until the sauce is shiny.

Rewarm the grapes over low heat. Add the tarragon and lemon juice.

To serve, remove the string from the halibut and place the fish in the centers of six dinner plates. Place 10 grape halves on top of each fillet, spoon the sauce around, and serve immediately.

Shellfish Ragout

SERVES 6

THE SHELLFISH

¼ cup canola oil

4 shallots, thinly sliced

4 thyme sprigs

1 pound cherrystone clams, scrubbed

1 pound steamer clams, scrubbed

1 pound mussels, scrubbed and
   beards removed

1 pound cockles, scrubbed

THE SAUCE

6 tablespoons unsalted butter

½ cup 3-inch-long julienne baby leeks
   (white and tender green parts)

Fine sea salt and freshly ground
   white pepper

⅓ cup reserved cherrystone broth

⅓ cup reserved steamer broth

⅓ cup reserved mussel broth

⅓ cup reserved cockle broth

1 tablespoon fresh lemon juice

Rock salt for serving

PREP: 10 minutes — **COOK:** 25 minutes

This is a simple dish using bivalves that, when they open from the cooking, release their own broth. You need only reduce it a little and whisk in butter to finish it. They're so efficient, they can act as their own serving dish as well.

For the shellfish, place a pot over medium-high heat and add 1 tablespoon of the canola oil, one-quarter of the shallots, and a sprig of thyme. Cook until the shallots have softened, about 2 minutes. Add the cherrystone clams, cover, and cook, stirring occasionally, until they begin to open, 5 to 7 minutes. Set the pan aside. Place another pot over medium-high heat, add another tablespoon of the oil, another quarter of the shallots, and a thyme sprig, and cook until the shallots have softened, about 2 minutes. Add the steamers, cover, and cook, stirring occasionally, until they open, about 2 to 3 minutes. Set aside. Cook the mussels and the cockles in the same manner in separate pots. Be careful not to overcook the shellfish, or they will be dry and tough.

One at a time, strain all the shellfish broths through a fine-mesh sieve, keeping them separate. Shell the cherrystone clams, discarding the muscle. Reserve six half shells and clean them well. Cut the cherrystone clams into ½-inch pieces. Shell the steamers, mussels, and cockles, discarding the muscles and shells. *(You can make the recipe to this point, up to 2 hours ahead; refrigerate the shellfish in their broths.)* Reserve ⅓ cup of each broth for the sauce, then return the shellfish to their individual broths and set aside while you make the sauce.

To make the sauce, place 1 tablespoon of the butter in a saucepan over medium heat, add the leeks; season with salt and pepper, and cook until the leeks are tender. Add the reserved broths (⅓ cup each) from the cherrystone clams, steamers, mussels, and cockles, and bring to a boil. Whisking constantly, add the remaining 5 tablespoons butter 1 tablespoon at a time. When the butter is fully incorporated, lower the heat and add the shellfish to the pan to warm them.

To serve, pour a layer of rock salt into the center of each plate and set a reserved cherrystone clam shell in the center. Add the lemon juice to the shellfish and stir to combine. Divide the shellfish among the shells. Spoon 2 tablespoons of the sauce over each.

Poached Pears with Poire William Caramel Sauce

SERVES 6

THE PEARS

3 cups sugar

6 cups water

1 vanilla bean, halved lengthwise

12 small or 6 large pears

THE SAUCE

1 cup sugar

½ cup heavy cream

¼ cup Poire William (pear brandy)

THE GARNISH

1 pint good-quality store-bought
   vanilla ice cream, slightly softened

3 tablespoons chopped pistachios

PREP: 25 minutes — **COOK:** 30 minutes

This is a delicious and easy dessert, especially if you have beautiful pears. At fancy ice cream cafés in France, poached pears, a quenelle of vanilla ice cream, and hot chocolate sauce is a common dessert. But Eric has put a caramel sauce with it, one flavored appropriately, even obviously, with pear brandy, and mixed pistachio nuts into the ice cream. Everything can be prepared as much as a day in advance.

For the pears, place the sugar, water, and vanilla bean in a large pot over high heat. Bring to a boil, stirring to dissolve the sugar, then lower the heat to a simmer.

Meanwhile, peel the pears, leaving the stems intact.

Add the pears to the simmering liquid. Cover with a circle of parchment paper to ensure even cooking and cook small pears for 15 minutes, large pears for 25 minutes, or until a small knife inserted in the bottom of a pear goes in with little resistance. Take the pan off the heat and cool the pears in the cooking liquid.

For the caramel sauce, heat the sugar over medium-high heat. Once the sugar melts, allow it to cook until it has a light caramel color. Take the caramel off the heat and add the heavy cream; be careful, the cream may sputter out of the pan. Stir to fully incorporate. Add the poire William and stir to combine.

To serve, place 2 small or 1 large pear, on each dessert plate. Combine the ice cream and pistachios in a mixing bowl, stirring to mix. Place a scoop of ice cream next to the pear(s) on each plate. Drizzle 2 tablespoons of the warm caramel sauce over the pears and ice cream, and serve immediately. (Refrigerate any remaining sauce for another time.)

For me, the vinaigrette is like a new mother sauce. For decades used primarily to dress salads, the vinaigrette emerged only twenty years ago as a modern sauce, following the advances of nouvelle cuisine. Until then, most sauces for meat were based on veal stock, and most sauces for fish were based on an emulsified butter sauce. For fish, you started with a *sauce vin blanc,* and from there used that as your canvas, adding basil puree for a basil sauce, ginger for a ginger sauce, et cetera. The notion of the vinaigrette has become that same sort of canvas on which to capture various flavors.

A vinaigrette is distinctive, unlike any other mother sauce. It feels lighter, more refreshing. The oil is neutral, and therefore captures and magnifies the flavor of the meat rather than masking it, as butter will do. And the high acid content spikes the dish, makes it lively and exciting. And they're so easy to make. Every kitchen has a neutral oil and an acid on hand, whether that acid is sherry vinegar or lime juice or balsamic.

I should be clear about saying "light." Light is an illusion. Calorie-wise, a vinaigrette won't be any less of a burden than a butter sauce— all fats have a similar calorie count per ounce. Vinaigrettes feel lighter, though, because you don't taste the richness of butter, and because the acid balances the richness of the oil. So a vinaigrette feels very lean.

But this is what is so unique and effective about the vinaigrette used as a sauce for meats and fish. Fats magnify flavor, but because the fat in a vinaigrette is a neutral oil, the flavors remain clear and authentic. The acidity, which enlivens the dish, can be varied depending on what you're cooking. Balance of the acid is critical. You can kill a piece of fish with too much acid. Not enough, and the dish will feel heavy and dull. So you must taste all the time. Cook a little scrap of the fish and taste it with some of your vinaigrette.

It's best to err on the side of too little acid rather than too much. You can always add acid if your sauce is not sharp enough, but if the sauce is too acidic, it's almost impossible to recover. You have to adjust the oil by three times the amount of acid, and this throws the composition of the sauce off.

The nature of the acid requires a little more thought. Traditional vinaigrettes are one part acid to three parts oil. But lemon juice is very sharp and so may need four parts oil for every one part lemon. Balsamic is soft and sweet and will need less oil. Also, you must cook to your own taste, and tastes often tend these days to reducing fat.

Learn to think of the vinaigrette as a valuable tool in your repertoire.

the vinaigrette

A basic vinaigrette is sherry vinegar, minced shallot and olive oil. Add salt to your vinegar first so that it dissolves, and then add the shallot and let it infuse for twenty minutes while the volatile acids dissipate, and finally add the oil. Beautiful and simple for fresh salad greens, but add some chopped basil and tarragon at the end, and it's a perfect sauce for any lean white fish. While aromatic vegetables like shallots need time to infuse, green herbs must be added at the last minute.

Mustard is often added to vinaigrettes to aid in emulsification, but add enough that you taste the mustard, and it becomes an excellent sauce for chicken or pork. Round this vinaigrette out with crème fraîche, and it's a great sauce for smoked salmon or for any smoked fish.

Vinaigrettes as sauce require some sensitivity and experience on the part of the cook, but if you are thoughtful and if you taste all the time, their ease and readiness make them the perfect sauce in the home kitchen.

After Eric decides on lamb for lunch, the next step is determining how to prepare it. A warm salad, he decides, and thinly sliced, "like a Thai beef salad." He knows he has some delicious organic soy sauce, so this will work. And, again like a Thai salad, he thinks of lime, and hot spices, chiles. As the chops come off the grill and drop their juices and fat, Eric adds this to the vinaigrette he's begun, capturing as much flavor as possible. After he's taken the meat off the bones, he returns the bones to the fire to cook them more to see if they will release more fat and juice for the vinaigrette. "We keep all the fat!" he says happily. "We're not cooking for the ladies."

Grilled Rack of Lamb and Cucumber Salad

SERVES 6

1 hothouse (seedless) cucumber,
    peeled and thinly sliced

12 lamb rib chops

6 tablespoons extra virgin olive oil

4 garlic cloves, chopped

3 thyme sprigs, leaves picked

1 rosemary sprig, leaves picked

Fine sea salt and freshly ground
    white pepper

Juice of 1 lime

3 tablespoons organic soy sauce

½ tomato, seeded and cut into ¼-inch dice

1 shallot, cut into tiny dice

1 teaspoon minced ginger

½ green banana pepper, cut into
    ¼-inch dice

½ teaspoon jalapeño pepper, cut into tiny
    dice (or a pinch of cayenne pepper)

6 mint leaves, cut into julienne

PREP: 30 minutes — **COOK:** 10 minutes

This succulent lamb, with its spicy lime-soy vinaigrette and cool cucumber seasoned with mint, is a beautiful first course or lunch entrée.

Make an overlapping circle of cucumber rounds in the center of each of six plates, using one-sixth of the cucumber for each one. Cover each plate with plastic wrap and refrigerate until ready to serve.

Place the lamb chops on a large platter and cover with 3 tablespoons of the olive oil, the garlic, thyme, and rosemary. Set aside to marinate while the grill is heating.

You can use either a charcoal grill or a grill pan. If using a charcoal grill, allow the coals to burn until the edges are gray, about 25 minutes. If using a grill pan, heat the pan over high heat for 5 minutes.

Season the lamb with salt and pepper. Place the lamb chops on the grill or in the grill pan and cook until seared on the first side, about 3 minutes. Turn them over and cook to medium-rare or a bit under, about 3 more minutes—the meat will continue to cook from the residual heat while it rests. Transfer to a platter and set aside.

For the salad, whisk together the lime juice, soy sauce, and all the juices that have collected on the lamb platter in a large bowl. Slowly whisk in the remaining 3 tablespoons olive oil. Add the tomato, shallot, ginger, banana pepper, jalapeño, and mint and stir to combine.

Cut the lamb off the bones and thinly slice. Add the lamb to the salad mixture and toss to combine. Season to taste with salt and pepper.

To serve, season the cucumber slices with salt and pepper. Place an equal portion of the lamb salad in the center of each cucumber crown.

Cod with Local Wax Beans, Chorizo, and Soy-Sherry Sauce

SERVES 6

¼ pound wax beans

2 tablespoons soy sauce,
   preferably organic

2 tablespoons sherry vinegar

5 drops Tabasco sauce

2 teaspoons minced ginger

2 teaspoons minced shallot

9 tablespoons unsalted butter

Fine sea salt and freshly ground
   white pepper

2 tablespoons canola oil

Twelve 3-ounce cod fillets

¼ pound chorizo, cut into 3-inch julienne

2 teaspoons chopped flat-leaf parsley

PREP: 20 minutes — COOK: 20 minutes

I think of cod as a "masculine" fish—meaning it has a very firm body and hearty character that you can put very strong flavors with, things like garlic and bacon. Scallops would be "feminine," requiring delicate accompanying flavors such as peas or asparagus. Here, I like spicy robust chorizo with the cod, paired with a soy-vinegar-ginger sauce—and plenty of butter, again because the cod is so hearty. Without even realizing it, I'm cooking Spanish. I love these powerful, vibrant flavors.

Snap the ends off the beans and halve them lengthwise. Blanch the beans in boiling salted water for 2 minutes, or until crisp-tender. Drain and shock in an ice-water bath to stop the cooking. Drain and set aside.

For the sauce, bring the soy sauce, sherry vinegar, Tabasco, ginger, and shallot to a boil in a small saucepan. Whisking constantly, add 8 tablespoons of the butter to the pan, a tablespoon at a time, making sure each tablespoon of butter has been absorbed before adding another. Season to taste with salt and pepper. Set aside.

Place two large nonstick sauté pans over high heat and add 1 tablespoon of the canola oil to each. Season the cod fillets on both sides with salt and pepper. When the oil is hot, add 6 fillets to each pan. Sauté for 3 to 5 minutes, or until the cod is golden brown on the first side. Turn the fillets over and cook for 30 seconds.

Meanwhile, heat the chorizo and beans in a pan with the remaining 1 tablespoon butter. Season to taste with salt and pepper. Add the parsley and toss to incorporate. Gently reheat the sauce, being careful not to let it boil.

To serve, place a piece of cod browned side down on each plate and top with a little of the chorizo-bean mixture. Top each with another cod fillet, browned side up. Drizzle the sauce around the cod. Serve immediately.

CHORIZO

Eric began to use chorizo here, and it would be like a theme everywhere we went. A chunk was always in the fridge or in the shopping cart or sliced on a board to snack on as we cooked or, as in this cod dish, in the food itself. In Portugal and in the northwestern region in Spain called Galicia, chorizo is often paired with seafood, especially in seafood stews, and so it is a natural extension of Eric's history that he pairs it with fish here (and later with mussels).

Chorizo, which is now available in many places throughout the United States, is a pork sausage powerfully flavored with paprika and garlic and hot spices. It can be fresh or dry, though Eric works only with dry chorizo—and the dryer the better.

It works double duty as an ingredient—when it cooks, the powerful meaty flavors leak into the dish to act as a seasoning device, and the fat, as it renders, enriches the dish.

Grappa-Marinated Peach and Basil Salad

SERVES 6

**6 peaches, peeled, pitted,
   and cut into ½-inch wedges**

2 tablespoons grappa

2 tablespoons sugar

7 basil leaves, cut into julienne

6 tablespoons crème fraîche (optional)

PREP: 15 minutes

When we cook at home, we do things easily and quickly. Traditionally, peaches should be blanched and shocked in ice water for easy peeling, but that takes too long, so we just peel these before we serve them sliced. Basil is plentiful, so we toss in julienned basil. When you cook at home, you use what happens to be available, and here we have some nice grappa. I put a little on a spoon with some peach and basil, and I taste. The grappa, *c'est bon*.

Place the peaches, grappa, sugar, and basil in a bowl and allow the fruit to macerate for 30 minutes in the refrigerator.

To serve, divide the peaches among six dessert bowls and, if you like, top each with a spoonful of crème fraîche.

The boundaries between soup and sauce are often blurred. Here is one straight forward soup plus two dishes that began as soup, but the soup turned out so interesting, Eric used it as a springboard to create an entrée, turning the soup into a sauce. This technique applies to almost any vegetable stock and indeed to almost anything that you might serve as soup, whether broth, bean or root vegetable puree, or green vegetable soup.

It's economical (as it doesn't rely on expensive, time-consuming stocks); it's healthful in that the flavor and richness come from the vegetable rather than from fat; and it's colorful— vegetable sauces are bright and bold rather than brown or creamy pale. Just about any green vegetable can be turned into a superlative sauce, especially for fish and delicate meats. Asparagus and scallops are a common pair, as are watercress and veal for example.

We tend to concentrate harder on the flavor and nuance of a sauce, so when we bring that focus to bear on soup making, the soups (and we who eat them) benefit.

Cranberry Bean Soup with Lemon Oil, page 46

Spicy Tomato Consommé, page 42

Spicy Tomato Consommé pictured on page 41

THE CONSOMMÉ

**5 pounds tomatoes, seeded and
roughly chopped**

1 lemongrass stalk, roughly chopped

1 scallion, roughly chopped

2 garlic cloves, roughly chopped

**¼ Scotch Bonnet pepper, seeded and
roughly chopped**

**Fine sea salt and freshly ground
white pepper**

½ cup mint leaves

THE GARNISH

9 grape tomatoes, halved

1 scallion, thinly sliced

PREP: 20 minutes, plus 3 hours resting time — **COOK:** 35 minutes

Place the tomatoes in a blender jar and pulse until they are still chunky but releasing their liquid. Line a fine sieve with a dampened double layer of cheesecloth and place it over a large container. Pour the tomatoes into the sieve and drain for 2 to 3 hours, or refrigerate overnight. The liquid that passes through the sieve will be clear.

Place the tomato water in a pot with the lemongrass, scallion, garlic, and Scotch Bonnet and bring just to a simmer; lower the heat if it begins to boil. Skim any foam that rises to the top, season with salt and pepper, and continue to simmer, skimming the foam as necessary. After 30 minutes, add the mint, turn the heat off, and allow the mint to infuse the consommé for 5 minutes.

Strain the consommé through a fine sieve lined with a double layer of cheesecloth. Adjust the seasoning.

To serve, place 3 grape tomato halves and a few slices of scallion in each soup bowl. Ladle the consommé into the bowls. Serve immediately.

TOMATO WATER

"Tomato water is an amazing product. I want to do a tomato water as a consommé," Eric announces. And so he does, simply infusing it with lemongrass as well as some garlic, a Scotch Bonnet pepper, scallion, and mint. He serves this hot, garnished with grape tomatoes and scallion, but it could be served cold depending on your mood and the weather. Although he adds very little olive oil, the tomato water feels rich and luxurious.

Striped Bass with Tomato-Verbena Water

SERVES 6

4 pounds tomatoes, seeded and
roughly chopped

4 fresh verbena leaves or
8 dried leaves

⅓ cup extra virgin olive oil

15 grape tomatoes, halved

½ cup peeled and diced
(¼-inch dice) cucumber

½ cup peeled and diced
(¼-inch dice) apple

1 tablespoon capers

2 tablespoons basil julienne

Six 7-ounce striped bass fillets

Fine sea salt and freshly ground
white pepper

PREP: 20 minutes, plus 30 minutes for infusing — **COOK:** 15 minutes

This is a refreshing summer entrée that combines vegetables, apple, and capers, marinated in olive oil, with a "sauce" of tomato water seasoned with verbena, a lovely lemon-scented herb native to South America. The fish is steam-roasted in a very hot oven.

Place the tomatoes in a blender jar and pulse until they are still chunky but releasing their liquid. Place a fine-mesh strainer lined with a double layer of dampened cheesecloth over a large container. Pour the tomatoes into the sieve and allow to drain for 2 to 3 hours, or refrigerate overnight. The liquid that drains will be clear.

Place the tomato water and verbena leaves in a small pot and bring to a boil. Skim any foam that rises to the top. Turn the heat off and allow the verbena to infuse for 15 minutes.

Meanwhile, place the olive oil, grape tomatoes, cucumber, apple, capers, and basil in a bowl and stir to combine. Season with salt and pepper to taste.

Preheat the oven to 500°F.

Season the striped bass on both sides with salt and pepper and place in a roasting pan that holds them comfortably. Bring a pot of water to a boil. Pour enough boiling hot water into the roasting pan to come one-quarter of the way up the sides of the striped bass. Roast for 6 to 8 minutes. To check for doneness, insert a metal skewer into the center of the fish and leave it there for 10 seconds; if the skewer is warm when you remove it, the fish is done.

To serve, gently reheat the sauce. Place a piece of fish in the center of each plate. Spoon an equal amount of the marinated vegetables over each piece of fish. Spoon about ¼ cup of the sauce around each fillet. Serve immediately.

The idea for the Parmesan-Cucumber Sauce came from two soups Eric had tasted, separated by a year. The first was in Bordeaux. It was a meat-based soup, not very good, but it contained Parmesan, and the effect intrigued him. One morning a year later, he woke up with the flash of an idea: Parmesan and cucumber, the white gazpacho. It was time to see if it would work.

I juiced two cucumbers and brought the juice to a simmer as he'd asked. He tasted, made an angry face. I tasted it—terrible. But by the time it finally reached the table, first as a sauce for littleneck clams, the cucumber juice had undergone an amazing transformation. It tasted clean—bright cucumber with an accent of nuttiness from both cucumber and the Parmesan; though enriched by cream, it seemed light and refreshing.

The soup and the sauce are virtually identical, with only small differences in the ratios of fats to liquid.

Cold Cucumber Soup

SERVES 6

2 hothouse (seedless) cucumbers, peeled
½ cup crème fraîche
½ cup heavy cream
½ cup finely grated Parmesan cheese
1 garlic clove, minced
¼ teaspoon Tabasco sauce
Fine sea salt and freshly ground
   white pepper
½ lemon

PREP: 20 minutes, plus 2 hours for marinating

Using an electric juicer, juice the cucumbers. Press the juice and pulp mixture through a fine-mesh sieve into a bowl. You should have 4 cups cucumber juice.

Add the crème fraîche, heavy cream, Parmesan cheese, garlic, and Tabasco. Place the soup in the refrigerator for 2 hours to marry the flavors.

To serve, strain the soup through a fine-mesh sieve. Season with salt and pepper to taste. Squeeze the juice from the lemon into the soup, and ladle into chilled bowls.

Steamed Littlenecks with Parmesan-Cucumber Sauce pictured on page 11

SERVES 6

2 hothouse (seedless) cucumbers,
   peeled and seeded
¼ cup crème fraîche
¼ cup heavy cream
1 cup finely grated Parmesan cheese
¼ teaspoon garlic mashed to a paste
¼ teaspoon Tabasco sauce
1 tablespoon canola oil
1 shallot, thinly sliced
30 littleneck clams, scrubbed
Fine sea salt and freshly ground
   white pepper
1 tablespoon fresh lemon juice

PREP: 20 minutes, plus 30 minutes for marinating — COOK: 7 minutes

Using an electric juicer, juice the cucumbers. Strain the juice through a fine-mesh sieve into a bowl. Measure 1¼ cups cucumber juice.

Add the crème fraîche, heavy cream, Parmesan cheese, garlic, and Tabasco. Set the sauce aside to allow the flavors to marry for 30 minutes.

Place a medium pot over medium heat and add the canola oil. When the oil is hot, add the shallot and cook until translucent; do not allow to color. Add the clams to the pot, cover, and cook until the clams are beginning to open, 3 to 5 minutes. Be careful not to overcook the clams, or they will become tough.

Meanwhile, check the cucumber sauce for seasoning and adjust with salt and pepper as necessary. To serve, place 5 clams in each bowl. Add the lemon juice and whisk until the sauce is frothy. Spoon about 3 tablespoons sauce over each bowl. Serve immediately.

Cranberry Bean Soup with Lemon Oil pictured on page 38

SERVES 6

½ cup extra virgin olive oil

Grated zest of 1 lemon

3 cups shelled fresh cranberry beans

6 garlic cloves, peeled

1 small tomato, cored

¼ onion

3 flat-leaf parsley sprigs

3 ounces prosciutto or good-quality
    smoked ham

6 cups chicken stock

12 thin slices French bread
    (about ¼ inch thick)

¾ cup heavy cream

4 tablespoons unsalted butter

Fine sea salt and freshly ground
    white pepper

PREP: 15 minutes — COOK: 1 hour

This is a straightforward bean soup. The fresh legumes are cooked in a stock flavored with prosciutto, garlic, tomato, onion, and parsley. If the soup will be served cold, it's important to season forcefully. What gives this soup its sparkle (all pureed soups need sparkle, usually in the form of acid and fat) is the lemon oil drizzled over it at the end. The garlic croutons provide a savory crunch that contrasts with the smooth rich soup.

Place the oil in a bowl and add the lemon zest. Set aside for at least an hour, or as long as overnight, to infuse.

Meanwhile, combine the beans, 5 of the garlic cloves, the tomato, onion, parsley, prosciutto, and 3½ cups of the chicken stock in a pot and bring to a boil. Reduce the heat to medium and simmer for an hour, or until the beans are tender. Skim any foam that rises to the top. Remove from the heat and let cool slightly.

Meanwhile, preheat the oven to 400°F.

Place the bread on a baking sheet and drizzle 3 tablespoons of the lemon oil over the slices. Bake for 5 minutes, or until toasted and golden brown. Rub each slice of bread with the remaining garlic clove.

Discard the tomato, onion, parsley, garlic cloves, and prosciutto. Transfer the beans and liquid to a blender, in batches if necessary, and blend until smooth. Return the soup to the pot, add the heavy cream and butter, stirring to blend, and season to taste. Add enough of the remaining 2½ cups chicken stock to achieve the desired consistency. If necessary, add some water.

The soup can be served hot or cold. If necessary, reheat the soup over low heat. Ladle soup into bowls and drizzle a few drops of lemon oil on top of each. Serve with the garlic croutons on the side.

Snapper with Caramelized and Braised Shallots pictured on pages 48–49

SERVES 6

1 cup shelled fresh cranberry beans

3 garlic cloves, peeled

1 small tomato, cored

¼ onion

2 flat-leaf parsley sprigs

1 ounce prosciutto or ham

2 cups chicken stock

35 medium shallots, peeled

2 cups water

**Fine sea salt and freshly ground
    white pepper**

**3 tablespoons unsalted butter,
    cut into small chunks**

¼ cup canola oil

Six 5-ounce snapper fillets (skin on)

PREP: 40 minutes — **COOK:** 1 hour and 20 minutes

The fish is simply sautéed—take care to get the pan very very hot and to press the fillets skin side down so they don't curl up—and served atop the cranberry bean puree, the caramelized shallots at its side.

Preheat the oven to 375°F.

Combine the cranberry beans, garlic cloves, tomato, onion, parsley, prosciutto, and chicken stock in a pot and bring to a boil. Reduce the heat to medium and simmer for an hour, or until the beans are tender. Skim any foam that rises to the top.

Discard the tomato, onion, parsley, garlic cloves, and prosciutto. Transfer the beans and any liquid to a blender and blend until smooth, adding more liquid as necessary.

Meanwhile, place 30 of the shallots in a baking pan, add the water, and season with salt and pepper. Scatter the butter around the shallots. Cover with aluminum foil and roast for 30 minutes, or until a knife is easily inserted in a shallot. Set the pan aside.

Thinly slice the remaining 5 shallots. Place a sauté pan over medium heat and add 2 tablespoons of the canola oil. Add the shallots and cook, stirring occasionally, until they are a deep caramel color, about 15 minutes. Stir into the bean puree. Set aside.

Place two large nonstick pans over high heat and place 1 tablespoon of the remaining canola oil in each pan. When the oil is very hot, nearly smoking, season the fillets on both sides and add 3 fillets to each pan skin side down. To keep the skin from curling, press down on the tops of the fillets with a large metal spatula during the initial stage of cooking, about 30 seconds. Continue to cook for 4 minutes, then turn the fillets and cook until a metal skewer inserted in one of the fillets comes out warm, about 2 minutes longer.

Meanwhile, transfer the braised shallots and their liquid to a saucepan and reheat the shallots. Reheat the bean puree.

To serve, place about ⅓ cup of the bean puree in the center of each plate, place a snapper fillet over the puree, and arrange 5 braised shallots around the fillet. Spoon about 3 tablespoons of the shallot braising liquid over each plate. Serve immediately.

THE SURPRISE OF SHALLOTS

What I love about this dish is the shallots, which
are not only in the sauce but are also braised
and served whole, adding a creamy sweetness
to the dish.

I'm using shallots all the time here. I had
never realized how important they were to me.
As a chef, I don't cut my own, so I don't think
about them, even though they're used throughout
the kitchen at Le Bernardin. Here, as a cook,
I chop them myself and come to realize how
much I love them and why.

Shallots bring something to a sauce, to a
dish, that onions don't. Onions have a much
higher water content. This is their distinguishing
characteristic. It's why minced shallots are used
in sauce making and onions aren't; onions would
release too much liquid and dilute rather than
enhance the sauce. The flavor isn't there, either.
Shallots are always bright, like a concentration
of the onion flavor. They tend to say what they
are instead of melting into a dish as onions do.

Eric often favors a light broth-like sauce
(here the shallot jus) where one might expect
something rich and creamy. He then delivers
the rich and creamy effect via the garnish,
here cranberry bean puree.

Snapper with Caramelized and Braised Shallots, page 47

One morning we drive out to Montauk Point to see the eastern tip of the island, the famous lighthouse, the surf along the rocky coast there, planning to do the day's shopping afterward. We pay at the gatehouse, park in the lot, and take the worn path to the water beneath the lighthouse.

The tide is coming in, just splashing over the rocks, and Eric sees that the rocks are covered with periwinkles, tiny snail-like mollusks. "We must do something with them," he says.

Periwinkles are eaten up and down the Atlantic coast of Europe, typically as bar food. They are served with a spicy aïoli, and eaten straight from their shells, plucked out with a pin.

As we begin to gather handfuls of periwinkles, Eric spots some tiny mussels. "Why can't I get these for my restaurant?" he asks, pleased by their size. He picks a couple off the rocks, turns them over. Mussels are filters and can carry toxins, sometimes causing shellfish poisoning. "They are too beautiful," Eric says. "We must take our chances." He grins. "The gods are with us." When you see periwinkles and mussels attached to rocks near your home, this is what you cook.

Montauk Periwinkles with Basil Aïoli

SERVES 6

THE PERIWINKLES

5 cups seawater plus 2 cups tap water or
   7 cups tap water plus 2 tablespoons salt

1 cup red wine vinegar

½ head garlic

4 thyme sprigs

2 flat-leaf parsley sprigs

2 tablespoons peppercorns

2½ pounds periwinkles (see Note)

THE AÏOLI

1 garlic clove

½ teaspoon fine sea salt, or more to taste

2 large egg yolks

⅓ cup canola oil

3 tablespoons extra virgin olive oil

1 tablespoon chopped basil

Freshly ground white pepper

PREP: 15 minutes — **COOK:** 40 minutes

The pleasure of the periwinkle, cooked in a court-bouillon of water, salt, vinegar, garlic, herbs, and pepper, is in their chewy texture—they're fun to eat. They have little flavor and require a rich tasty sauce.

For the periwinkles, combine the water, red wine vinegar, garlic, thyme, parsley, and peppercorns in a pot and bring to a boil. Cook for 15 minutes. Lower the heat to a simmer, add the periwinkles, and cook for 25 to 35 minutes.

Meanwhile, prepare the aïoli: Place the garlic clove and salt on a cutting board and mash to a paste using the side of a large knife. Transfer the garlic paste to a medium bowl, add the egg yolks, and whisk to combine. Place the bowl inside a pot lined with a towel to anchor it and free both hands. Whisking constantly, slowly drizzle the canola and then the olive oil into the bowl, continuing to whisk until a thick emulsion forms. Alternatively, using a mortar and pestle, mash the garlic clove and salt with the pestle until it forms a paste. Add the yolks and pound with the pestle until well combined. Constantly grinding with the pestle, slowly add the canola oil, then the olive oil. Continue grinding with the pestle until you achieve the desired consistency. Add the basil to the aïoli and stir to incorporate. Season to taste with salt and pepper. Cover and refrigerate until ready to serve.

To serve, drain the periwinkles and discard the vegetables and herbs. Serve on a platter, with small pins or skewers for the periwinkles, and the aïoli, for dipping, on the side.

NOTE: If you don't live where periwinkles do, you can order them (see Sources, page 320). The quality is very good, and they will likely be a bit larger than those you collect yourself; they will also probably be meatier and easier to remove from the shells.

AÏOLI, BY MORTAR AND PESTLE

Aïoli, the garlicky mayonnaise, is traditionally
made using a mortar and pestle, not with a whisk
or, more common today, a food processor. It's a
tiring but enormously satisfying method. If your
mortar is not heavy enough, you'll need two
people, one to drizzle the oil into the mortar
and the other to hold the mortar and grind
and stir like mad with the pestle. It's good too
to trade off, unless you want forearms like
Popeye's.

   The result is like no other aïoli. The garlic
gets seriously smashed, and so do the herbs,
truly incorporating themselves into the emulsified
oil; a food processor would mince the herbs and
garlic. The texture of the finished sauce is rich
and dense and smooth. "You never get that kind
of consistency with a whisk," Eric says.

Eric couldn't resist buying the monster lobster in a Montauk fish store. But this also meant he had to kill it. He doesn't like to kill anything, has assistants do it for him if he can. But he'd chosen this ancient creature, far older than he, and it was up to him to do the unpleasant task. He did it out by the pool, and I watched from the distance. It was like a wrestling match—the lobster was so huge, its shell so thick, and it seemed to know what was going on.

Eric won after a struggle.

Because the shell was so thick, this would be a suitable lobster for grilling. Eric brushed it with butter and seasoned it with dried herbs and curry powder (see page 55). Then he fashioned a sauce of lemon, tomatoes, herbs, and olive oil, really a refreshing salsa, and spooned it over the meat that was so plentiful (and tasty and tender) that he sliced the tail like a beef tenderloin.

Mussels with Spicy Italian Sausage

SERVES 6

2 tablespoons extra virgin olive oil

2 shallots, thinly sliced

2 garlic cloves, thinly sliced

Fine sea salt and freshly ground
white pepper

2 links spicy Italian sausage, casings
removed and roughly chopped

1 cup dry white wine

1 rosemary sprig

3 pounds small mussels, scrubbed and
beards removed

1 tablespoon chopped flat-leaf parsley

2 tablespoons fresh bread crumbs, toasted

PREP: 15 minutes — **COOK:** 15 minutes

A simple ragout of shellfish and sausage, so easy to prepare it's almost a heat-and-serve dish. Cook the shallots and garlic, then the sausage, add the wine and rosemary, then the mussels, which will release their juices into the pan, and finish with the parsley and bread crumbs—a rustic, spicy, brothy dish to be eaten with good crusty bread.

Place the olive oil in a large heavy-bottomed pot over medium heat. When the oil is hot, add the shallots and garlic, season with salt and pepper, and cook until the shallots are translucent but still have a bit of crunch, about 3 minutes.

Add the sausage to the pan and cook, stirring to crumble it, for 5 minutes, or until thoroughly cooked. Add the wine and rosemary and bring to a boil. Lower the heat to medium, add the mussels, cover the pan, and steam until the mussels open, 3 to 5 minutes.

Sprinkle the parsley and bread crumbs over all. Divide the mussels among six bowls and ladle the broth and sausage over them. Serve with crusty bread.

Grilled Lobster with Sauce Vierge

THE LOBSTER

One 9- to 10-pound lobster (see Note)

½ pound (2 sticks) unsalted butter, melted

1 tablespoon herbes de Provence

1 teaspoon curry powder

Fine sea salt and freshly ground white pepper

THE SAUCE

1 lemon

¾ cup extra virgin olive oil

2 tablespoons fresh lemon juice

2 yellow tomatoes, seeded and cut into small dice

2 red tomatoes, seeded and cut into small dice

1 shallot, minced

½ garlic clove, minced

3 tablespoons chopped basil

1 tablespoon chopped tarragon

Fine sea salt and freshly ground white pepper to taste

PREP: 15 minutes — **COOK:** 20 minutes

Prepare the grill: Allow the coals to become burned through, about 20 minutes.

To kill the lobster, plunge a heavy knife through its head just above the eyes, making sure the knife goes all the way through the head, then pull the knife in a downward motion through the eyes. Split the lobster in half. Remove the green tomalley. Brush the meat with the melted butter and sprinkle the herbes de Provence and curry powder evenly over the lobster tail. Season with salt and pepper.

Meanwhile, to make the sauce, cut off the ends of the lemon. Stand it on end and, using a paring knife, cut off the peel and white pith. Slice the sections from between the membranes and cut into small dice, discarding any seeds. Combine the lemon and all the remaining ingredients in a bowl and stir to combine.

Place the lobster shell side down on the grill, close the lid, and cook for 20 to 25 minutes, or until the meat is opaque.

To serve, remove the lobster and crack open the claws. Evenly divide the meat from the claws among six plates. Remove the tail meat and cut crosswise into ¼-inch slices. Pass the sauce at the table. Serve immediately.

NOTE: You can prepare the dish with smaller lobsters, adjusting the grilling time accordingly. A 2-pound lobster will cook in about 7 minutes.

Wherever I go, I always end up on the fish station. At my first restaurant job, La Tour d'Argent, I did all the stations but ended up as poissonier. Poissonier at Robuchon for two years. The first six months at Palladin, fish station. Bouley, fish station. And for more than ten years I have been at Le Bernardin, which is one giant fish station.

To be a *chef poissonier* in a traditional French brigade is to hold a position like no other cook. *Chef garde-manger*, because of the variety of skills required for that station, has traditionally been the one on the track to sous-chef. *Chef saucier* has more prestige, but I've always thought of the *poissonier* as the most sexy, the most elegant chef in the kitchen.

The poissonier is an entity unto him- or herself, in charge of receiving fish deliveries, evaluating quality, handling and butchering the fish, saving bones and scraps for sauce, mastering the sauces (which are typically the most subtle and nuanced), and understanding a range of technical skills and knowledge required for cooking all kinds of fish. No other station requires such self-reliance, precision, and expertise.

The skills the poissonier must master are among the most complex and are therefore more engaging. The preparation of each fish is unique. A rabbit is different from a cow, but not that different. But you handle a lobster differently than you do a scallop, differently from a sole, differently from a grouper. Each one requires experience. You learn only by working with each product.

You must be very, very clean, because you're always working in scales and blood. Fish is also very delicate, and it demands a sensitive touch in both cooking and saucing. (Saucing fish requires more subtlety than saucing red meat does.)

What I like most about poissonier is the cooking. Your gestures must be gentle and precise because that is the nature of the product you're working with. Your timing has to be exact. Cooking fish is almost like meditation—you must focus everything on the cooking. Everything goes into the process.

If you're cooking tuna, you'll have to have butchered it correctly to begin with or no amount of skill will allow you to cook it properly—if it is too thin, it will overcook; if it is too thick, the exterior will be overdone, the interior cold.

Sautéed Pompano on Pureed Chickpeas with Citrus Sauce, page 61

If you're sautéing halibut, you want a crust on one side, but you don't want a thick one. And your temperature must be precise or you'll overcook the fish. So perhaps you should have been poaching or steaming that halibut instead.

Fatty fish must be cooked at very high temperatures or the fat will melt out; lean fish at a slightly lower heat. Fish must be completed at the last minute, and you don't rest fish as you do meat. Yes, if you're cooking large whole fish, resting can be beneficial, but generally fish that rests tends to dry out.

You can't know any of this without actually working with the fish itself. You may have ten thousand cookbooks and all the knowledge, but it will be only theory. It took me two years working hard every day, searching myself, before I became a *chef poissonier*. I'm still learning after more than twenty years of cooking fish. It's like painting for Valentino. He can learn how Dalí was painting, how Picasso was painting, but if you don't do it yourself, over and over, you will never marry the theory with the gesture.

Sautéed Baby Calamari with Pepper Oil and Garlic

SERVES 6

1 red bell pepper

½ cup extra virgin olive oil

4 garlic cloves, peeled

1 thyme sprig

2½ pounds baby calamari

Pinch of cayenne pepper

Fine sea salt and freshly ground
   white pepper

2 tablespoons chopped flat-leaf parsley

½ lemon, seeds removed

PREP: 15 minutes, plus 25 minutes for infusing — **COOK:** 10 minutes

The distinguishing element of this is the oil, infused with sweet bell pepper, garlic, and thyme, to which cayenne is added for spiciness and lemon and parsley for final seasoning. Make the oil early in the day, have your parsley, lemon, and cleaned calamari at the ready, and the dish can be a first course in five minutes.

Trim the ends off the pepper. Slice it open down one side and open it out flat. Discard the seeds and slice off any white flesh from the inside of the pepper. Cut ¼ cup of tiny pepper dice. Reserve the scraps.

Place the oil in a small pan over medium heat. Add the pepper scraps, 2 garlic cloves, and the thyme, raise the heat to high, and bring to a boil. Turn off the heat and let the oil infuse for 25 minutes. Strain the oil and reserve. *(This can be done early in the day.)*

To clean the calamari, cut off the tentacles. Remove the beaks and set the tentacles aside. Remove the cartilage from inside the bodies and squeeze out the innards, discarding both. Cut a slit down the side of each body and lay it out flat on the work surface skin side up. Scrape the skin off and discard. Cut the calamari bodies into 2-inch by ¼-inch strips. Cut the tentacles in half. *(This can be done early in the day. Store refrigerated over ice.)*

Place a large nonstick sauté pan over high heat and add 2 tablespoons of the pepper oil and the remaining 2 garlic cloves. When the oil is hot, add the diced pepper. Cook for 30 seconds. Add the calamari and, stirring vigorously so it will cook evenly, season with the cayenne, salt, and pepper, and cook until it becomes opaque, 1 to 2 minutes. Be careful not to overcook it, or the calamari will be tough. Sprinkle the parsley over the calamari and stir to combine. Squeeze the lemon juice over it and toss to combine. Turn off the heat. Adjust the seasoning with salt and pepper.

To serve, divide the calamari among six plates. Serve immediately.

Pan-Roasted Monkfish with Lemon Carrots and Mint Pesto

4 medium carrots

3 tablespoons extra virgin olive oil

1 teaspoon ground cumin

½ teaspoon fennel seeds, crushed

¼ teaspoon turmeric

3 pinches cayenne pepper

Pinch of saffron threads

1 garlic clove, minced

2 teaspoons minced Lemon Confit (page 21)

Fine sea salt and freshly ground white pepper

3 cups chicken stock

3 tablespoons cold unsalted butter, cut into small chunks

½ cup packed mint leaves

2 tablespoons canola oil

Six 6-ounce monkfish fillets

3 rosemary stalks, cut in half

PREP: 20 minutes — **COOK:** 30 minutes

This is a killer dish because of the pesto sauce, which uses exciting seasonings—garlic, fennel seed, turmeric, cumin, cayenne—to sharpen and contrast with the sweetness of the carrots. For the pesto, butter is added to a portion of the broth and emulsified in a blender, then mint leaves are added and pureed. The broth can be prepared ahead, and the pesto made while the monkfish is finishing in the oven.

Preheat the oven to 500°F.

Peel the carrots and slice them very thin. Heat 1 tablespoon of the olive oil in a large pot over medium heat. Add the carrots, cumin, fennel seed, turmeric, cayenne, saffron, garlic, and lemon confit. Cook and stir for about 4 minutes, or until the carrots are crisp-tender. Season with salt and pepper to taste.

Add the chicken stock and simmer until the carrots are tender, about 10 minutes. Remove from the heat and strain, separately reserving ¼ cup of the broth for the pesto and the remaining broth. Set the carrots aside.

For the pesto, transfer the reserved ¼ cup warm broth to the jar of a blender. With the blender on medium speed, add the butter and blend until incorporated. Turn the blender to high and slowly add the mint leaves. When the mint is pureed, add the remaining 2 tablespoons olive oil and blend until incorporated. Season to taste with salt and pepper. Set aside.

For the monkfish, heat 1 tablespoon of the canola oil each in two large ovenproof sauté pans over high heat. Season the monkfish fillets generously with salt and pepper. When the oil is hot, almost smoking, add 3 fillets to each pan and sear until golden brown on the first side, about 5 minutes. Turn the fillets over, place a piece of rosemary stalk on each one, and place the pans in the oven to finish cooking, about 4 minutes, or until a metal skewer inserted in the thickest part of the fish comes out warm.

Meanwhile, reheat the carrots over low heat. Reheat the broth.

To serve, make a bed of carrots in the center of each plate. Spoon the broth around the carrots. Slice the monkfish fillets on the bias into 4 or 5 slices each and place on the carrots. Drizzle 1 tablespoon mint pesto into the broth on each plate. Serve immediately.

Flash-Marinated Fluke with Lemon Confit

SERVES 6

Six 5-ounce sushi-quality fluke fillets

3 tablespoons extra virgin olive oil

Fine sea salt and freshly ground
   white pepper

1½ teaspoons minced shallot

¾ teaspoon tiny dice of Lemon Confit,
   (page 21)

6 mint leaves, cut into julienne

1 teaspoon fresh lemon juice

PREP: 20 minutes — **COOK:** 5 minutes

Fluke fillet, left raw, sliced, and seasoned at the last minute with oil, shallot, lemon confit, lemon juice, and mint—this is a simple, beautiful, startlingly fresh preparation whose success is determined by the quality of the fish.

For the fluke, cut each fillet on the bias into ¼-inch by 2½-inch pieces. On each chilled plate, arrange the slices from one fillet in a rectangle . If not serving immediately, wrap in plastic and refrigerate for up to 2 hours.

To serve, brush the fluke lightly with the olive oil. Season with salt and pepper. Sprinkle ¼ teaspoon of the shallots, ⅛ teaspoon of the lemon confit, one-sixth of the mint, and about 4 drops of lemon juice over each rectangle of fluke. Serve immediately.

ON BUYING AND SERVING: RAW FISH

Most fish can be eaten raw, especially, but not limited to, white, nonfatty fish (such as striped bass, fluke, halibut, and red snapper) and tuna and salmon. But some you should not eat raw, such as tropical fish (parrot fish, for instance), nor flesh that has blood in it (always be sure to cut out the blood line of a fish if you are serving it raw). Others (skate or grouper) must be cooked in order to become tender.

Fish to be served raw must be impeccably fresh. You can see and smell freshness. Fresh fish is moist and brightly hued, not dry or dull looking. It's firm, slightly elastic, not squishy or flaccid. The odor should be fresh and appealing, without a hint of unpleasantness. If it smells like cat food, give it to your cat.

Get to know your fishmonger. Tell your fishmonger what you are looking for and ask if he or she can get it for you—be sure to mention that you intend to serve it raw and would like sushi quality.

When fish is very, very fresh, it almost demands to be eaten raw because of it exceptional texture and flavor. Very fresh beautiful fish can be served in a ceviche preparation (using acid as a form of cooking that doesn't alter texture but enhances the flavor; see page 118) or simply with a dressing as with this fluke.

Fish may be the best product in the United States because, for the time being, much of it remains wild, not farmed.

Sautéed Pompano on Pureed Chickpeas with Citrus Sauce pictured on page 56

SERVES 6

THE CHICKPEAS

½ pound dried chickpeas, soaked
   overnight in 4 cups cold water

3 tablespoons extra virgin olive oil

3 tablespoons chopped cilantro

3 tablespoons chopped flat-leaf parsley

3 tablespoons chopped scallions
   (white part only)

Fine sea salt and freshly ground
   white pepper

THE SAUCE

1 tablespoon fresh lime juice

1 tablespoon fresh orange juice

1 teaspoon fresh lemon juice

1 teaspoon Dijon mustard

Pinch of fine sea salt

Pinch of freshly ground white pepper

½ shallot, minced

1 tablespoon tiny dice of Lemon Confit
   (page 21)

½ teaspoon grated lime zest

½ teaspoon grated orange zest

3 tablespoons extra virgin olive oil

3 tablespoons canola oil

2 tablespoons tiny dice of seeded tomato

1 tablespoon chopped cilantro

1 tablespoon chopped flat-leaf parsley

THE POMPANO

2 tablespoons canola oil

Twelve 3-ounce pompano fillets

Fine sea salt and freshly ground
   white pepper

PREP: 30 minutes, plus overnight soaking for the chickpeas — **COOK:** 1 hour

Here dried chickpeas are soaked overnight, then cooked and pureed. The fish, quickly sautéed, rests upon the puree, served with a citrus sauce, which is more or less a vinaigrette (a good strategy for saucing fish if you don't have fish stock on hand, page 205).

Drain the chickpeas, place in a medium pot, and add 4 cups fresh water. Bring to a simmer over medium heat and cook until the chickpeas are tender, about an hour.

Drain the chickpeas and reserve the cooking water. Transfer the chickpeas to a bowl and mash them, using a potato masher or a fork, to a chunky consistency. Add the oil and herbs and season to taste with salt and pepper. Set aside.

For the sauce, combine the lime, orange, and lemon juices in a bowl. Add the mustard, salt, and pepper and whisk to combine. Whisk in the shallot, lemon confit, and orange and lime zest. Whisking constantly, add the olive oil and then the canola oil in a slow, steady stream. Stir in the tomatoes, cilantro, and parsley. Set aside.

Place two large nonstick skillets over high heat. When they are hot, add 1 tablespoon of the canola oil to each pan. Season the pompano with salt and pepper and place 6 fillets skin side down in each pan. These cook very quickly, so you must be careful not to overcook them: after 2 minutes, check to see if the skin is golden brown. As soon as it is, turn each fillet over and cook for another 30 seconds.

Meanwhile, reheat the chickpea puree in a small pan.

To serve, spread about ½ cup of the chickpea puree down the middle of each plate. Top the puree with 2 pompano fillets skin side up, arranging them to form a cross. Drizzle the sauce over the fish. Serve immediately.

Shimon had been talking about chickpeas, a staple of Israeli cooking (hummus, falafel), and Eric, curious, created a dish with them.

"I like the challenge of this book," he said. "I'm not doing blanquette de veau and I'm not doing cassoulet; I'm not doing the things I usually do. Like the chickpeas—you don't know how it's going to turn out. How often do I eat chickpeas? Never in my life. Never."

Valentino usually has his morning coffee around noon. Hours later, when he is ready to start work, he pads into the kitchen with pens or brush and black ink and a glass of Champagne. He beholds the knives, the vegetables, the herbs, whole fish, the meat, legs of lamb, a rabbit. "Everything in the world is here," he says.

The muscles Valentino uses in his art parallel those Eric uses in his work, as Eric had originally contended. Part of it is physical, part is spiritual. Valentino's paintings are about process; he adds ingredients here, some color there, tasting with his eyes. He will say to me as I regard his work, "It's not finished. This one needs hands. And not just normal hands, but very, very beautiful hands." He shakes his long wavy hair. "So beautiful you cannot believe." Valentino has lived as an artist for more than thirty years. He seldom speaks in English, but when he does, it is typically epigrammatic. "Observing, contemplating life: *That is painting*." "My father taught me two things. Never to talk about the women you have been with. And never to swear." "Every recipe is a poem." And, with an unusual edge of warning in his voice, "Be sure you are hungry for what you eat."

A piece of clean slate inspires a tapas platter. Eric sets crumbled goat cheese and sweet yellow watermelon on the slate, then scatters salt, some tomatoes, a caperberry with a long stem. Shimon and Tammar become entranced and they begin to shoot it. "It's fantastic," says Valentino. He peers through their camera, then begins to sketch this still life. It's a marvel to see—cook, photographer, painter, focusing differing gazes, their separate crafts, on the same object, all of them connected by the food.

Tapas Still Life

SERVES 6

Six ½-inch-thick slices country bread

1 garlic clove, peeled

1 small tomato, halved

2 tablespoons extra virgin olive oil

6 thin slices prosciutto

2 ounces fresh goat cheese

1 tablespoon olive paste

½ seedless yellow watermelon, rind
   removed, cut into 18 bite-size chunks

18 tiny basil leaves

12 caperberries

18 oil-cured black olives

9 grape tomatoes, halved

½ teaspoon gray sea salt

PREP: 10 minutes — **COOK:** 5 minutes

Toast the bread slices in the oven or a toaster oven until golden brown. Rub the garlic over one side of the toasts while they are still hot, then rub the tomato over them, squeezing the pulp and juices on the toast. Drizzle the olive oil over the toasts. Drape 1 slice of prosciutto over each one.

Place a small piece of crumbled goat cheese and a dash of olive paste on top of each watermelon chunk. Top each with a tiny basil leaf.

Arrange the bruschetta, watermelon, caperberries, olives, and grape tomatoes on a platter. Season the grape tomatoes with salt.

Figs Wrapped in Bacon

Serves 6

18 figs, peeled

20 bacon slices

**Fine sea salt and freshly ground
white pepper**

1 shallot, thinly sliced

2 tablespoons balsamic vinegar

PREP: 20 minutes — COOK: 20 minutes

A salty-sweet canapé—an updated version of the country-club standard, water chestnuts with bacon—enhanced by balsamic and caramelized shallots.

Preheat the oven to 350°F.

Wrap each fig in a strip of bacon, trimming the bacon as necessary, and secure with a toothpick. Season with salt and pepper. Place on a small baking sheet and bake for 10 minutes, or until the bacon is crisp and the figs are tender.

Meanwhile, place the remaining 2 slices bacon in a sauté pan over medium heat and cook until they render their fat. Add the shallot and season with salt and pepper. Cook until the shallot is caramelized, 8 to 10 minutes. Remove the bacon (a treat for the cook) and excess fat from the pan. Deglaze the pan with the balsamic vinegar. Set aside.

Serve warm on a platter, with the shallot slices draped over the figs.

Black Pepper and Cognac Shrimp pictured on page 14

Serves 6

2 tablespoons canola oil

1 onion, thinly sliced

Fine sea salt

2 pounds large shrimp in their shells

1 tablespoon coarsely ground black pepper

3 thyme sprigs

½ cup Cognac

**8 tablespoons (1 stick) cold unsalted
butter, cut into 1-inch chunks**

1 tablespoon chopped tarragon

1 lemon, cut in half and seeded

PREP: 10 minutes — COOK: 10 minutes

This is a simple dish meant to be eaten as an hors d'oeuvre. The shrimp, still in their shells, are seasoned and sautéed; then brandy and butter are added to the pan. The shells flavor the sauce. A lot of freshly ground pepper gives it some bite.

Eric made this dish for us to eat in the kitchen while we cooked the rest of the dinner. As we peeled and ate, Eric wasn't satisfied. The dish was missing something. Aha—lemon! Eric had meant to finish the dish with fresh lemon juice. He was right—then it was perfect.

Place the canola oil in a large sauté pan over medium-high heat. Add the onion and cook until translucent, about 5 minutes, seasoning with salt to taste.

Add the shrimp, pepper, and thyme. Cook until the shrimp turn bright orange, about 2 minutes. Be careful not to overcook.

Add the Cognac and carefully ignite it with a match. Add the butter and stir with a wooden spoon until the butter is incorporated. The sauce should be creamy. Add the tarragon and squeeze the lemon juice over the shrimp.

Serve immediately with crusty bread. Provide a bowl for the shells.

Roasted Duck and Foie Gras with Sautéed Melons and Figs

SERVES 6

THE DUCK

One 5- to 6-pound duck

5 garlic cloves

2 rosemary sprigs

¼ onion

Fine sea salt and freshly ground
white pepper

1 slice hearty bread

½ cup brandy

¼ cup balsamic vinegar

2 cups cold chicken stock

THE FOIE GRAS

One 2- to 2¼-pound Grade A foie gras

4 shallots, thinly sliced

12 figs, peeled

6 cantaloupe wedges (about 1 inch thick)

Fine sea salt and freshly ground
white pepper

SPECIAL EQUIPMENT

Kitchen string

PREP: 20 minutes — **COOK:** 1 hour and 40 minutes

Preheat the oven to 400°F.

To prepare the duck, set the heart, gizzard, and liver aside. Cut off the wing tips and reserve with the organs. Rinse the duck with cold water and pat dry with paper towels. Stuff the garlic, rosemary, and onion into the duck's cavity. Season with salt and pepper. Place the piece of bread in the opening, using it as a cork to seal in the flavors. Tie the legs together with kitchen string.

Heat a large heavy-bottomed casserole over medium heat. Add the duck and sear on all sides until golden brown, about 10 minutes.

Transfer the pan to the oven and roast the duck for 30 minutes; it should still be rare. Transfer the duck to a platter and allow to rest for 10 minutes; set the pan aside. (Leave the oven on.) Cut off the legs of the duck and cut each leg apart at the joint. Remove the breast meat. Set the duck aside. Discard the stuffing, and reserve the ribs and back bones. Discard all but ¼ cup fat from the pan.

Chop the bones and add them to the pan. Place the pan over medium-high heat and add the reserved heart, liver, gizzard, and wing tips. Cook for 10 minutes, or until the bones are browned and caramelized. Deglaze the pan with the brandy, scraping up any browned bits from the bottom. Add the balsamic vinegar and bring to a boil. Add the chicken stock, whisking constantly to emulsify the sauce. Lower the heat and simmer for 20 minutes longer. Strain the sauce through a fine-mesh sieve into a small saucepan. Adjust the seasoning with salt and pepper and set aside.

Meanwhile, to clean the foie gras, split the foie at the natural separation. Remove the large central vein and any smaller veins you can reach using a paring knife. Place another large heavy-bottomed pot over medium-high heat. When the pan is hot, add the foie gras and sear on all sides, for a total of about 6 minutes. Spoon off 2 tablespoons of the fat and reserve. Add the shallots to the pan, reduce the heat to low, and cook for 5 minutes.

Add the figs to the pan, place in the oven, and cook for 20 minutes, or until the foie gras is medium rare.

Meanwhile, for the melon, place a large sauté pan over medium heat and add the reserved 2 tablespoons foie gras fat. Add the melon and season with salt and pepper. Cook, turning once, until the melon is golden brown, about 2 minutes per side. Set aside.

Shortly before serving, place the duck pieces on a baking sheet and reheat in the oven. Reheat the sauce over low heat. If necessary, gently reheat the melon.

To serve, place one slice of melon on each plate. Slice the foie gras into ½-inch-thick slices across the lobe and place 2 slices on each plate. Carve the breast meat from the duck, across the grain and on the bias, and place 2 slices on each plate. Carve the meat from the legs and thighs and divide among the plates. Place 2 figs on each plate, spoon about 2 tablespoons of sauce over each plate, and serve immediately.

Eric has a duck and a whole Grade A foie gras, some figs, and melons. He's been doing nothing but simple and rustic, but today is Valentino's fifty-first birthday and Eric wants to cook classic. This is part of who he is as a cook, too. And a classical cook loves fat.

"There's nothing wrong with it if you eat it in the right amount," he says." He decides to finish everything in the same pan so that the figs and melon and foie gras and shallots all melt in there, almost confit right in the pan.

"This is home cooking?" I ask as Eric chops duck bones to make the sauce.

"Classical food I can't screw up, I'm sorry."

He scrapes browned bits off the bottom of the pan with a wooden spoon (he says he's always happy when he's holding a wooden spoon). "I do it out of fear. Jean-Louis and Joël would never forgive me."

Eric's method is to cook the duck rare by searing and roasting it; then he removes the meat from the bones so that he can use them to enrich chicken stock. When the stock is finished and strained into a small saucepan, he can put the foie in the oven to roast, giving him time to sauté the melons and figs and to finish the duck.

This is a special-occasion meal that requires some concentration and care.

After a long night, with a rich dinner, including plenty of Champagne, wine, and Cognac, Eric wakes hungry. He scoops up some of the foie gras fat, drops it into a nonstick pan, and gently fries three eggs, sunny side up. Heaven.

beach picnic

Why, I want to know, do people insist on beach picnics? If I want to eat good food that has been carefully prepared, the last place I want to do it is on a hot beach with sand blowing in the food and seagulls squawking, circling. Bugs and flies. Glasses tilt in the sand. Someone's always facing uphill.

You are being too negative, Michael. You should relax a little. I like a picnic once in a while. I grew up picnicking in the mountains on long hikes. We'd bury the Bordeaux in the ground to keep it cool. Now we're in the Hamptons, so we go to the beach. This meal is about transportable food; food that's prepared ahead of time, doesn't need to be served hot, and makes a great lunch buffet. It's important to have this kind of cooking in your repertoire.

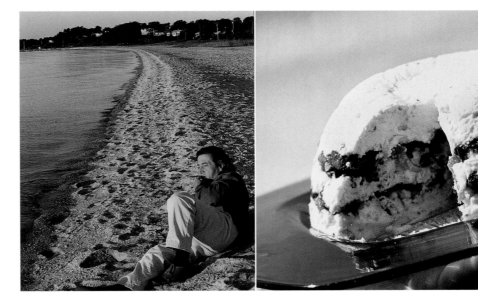

Goat Cheese and Ricotta Terrine

SERVES 6

1 cup fresh ricotta cheese

1 cup (about 8 ounces) fresh goat cheese

**Fine sea salt and freshly ground
white pepper**

1 tablespoon thinly sliced chives

¼ cup Basil Pesto (recipe follows)

**3 tablespoons finely chopped
sun-dried tomatoes**

20 Kalamata olives, pitted and chopped

**3 tablespoons pine nuts, toasted
and chopped**

PREP: 20 minutes — COOK: At least 2 hours

Ricotta–goat cheese terrine is light, refreshing, and visually appealing, with its layers. The goat cheese adds some sharpness to the mild ricotta. The ricotta makes the dish light. The fat of the cheeses carries the flavors of the basil and pine nuts and olives and sun-dried tomatoes.

Combine the ricotta cheese and goat cheese in a medium bowl and stir to blend. Season to taste with salt and pepper. Add the chives and stir to combine.

To assemble the terrine, line a small bowl (5 inches wide) with plastic wrap, leaving enough overhang to cover the terrine once you are finished. Put one-third of the goat cheese mixture in the bowl and smooth the top. Spread half the pesto over the goat cheese. Scatter half each of the sun-dried tomatoes, olives, and pine nuts evenly over the pesto. Repeat with another layer of cheese, spread the remaining pesto over it, and scatter the remaining tomatoes, olives, and nuts over the pesto. Top with the remaining cheese mixture. Fold the plastic wrap over the top and place in the refrigerator to set for at least 2 hours.

To serve, unwrap the top of the terrine, invert it onto a serving platter, and pull off the plastic wrap. Serve with crackers or crusty bread.

BASIL PESTO

MAKES ¾ CUP

2 tablespoons chopped garlic

¾ cup extra virgin olive oil

2 cups firmly packed basil leaves

½ teaspoon fine sea salt

Place the garlic and olive oil in a blender. Blending at high speed, slowly add the basil leaves until all are incorporated. Add the salt. Transfer the pesto to a container and place plastic film directly against the surface to prevent discoloration. *(The pesto can be refrigerated for up to 1 day.)*

Olive and Pesto Pasta Salad

SERVES 6

THE PASTA SALAD

1 pound tagliatelle
   (you can substitute fettuccine)

1 tablespoon extra virgin olive oil

½ cup Basil Pesto (page 69)

½ cup Tomato Compote (recipe follows) or
   high-quality prepared tomato sauce

½ cup olive paste

½ teaspoon finely chopped Lemon Confit
   (page 21)

2 tablespoons fresh lemon juice

1 teaspoon Tabasco sauce,
   or more to taste

Fine sea salt and freshly ground
   white pepper

PREP: 35 minutes — COOK: 1 hour if making the tomato compote; 10 minutes if using prepared tomato sauce

The first step to a great cold pasta salad is so elementary that it is the most overlooked: Start with great pasta. Then cook it perfectly in properly salted water, or you won't have a good finished dish. Also key is the length of marination. The pasta should be tossed with its ingredients an hour before serving. Because this dish is served cold, it's critical that the flavors be powerful. The amount of salt should be on the higher side for the same reason.

If you make the tomato compote, you will have a good amount left over; it can be refrigerated for several days and used in another dish.

Bring a large pot of water to a boil. Add salt, then add the pasta and cook until slightly less than al dente, 5 to 8 minutes, depending on the pasta. Drain and rinse quickly under cold running water. Place the pasta in a large bowl and toss with the extra virgin olive oil. *(The pasta can be cooked in advance and refrigerated until ready to assemble the salad.)*

Up to 1 hour before serving, add the pesto, tomato compote, olive paste, lemon confit, lemon juice, and Tabasco sauce to the pasta and toss to combine all the flavors. Season to taste with salt and pepper. Cover and marinate in the refrigerator for 30 minutes to 1 hour. The salad should be served very cold.

TOMATO COMPOTE

MAKES 2 CUPS

2 pounds tomatoes, peeled, seeded,
   and cut into ½-inch dice

¼ cup diced shallots

2 tablespoons chopped garlic

Fine sea salt and freshly ground
   white pepper

Place the tomatoes, shallots, and garlic in a pot over medium heat. Season to taste with salt and pepper. Cook for 1 hour, or until tomatoes are still a little chunky and the liquid has evaporated; the compote should have the consistency of a very thick sauce. Adjust the seasoning with salt and pepper. *(The compote can be prepared up to a day in advance, covered, and refrigerated.)*

Caramelized Onion Tart pictured on page 73

SERVES 6

THE CRUST

1¼ cups all-purpose flour,
    plus more for dusting

1 teaspoon fine sea salt

8 tablespoons (1 stick) cold
    unsalted butter

1 large egg yolk

¼ cup ice-cold water,
    plus more if necessary

THE FILLING

2 tablespoons canola oil

6 cups thinly sliced onions

1 teaspoon thyme leaves

Fine sea salt and freshly ground
    white pepper

6 anchovy fillets

20 Niçoise olives, pitted and halved

PREP: 20 minutes — **COOK:** 1 hour and 5 minutes

This preparation, with olives and anchovies, is typical of Nice and Provence. The onions are first sautéed gently until they've lost most of their moisture and are evenly caramelized, then they are simply transferred to an unbaked tart shell, the anchovies and olives added, and the tart baked. A simple do-ahead dish.

For the crust, place the flour and salt in a medium bowl and stir to combine. Add the cold butter and use a fork or your fingertips to work the butter into the flour; there should still be some pieces of butter visible. Add the yolk and 2 tablespoons of the water and stir with the fork until the dough starts to come together. If necessary, add some or all of the remaining water. Quickly knead the dough just until it comes together; be careful not to overwork it. Shape the dough into a disk, wrap in plastic film, and refrigerate for at least 3 hours, or overnight.

For the filling, place a large nonstick sauté pan over medium-high heat and add the canola oil. Add the onions and thyme, season with salt and pepper, and cook until the onions are limp and translucent, about 10 minutes. Lower the heat and continue to cook, stirring occasionally, until the onions turn a deep caramel color, about 30 minutes. Transfer to a bowl and refrigerate until cold.

Preheat the oven to 400°F.

To make the tart, on a lightly floured surface, roll the dough to a thickness of ⅛ inch. Fit it into a 9-inch tart pan with a removable bottom. Trim off the excess dough. Spread the onions in the bottom of the tart shell. Arrange the anchovies on the onions, like the spokes of a bicycle wheel. Arrange the olives evenly over the onions.

Bake the tart for 30 minutes, or until the crust is golden. To ensure even cooking, turn the tart around halfway through cooking.

Serve the tart warm or at room temperature. Remove the sides of the tart pan and cut into slices.

Arugula Salad with Goat's Milk Yogurt Dressing

SERVES 6

½ cup goat's milk yogurt

1 teaspoon minced shallot

¼ teaspoon minced garlic

Fine sea salt and freshly ground
white pepper

1½ teaspoons thinly sliced chives

2 large bunches arugula, stems removed
and thoroughly washed

¼ cup pine nuts, toasted and
coarsely chopped

PREP: 10 minutes

This easy salad combines two powerful and intriguing flavors—peppery arugula and earthy, acidic goat's milk yogurt, enhanced by garlic, shallots, chives, and pine nuts. Wait to dress it at the last minute if it will be traveling.

In a small bowl, whisk the yogurt, shallot, and garlic to combine. Season with salt and pepper. Whisk in the chives. Cover and refrigerate. *(This can be done early in the day.)*

To serve, place the arugula and pine nuts in a large bowl. Lightly season with salt and pepper. Add enough dressing to lightly coat the arugula (you may not need all of the dressing) and toss. Serve immediately.

Caramelized Onion Tart, page 71

summer's end

In Andorra, where I grew up, everyone cooked outside on slate, not on a grill. I'd love to see more people using this method here: just a simple piece of half-inch-thick slate that you can buy at a garden store is a great cooking tool. You can put it on your grill, or you can rest it directly on the coals. If you camp, it's a great portable cooking surface.

It's especially good for cooking fish outside because you can control the heat better—it's evenly distributed, and you don't have harsh flames or carbon-filled smoke coating the flesh. Similarly, you can put meats that have been marinated in oil directly on it and not worry about the meat being engulfed in flames as the fat ignites. The oil stays on the stone and helps the meat cook evenly. And you still have the smoky open-flame flavor. Another advantage is that you can flavor the slate itself by rubbing a sturdy herb, like rosemary, and garlic onto the oiled surface before cooking, say lamb chops. But mostly I love the way the stone communicates the heat.

The common wisdom in Andorra is to coat the slate with oil the first time you use it, and to start it at a lower heat, and that will help temper it and prevent its cracking.

For our last night in Sag Harbor, we want something special yet easy: A mixed grill is the perfect solution. We could have done steaks for everyone, but it is much more interesting to have a variety of meats, with different flavors and textures. The trick, of course, is to cook each item perfectly, given that each requires a slightly different heat and cooking time. Fortunately, the hearty meats that work well on a grill also rest very well; undercook them slightly, and they can sit covered for a half hour. Choose what you like—a selection of pork, beef, and veal, or chicken and sausages, or chicken with a variety of beef cuts to taste and compare—strip, rib eye, and skirt steaks—as we did.

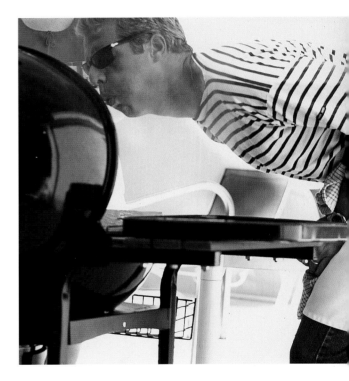

Sautéed Summer Vegetables with Garlic and Herbs

SERVES 6

2 medium zucchini

2 medium eggplants

2 large tomatoes

2 red bell peppers

6 tablespoons olive oil

12 garlic cloves, peeled

Fine sea salt and freshly ground white pepper

12 rosemary sprigs

12 thyme sprigs

PREP: 10 minutes — **COOK:** 30 minutes

Sautéing zucchini is simple, but even here some technique and care is involved for the best result. Because it's mild tasting, you must start the squash over medium-high heat, to get a quick sear on the surface; this gives them flavor. Then, turn down the heat to finish cooking them, making sure the garlic and herbs flavor the oil but do not burn.

Cut the ends off the zucchini and the eggplant and cut each lengthwise into 3 equal slices. Cut 3 thick slices from each tomato, discarding the tops and bottoms. Cut off the tops and bottoms of the red peppers and remove the seeds. Cut each pepper into 3 equal pieces.

Place two large nonstick sauté pans over medium-high heat. Add 2 tablespoons of the olive oil and 3 garlic cloves to each pan. Season the zucchini, eggplant, tomatoes, and red peppers with salt and pepper. Place the zucchini in one pan, the eggplant in the other, and add 3 rosemary sprigs and 3 thyme sprigs to each pan. Lower the heat to medium and cook turning once, until the vegetables are golden brown on both sides, about 5 minutes per side. Using a slotted spoon, transfer the vegetables to a serving platter.

Discard the garlic, rosemary, and thyme in the pans. Add 1 more tablespoon of the olive oil and 3 garlic cloves to each pan. When the oil is hot, place the red peppers in one pan and the tomatoes in the other, add 3 rosemary sprigs and 3 thyme sprigs to each pan, and cook, turning once, until the vegetables are golden brown on each side, 3 to 5 minutes per side. Transfer the vegetables to the platter. Serve warm or at room temperature.

Marinated Mixed Grill

SERVES 6

One 3½- to 4-pound chicken, cut into 8 pieces

6 tablespoons extra virgin olive oil

3 sage leaves, torn

4 teaspoons thyme leaves

4 teaspoons rosemary leaves

4 garlic cloves, thinly sliced

¼ teaspoon tiny dice of Scotch Bonnet pepper

One 12-ounce boneless rib eye steak

One 12-ounce T-bone steak

One 10-ounce skirt steak

Fine sea salt and freshly ground white pepper

PREP: 10 minutes — **COOK:** 25 minutes

Prepare the grill: Allow the coals to burn for 20 minutes.

Place the chicken on a platter and drizzle 2 tablespoons of the olive oil over it. Toss with the sage leaves, 1 teaspoon of the thyme leaves, 1 teaspoon of the rosemary leaves, one-quarter of the garlic, and a pinch of the Scotch Bonnet peppers.

Place the rib eye, T-bone, and skirt steak on a separate platter and toss with the remaining ¼ cup olive oil and the remaining thyme, rosemary, garlic, and Scotch Bonnet.

Season the chicken with salt and pepper. Place the chicken on the grill and cook for 10 to 12 minutes on each side; the skin should be crisp. Transfer the chicken to a serving platter.

Season the steaks with salt and pepper on both sides. Place the T-bone steak on the grill and cook for about 3 minutes. Add the rib eye steak and cook for 2 minutes, then turn both steaks. Cook for another 2 minutes, or for medium-rare, until desired doneness. Transfer them to a platter to rest and allow the juices to flow back into the meat. Place the skirt steak on the grill and cook for 2 minutes, then turn and cook for another minute.

Cut the steaks into ½-inch-thick slices. Arrange all the beef and chicken on a platter and serve.

Strawberry Soufflé *pictured on page 78*

SERVES 6

THE PASTRY CREAM

3 cups milk

1 vanilla bean, halved lengthwise

5 large egg yolks

½ cup sugar

⅓ cup cornstarch

2 tablespoons unsalted butter

THE SOUFFLÉS

6 tablespoons unsalted butter, melted

¼ cup sugar, for coating the ramekins,
    plus 3 tablespoons, or more to taste

2 pints strawberries, hulled and halved

2 tablespoons framboise liquor

10 large egg whites

Pinch of fine sea salt

SPECIAL EQUIPMENT

Six 6-ounce ramekins

PREP: 20 minutes — **COOK:** 45 minutes

The sweet soufflé is an overlooked dessert. It shouldn't be—it's both special enough for a dinner party and very easy. Almost everything can be done ahead of time: coating the dishes, whipping the whites, and making the strawberry puree. Before you begin to clear the table, fold the ingredients into the egg whites, dollop the mixture into the prepared dishes, and pop them in the oven. They'll be ready by the time the table is cleared and coffee is poured.

For the pastry cream, combine the milk and vanilla bean in a medium pot and bring to a simmer. Remove from the heat and set aside for 5 minutes to infuse.

Whisk together the yolks and sugar in a medium bowl. Add the cornstarch and whisk to incorporate. Temper the eggs by slowly adding ¼ cup of the hot milk to them and whisking to incorporate. Place the pot of milk over high heat and add the tempered eggs. Whisking constantly, bring to a boil and boil just until thickened. Add the butter and stir to incorporate. Transfer the cream to a bowl and place a piece of plastic film directly against the surface of the cream. Refrigerate to cool quickly.

Prepare the ramekins by brushing them with the melted butter, using upward strokes on the sides. Pour some of the sugar into each ramekin, turn the ramekin to coat the inside, and shake upside down to remove the excess. *(This can be done early in the day; refrigerate if not using immediately.)*

To prepare the puree, place the strawberries in a blender and blend at high speed until pureed. Pass the puree through a fine-mesh strainer into a saucepan. Taste the puree; if it seems a bit tart, add sugar to taste. Place the pan over medium heat, bring to a simmer, and simmer until the puree is reduced and thickened, about 30 minutes. Add the framboise. Set aside to cool.

Preheat the oven to 400°F.

Combine the pastry cream and 1 cup of the strawberry puree in a bowl and whisk to blend. Set aside.

Place the egg whites in a large bowl, add the salt, and whip them until they form soft peaks. Add the 3 tablespoons sugar in a steady stream and continue to whisk until the whites form stiff peaks when the whisk is lifted from the bowl. Be careful not to overbeat, or they will become dry. Add a little of the egg whites to the strawberry pastry cream and stir to incorporate. Carefully fold in the remaining egg whites with a rubber spatula.

Fill the prepared ramekins and smooth the tops with a spatula. Bake for 12 to 15 minutes, or until the soufflés have risen about 2 inches, are golden on top, and a skewer inserted in the center comes out clean.

Meanwhile, reheat the remaining strawberry puree in a small saucepan.

Serve the soufflés immediately. At the table, insert a spoon into the center of each one and drizzle in 1 tablespoon of the reserved sauce.

"How is it, Valentino?" Eric asks during the main course.

Valentino closes his eyes as if in prayer: "There are no words."

And later, we all crowd around the oven door, like kids with a science experiment, watching the gorgeous soufflés rise.

"Sensuousness is the most important thing in cooking," Eric says. "You can have technique but . . ."

Valentino seems to finish Eric's thought: "You can go to school to learn how to make good paintings, but if they're only technique, they won't have any poetry. They won't make people happy."

Eric says, "It's why cooking is an art. Cooking is not about construction, it's about flavor. You have to have sensitivity to the food, intuition. Without that, you are just a technician, you have nothing to say."

"A *cook*," Eric concludes, "is an instrument of nature."

Strawberry Soufflé, page 77

BE A CHEF AND YOU CAN BE ANYTHING

The best cooks I've known have also been the most beautiful to watch in action. Offering clean, beautiful presentations of perfectly cooked food, hundreds of plates each evening, they are truly dancers: combining speed with grace, economy of movement, a physical control and balance that is both athletic and intellectual, often in a brutally hot small kitchen while lesser cooks around them spill sauces, overcook food, and burn themselves. Put several great cooks on a line together and it's the "kitchen dance" cooks often refer to, a sight as compelling as ballet, or theater, or sport.

Eric has this grace, but there's something more—an innate elegance—and I'm not the only one who's struck by this. Even his cooks joke that he's "light in his loafers." This may be fundamental to being a great cook. I think Eric was born with it.

Eric Ripert, gangly youth of fifteen, no good in school, an awkward athlete, was sent to vocational school to learn a trade, cooking. He couldn't stand the kitchen there. "Mediocrity," he says now. He knew the food was garbage. He wanted instead to be a waiter. In the dining room, he saw grace and wanted to pursue it. "I loved the refinement of table service," he says. But the day his mother came with other parents for lunch, Eric spilled a tray of food on a respected general. He was banished to the kitchen.

This was all right with his mother, a distributor for a high-end fashion label. "Be a waiter and that's all you'll ever be," she advised him. "Be a chef and you can be anything."

Eric took her advice. He'd always loved to eat. And he'd cooked at his mother's apronside, devoured Grandmère Ripert's croque-monsieur, Grandmère Maguy's ravioli. Now he would take these loves and do something with them. "For me, it was Bocuse, or it was not worth doing."

How did he know this in his pimply youth? I don't know the answer except insofar as I've seen it in other people who have achieved high distinction in their profession: They recognized excellence early, then strove to emulate it.

Eric applied only to the best Paris restaurants, those carrying three Michelin stars. Tour d'Argent, one of the oldest, responded. Ripert didn't know what chervil was. The chef told him to make a thirty-yolk hollandaise and he asked, *"Qu'est-ce que c'est?"*

And so he began. He cooked staff meal there, that was his job, a hundred meals a day. When the *truite à la Hussarde* was soggy and ugly, the chef shoved all the trays off the holding counter, sending dozens of lunches cascading onto counters and floors. He learned to sauté the trout so they were crispy and beautiful. He learned the basics. And in a year he headed to Jamin, run by a chef some consider to be among the best of the century.

"Most of what I have, I owe to him," Eric says of Jamin's chef-owner, Joël Robuchon. "At the time, I thought he was God." He says Robuchon was, and is, more than a mentor. But when asked to talk about his three years with the chef, Eric, normally ebullient, grows hushed. "Robuchon," he says. "Whenever I remember Robuchon, I always see this dark, dark street."

"On Sunday afternoon, your stomach is like *woooo*," he says, recalling the anticipation of the coming work week. "You go for dinner Sunday night, and are too wound up to even see it. And then you go to bed and you don't sleep all night. You're making all the setups—'Tomorrow I'm going to start this and I'm going to start that, and I hope I'm going to get the fish early and I'm going to start that.' And you wake up—and you're *exhausted*. . . . Many times I thought I'd take the car to the airport and get out of there."

The care of the food was all but sacred, and Robuchon controlled your every moment and every movement. You didn't carry a red pepper to your station in your hand—you carried it on its own tray. Robuchon bought Bresse chickens every day, took the main shoulder muscle off each drumstick and the two oysters (the nuggets of meat on either side of the backbone)—the rest of the chicken was for staff meal. When oyster mushrooms were used, they weren't sautéed en masse—each was sautéed individually.

As poissonier, Eric made seven or eight sauces for each service—lunch and dinner, Monday through Friday—including lobster, fennel, fumet, verjus. Robuchon tasted each, and if he didn't like one, he would tell Eric to throw it out, without saying what was wrong. Eric would have to learn for himself. During service, silence from the chef was your reward; otherwise, he would harass you. Plating during service was so difficult that sometimes Robuchon himself couldn't do what he demanded of his chefs, Eric recalls.

For the oysters with a scallop enclosed in steamed spinach, served with leeks, hair-fine red pepper julienne, and foamy fennel beurre blanc, for instance, in the frenzy of service Eric would have to complete an already complicated plate with two dozen tiny dots of bright red coral sauce around the periphery of the plate, placing them not with a tiny squeeze bottle but rather off the tip of a spoon—with Robuchon shouting all the while. While such behavior is common in kitchens, Eric says that if a grain of rice came back on a plate, you were humiliated. VIP diners, Ripert says, knew among themselves, to eat every morsel "or they could destroy a cook."

"It was fear," Ripert says. "That fear eats people from inside."

And yet Robuchon treated Eric differently from the other cooks, almost paternally. Robuchon liked Eric, who was young and mischievous. He tugged at his hair, called him Coco, didn't humiliate him the way he did the other cooks. Eric could even tease the great chef.

"I wasn't the best cook there," he says. "There were many who were older and more experienced. But I charmed him."

Today, Eric remains close to Robuchon, even though he says, "When I talk about working for Robuchon, I feel like we're talking about the war." Ultimately, he says, he endured because it was a great honor to work there. It was something he knew he had to do in order to be a great chef. And he's glad he did.

Robuchon sent Eric to work for Jean-Louis Palladin in Washington, D.C., the raving, life-loving chef from Gascony who'd earned his reputation at age twenty-eight by becoming the youngest chef ever to earn two *Michelin* stars. Known throughout the cooking world simply as Jean-Louis, the bushy-haired nearsighted chef flourished in meat and offal cookery, in the powerful flavors of southwestern France.

"To me, no one equals the force he had, those flavors, the intensity," Eric says of his friend, who died in the late fall of 2001. While everything, even military duty, was a vacation compared with Robuchon, Eric worked hard for Jean-Louis and deepened his knowledge of cooking. "I learned technique from Robuchon," he says, "but Jean-Louis is my taste and spirit."

Moving from Jamin to Palladin was like being transported from a Catholic boys' school to Woodstock, Eric says. "It was the discovery of myself, the opening of my instinct. I never knew that I had talent. In France, it was taboo to say, 'I have talent.' But I discovered that what I did have was discipline. And knowledge. And with these, I developed instinct. I touch an onion, and something happens inside me. I understand the nature of that onion. I have sensitivity in my hands. The hand and the mind have to work together."

Eric had always dreamed of living in New York City—at age ten he fantasized about staying in the Waldorf, pored over New York travel brochures—and after his contractual eighteen months with Jean-Louis ended, he went to work for David Bouley, who had been a *stagiaire* at Robuchon. In 1991, Gilbert Le Coze, executive chef and owner, with his sister, Maguy, of Le Bernardin, was looking to replace chef de cuisine Eberhard Mueller. He called Eric.

Eric declined the offer. But Le Coze pursued him, and when his obligation to Bouley was completed, Eric, then twenty-six, finally accepted. He planned to take a two-week vacation before he began work. Le Coze shocked him by asking to come along. Eric agreed that they could travel in Spain together. By their return, they had cemented a friendship that would become more an older-brother–younger-brother relationship than boss-employee.

But Gilbert suddenly died of a heart attack in July 1994, at age forty-eight. "I felt like I lost someone in the family," Eric says. "We were friends, but it was a bit more. Gilbert had no children, I lost my father when I was young. It was like someone in my family passed away."

Eric had by then been in charge of the kitchen for three years, accustomed to performing under extraordinary stress. Maguy Le Coze had been very close to her brother and needed time to regroup. Food critics would soon descend, and there were rumors Le Bernardin would lose coveted *New York Times* stars. Eric kept the business going while Maguy grieved. Then, in September, he took off two weeks, before what both knew would be a stressful season. Before he left, Maguy told him that she wanted a completely new menu, one that was all his. He was ready.

"I knew what I had to do," he recalls. "I was completely focused."

Then twenty-nine, Eric was perfectly prepared for this moment. *The New York Times* ran its review in the spring of 1995: "Four stars are easier to get than to keep," Ruth Reichl wrote, making Eric the youngest chef by far to carry four stars, and he never looked back. In a matter of months, he was launched from invisible *chef de cuisine* into the realm of celebrity—acquiring a status that would inevitably carry him away from cooking itself.

Eric is spiritual in overt ways, though he is wary of talking about it—he doesn't want to sound like a flake. He meditates daily, reads Buddhist and Christian literature, is active in Freemasonry. He wears a protective copper medallion with the image of Christ and two angels on it. It was given to him when he was a teenager by a mystic who said it would protect him; he failed to wear it only once—the night he was mugged in a Paris Métro station. He believes in reincarnation, and he says that his soul is either Spanish or Latin: "You can never know a hundred percent," he admits.

When such beliefs are a part of who you are, they inform all your endeavors. Eric doesn't quite realize it yet, but his return to real cooking, his hope of combining the art he loves with the work he loves, this cooking in summertime Sag Harbor, is really the beginning of a spiritual journey.

{ **winter** }

Puerto Rico—A Spiritual Journey

"I can't go a year without visiting Puerto Rico," Eric says, explaining why we've come to San Juan in January to cook. "Puerto Rico is about the sea and the rain forest. I get rejuvenated here. I was born in Antibes in the South of France, and I've cooked all my life in French restaurants, but my spirit is Spanish-Latino. I feel at home here."

Sancocho, page 140

FLAME FOR THE COOKING SPIRITS

We arrive at the house in the mountain rain forest called El Yunque—an arrival, like most, that seems full of energy and promise. The open, airy house is ensconced in dense foliage. Wild orchids bloom, and the air is warm and moist.

Alfredo Ayala is a local chef and restaurateur Eric met long ago at Robuchon and has remained close friends with since. He has prepared a food table for us: oranges, blood oranges, mangoes, tiny limes and lemons, a variety of bananas (big and little, ripe and green), pineapple, passion fruit, guava paste and bitter orange paste, baby potatoes, spring onions; the abundant root vegetables that grow here—yautia, apio, batata, ñame; and seasonings like achiote, red seeds with a flavor not unlike cumin, used to make a bright red oil, various local and Indian spices, and herbs—the native oregano with big tough leaves, tarragon, and *cilanruel,* a strong form of cilantro. For Eric, it's like having a palette of colors. He can see the landscape of food he has to work with.

Eric lights the candles on the table. You see candles all over Puerto Rico, colorful ones in tall slender jars, and many have special purposes, the writing on them like that on holiday greeting cards (one promises to keep the house safe, another honors the Virgin Mary, another guarantees wealth and happiness); others are plain. "Flame breaks through the darkness, helps to connect you with the spirits," Eric says as he lights these.

We were not ten minutes from the airport,
heading toward the house, when Eric stopped
our two-vehicle caravan and pulled off the road
into the sand across from a shack on the beach.
His exuberance was palpable.

"I feel like I've lived here my whole life, " he
says. "Everywhere there is music in the air. It's
alive. I love the street food. You see women in
shacks on the beach with rollers in their hair,
deep-frying alcapurria and tostones and dancing
to the music."

We watch as an expressionless woman turns oblong fritters in a big black iron pot, filled with cooking fat, on a grate over a wood fire. Another half dozen of these things hang on a skewer over the fat, to stay hot. Alcapurria: Yautia, a starchy root vegetable, like a moist yam, is grated and seasoned; it's soupy-thick, like a batter. The women drop some batter onto a banana or sea grape leaf, place a spoonful of land crab meat or a beef mixture into the center, fold the leaf to shape the filling, and let it slide off the leaf into sizzling hot fat. Eric buys us all enormous green coconuts, their tops macheted off, a straw inserted for drinking the sweet water.

He says, "When I retire, I'll get a restaurant like this."

Here is where you come to be inspired. The food I love is rustic. I want to do shepherd's pie with blood sausage. My friend Alfredo has made *pique*. Pique is a sweet spicy condiment concocted from pineapple stock and fermented chiles and garlic and herbs. It's like a drug. It's delicious. If we get good-quality snapper, we'll do it raw and use pique. I put it on fish at Le Bernardin, and nobody knows why their dish tastes so good. I must find good bacalao, salt cod. And we'll make *sancocho*, a stew of beef brisket, pigs' feet, pork shoulder, and green bananas. We can do a fancy foie gras, but then we do it with mango and a rum and lime gastrique.

I cook according to the landscape, and this landscape is all about vibrant flavors—lime and ginger and chiles and sweet coco milk and bananas. It's about improvisation and cooking what this earth and this sea give you. So we'll do a snapper with lime and coco milk. And ginger oil. Ginger oil will be everywhere.

Pique

MAKES 1 QUART

2½ cups water

6 ounces pineapple skin (from 1 pineapple)

8 tiny green hot peppers, such as
   Thai chiles

4 tiny red hot peppers, such as Thai chiles

1 garlic clove, peeled

1 oregano sprig

1 teaspoon peppercorns

½ teaspoon sugar

Pinch of fine sea salt

2 tablespoons extra virgin olive oil,
   or as needed

SPECIAL EQUIPMENT

Heatproof narrow-necked bottle

PREP: 10 minutes, plus 1 week standing time — COOK: 20 minutes

This amazing concoction seems to grow right out of the earth here. It is as natural as the air and has the spirit of fire. It begins with pineapple scraps. You boil the skin of a pineapple and then pour the liquid into a bottle packed with hot, hot, hot peppers, garlic, oregano, peppercorns, and top it off with a barrier of olive oil in the bottleneck. Set it in the sun to ferment for a week, and it's good to go. Pour it on sancocho. Pour it on beans, on rice. Over alcapurria. On fish. It's a colorful flavor, sweet and hot and full of life.

"Pique and ginger oil go everywhere," Eric says the first night.

Combine the water and pineapple skin in a saucepan and bring to a boil. Take off the heat and infuse for 5 minutes, then strain. Discard the pineapple skin.

Bring a large pot of water to a boil. Submerge a heatproof bottle in the water to sterilize it. Remove with tongs and let dry on a rack.

Make a ½-inch slit near the stem in each of the hot peppers, Add the peppers, garlic, oregano, peppercorns, sugar, and salt to the bottle. Cover with the pineapple-infused water. Slowly add the olive oil. The olive oil should completely cover the pique; if it does not, add more to cover.

Leave the bottle open for 1 week on your countertop, covered loosely with cheesecloth. Throughout the week, bubbles will rise to the top. After a week, the bubbles will have subsided. Seal the bottle and refrigerate. Pique should keep for up to a month.

Ginger Oil

MAKES 1½ CUPS

½ pound ginger, peeled and minced

1 cup canola oil

PREP: 10 minutes

Ginger oil is something that everybody should have in reach as a part of one's seasoning array, right next to lemon confit. It's these little flavor boosters that make your dishes sparkle, that push an ordinary dish to a new level.

Ginger oil, like any flavored oil, is an essence, the essence of ginger, a powerful but not overpowering flavor. You have to be careful when using it—too much and the dish can taste soapy—and you wouldn't want to sauté with it. But as a flavoring device at the end of cooking, it's magical. Or use it as seasoning on raw fish. It's beautiful on salad, on vegetables. Add it to soups and stews, such as a pot-au-feu. Drizzle it over rice. It gives a dish that Why-do-I-like-this? intrigue.

Put the ginger in a clean jar and add the oil. Let stand at room temperature for at least 2 hours, or refrigerate overnight, before using.

Store the oil in the refrigerator, for up to 2 weeks.

Coconut Milk

MAKES ABOUT 1 CUP

1 coconut

¼ to ½ cup tepid water (if necessary)

PREP: 15 minutes

You can use coconut milk in a can, but it's not the same as fresh coco milk, which is not difficult to make. Find coconuts that are very fresh, with plenty of liquid inside. Crack them open, reserve the liquid, and peel the flesh. Alfredo's technique of holding the coconut over a flame makes it easy to peel. Then blend or puree the flesh with the coconut water and strain.

To open the coconut, place an ice pick or screwdriver in one of the eyes of the coconut and hit with a hammer. Allow the coconut liquid to drain into a bowl; reserve.

Split the coconut in half. To remove the flesh, either hold the pieces shell side down over a gas flame for 2 minutes or roast on a baking sheet in a 400°F oven for 5 minutes. The flesh will separate from the shell. Peel off the brown skin and roughly chop the flesh.

Place the coconut flesh in a blender with the reserved liquid and pulse to puree. If the mixture seems too dry, add the water and pulse until incorporated. Pass through a fine-mesh sieve, pressing hard to extract all liquid. Store, refrigerated, for up to 2 days.

COCO MILK

I love coco milk in cooking. It's an amazingly versatile product. You can cook in it, poach in it, add it to sauces, soups, and stews. Coco milk can be a substitute for cream. It's sweet without being sugary, rich without being heavy, and it has a subtle intriguing flavor. You can use it like butter in a sauce, to enrich it. It rounds out flavors, takes the edges off. When you are making a traditional stew, for instance, and it's a bit too sharp, traditionally you would make a gastrique—a sweet-sour sauce—and then *monter au beurre*, emulsify butter into the stew. Coco milk can replace the gastrique and the butter.

And it takes acidity well. When you make a blanquette de veau, for instance, a traditional veal stew, you add lemon juice at the end. Adding it too early can sour the cream in a sauce, make it taste almost cheesy. I will be banished from France for saying this, but coco milk would work beautifully in a blanquette de veau.

The flesh of the coconut is excellent as well. I love the bite, the feel on my gums. Coconuts make my mouth water. I like to use coco milk, but I have waited until now, when we are in Puerto Rico, where coconuts are part of the landscape.

We'd traveled all day and I was working with an unfamiliar stove, so for our first night I needed to make a simple dish. The key to both the simplicity and the amazing flavor of this dish is the gentle poaching in a coco milk *nage*. The nage—cooking liquid that becomes a loose abundant sauce—is first flavored with shallot, garlic, and lemongrass. I season the fillets with salt and pepper, but also with a light dusting of curry powder, then add the fillets to the hot broth and pop the dish into a hot oven for five or ten minutes, and it's done. Squeeze some lime juice over it, sprinkle with cilantro, and serve with white rice.

For dessert, simple again—fruit with fresh herbs, enhanced with a splash of alcohol. The fruit is so beautiful here you don't need to do anything to it, and the Puerto Rican tarragon is powerful and sweet.

Poached Snapper with Coconut Milk and Tomatoes

1 tablespoon canola oil

3 shallots, minced

2 garlic cloves, minced

1 tablespoon minced lemongrass
(tender inner leaves only)

3 ripe tomatoes, seeded and
cut into ¼-inch dice

1 cup coconut milk, fresh (page 98)
or canned

Six 5-ounce red snapper fillets

Fine sea salt and freshly ground
white pepper

1 teaspoon curry powder

1 lime, halved, one half cut into
6 thin slices, the remaining half
reserved for juice

12 cilantro leaves

4 cups hot cooked white rice

PREP: 20 minutes — **COOK:** 10 minutes

When you arrive in a new place, you take your inspiration straight out of the air. Here the tropical moistness makes you think of lime juice and coco milk, tropical flavors, perfect for one of Puerto Rico's most abundant and treasured fish.

Preheat the oven to 400°F.

Warm the canola oil in a medium pot over medium heat. Add the shallots, garlic, and lemongrass and cook until tender and softened, 5 to 7 minutes; do not allow it to color. Add the tomatoes and coconut milk and simmer until the tomatoes release their juices and are soft, about 5 minutes.

Place the tomato mixture in a casserole or baking dish large enough to accommodate all the snapper fillets in a single layer. Generously season each fillet with salt and pepper and a pinch of curry powder. Place the snapper in the casserole. Top each fillet with a lime slice and 2 cilantro leaves.

Bake for 7 to 8 minutes: To test for doneness, insert a metal skewer in the thickest part of the fish for 5 seconds. Hold the skewer against the inside of your wrist; if the skewer is warm, the fish is done.

To serve, spoon about ¼ cup of the tomato mixture onto each warmed plate and top with a snapper fillet. Squeeze lime juice over each plate. Serve with the rice on the side.

Mango, Passion Fruit, and Tarragon Salad

3 mangoes, cut into ½-inch cubes

1 passion fruit, halved, flesh scooped out,
and shells discarded

1 blood orange, peeled and sectioned
(you can substitute a mandarin orange
or clementine)

1 tablespoon anisette or other licorice-
flavored liqueur

1 tablespoon tarragon leaves

1 tablespoon grenadine syrup

PREP: 15 minutes

Combine the mangoes, passion fruit, and blood orange sections in a large bowl and toss to mix. Drizzle the anisette over the fruit and toss to combine. Scatter the tarragon over the fruit salad. Refrigerate for 20 to 30 minutes.

Just before serving, drizzle the grenadine over the salad. Serve chilled.

A quiet afternoon, Eric's gears grinding away, imagining what to cook; Andrea organizing the kitchen like a sauté station, knives, oils, and seasonings aligned, counters wiped down; Valentino sketching in the humid air. The terrain reminds Valentino of where he grew up, on the coffee plantation, and this energizes him. He faces south toward the mountain, then west, then north, then east, changing seats and vantages, indoors and out, but he doesn't change the thick sheet of paper he's sketching on. The kitchen and cupboards, the mountain foliage, the orchids creeping in the window, they all morph into a single image.

"Everything is happening at the same time," he says. "Things are appearing and going away."

The same dynamic works in Eric's mind as he surveys the cornucopia table, candles flickering, but there's an urgency in his demeanor that Valentino doesn't share. He has brought a basket of pear tomatoes to the kitchen. His mind is stuck on a soy-lime flavor for the crab. "If I do that, I can't use avocado." He shakes his head. "I'm wasting time because I'm indecisive. Andrea, we just do a tomato vinaigrette."

Andrea makes it, and it's beautiful and so simple as to seem incredible: three tomatoes blended with olive oil, pressed through a strainer, mixed with vinegar, and seasoned with salt and pepper. That's it—tomato vinaigrette, a.k.a. gazpacho sauce.

From out of nowhere, it seems, Eric decides to use green tomato for the crab, finely diced and marinated with oil, lemon confit, pique, salt, and pepper. It will be almost crunchy, resting brightly on the cylinder of crabmeat, which is simply mixed with mayo. (Eric likes jarred American mayonnaise. "It's very good," he says, smiling at the plain fact of it.) Crab with a green tomato top, a plate sauced with Andrea's tomato vinaigrette, and avocado.

Tomatoes at the market, they're usually green. Maybe it's so hot here they have to pick them that way or they become damaged on the way to the market. They have a wonderful crunchy texture then but they don't have much flavor, so we have to add the flavor by marinating them with lemon confit, oil, salt. The tomato vinaigrette is very simple and delicious. I'm glad I didn't waste our time with a soy-lime vinaigrette; I don't know what I was thinking. Sometimes you fix on something and have to know when to let it go.

Crab Salad with Chilled Gazpacho Sauce

SERVES 6

3 large tomatoes, seeded and
   roughly chopped

3 tablespoons extra virgin olive oil

2 tablespoons sherry vinegar

Fine sea salt and freshly ground
   white pepper

2 green tomatoes

3 tablespoons bottled lemon oil

1 tablespoon minced Lemon Confit
   (page 21)

1 teaspoon Pique (page 96)

3 tablespoons Vinaigrette (page 205)

3 tablespoons mayonnaise

¾ pound lump crabmeat, picked over
   for shells and cartilage

2 tablespoons thinly sliced chives

2 avocados

Gray sea salt and freshly ground
   white pepper for garnish

SPECIAL EQUIPMENT

Six 2-inch by 1½-inch-high ring molds

PREP: 25 minutes

For the sauce, combine the chopped tomatoes and olive oil in a blender and pulse to puree. Don't incorporate too much air, or the puree will lose its bright red color. Pass the puree through a strainer, pushing against the solids to extract as much tomato pulp as possible. Add the vinegar and season to taste with salt and pepper. Cover and refrigerate.

Using a vegetable peeler, peel the green tomatoes. Remove the cores and halve them crosswise. Scoop out the seeds and finely chop the tomatoes. Transfer them to a bowl and add the lemon oil, lemon confit, and pique. Season to taste with salt and pepper. Cover and refrigerate until ready to serve.

In a large bowl, combine the vinaigrette and mayonnaise and whisk until smooth. Add the crabmeat and chives and gently stir to combine. Season to taste with salt and pepper. Cover and refrigerate until ready to serve.

Just before serving, halve, pit, and peel the avocados. Cut each half into 3 slices. Cut each slice crosswise on the diagonal.

To serve, place a ring mold just left of center on each plate. Divide the crab mixture evenly among the molds. Top with the green tomato salad. Spoon the gazpacho sauce around the mold on each plate. Place one-sixth of the sliced avocados just right of center of each. Season the avocado with gray salt and pepper. Remove the ring molds and serve immediately.

Rabbit Curry with Caribbean Garnish

SERVES 6

THE RABBIT

Two 3- to 4-pound rabbits

¼ cup canola oil

2 onions, 1 thinly sliced, 1 diced

8 garlic cloves, 3 halved, 5 thinly sliced

6 cups water

Fine sea salt and freshly ground
   white pepper

3 tablespoons curry powder

All-purpose flour for dusting

2 tablespoons minced ginger

1 cup coconut milk, fresh (page 98)
   or canned

1 tablespoon finely grated lime zest

THE GARNISH

½ cup diced (¼-inch) pineapple

1 mango, cut into ¼-inch dice

1 banana, cut into ¼-inch dice

½ cup diced (¼-inch) seeded tomato

½ cup sliced almonds,
   toasted in a dry skillet

½ cup shredded coconut,
   toasted in a dry skillet

4 cups hot cooked white rice

PREP: 30 minutes — **COOK:** 2 hours

Cut each rabbit into 5 pieces: 2 shoulders, 2 legs, and the saddle. Remove the rib cage from each saddle and roughly chop the bones. Reserve the bones. Cut the saddles in half.

Place a medium heavy-bottomed pan over medium-high heat, add 2 tablespoons of the canola oil, and heat until hot. Sear the rabbit bones, turning occasionally, until golden brown, about 10 minutes. Lower the heat to medium, add the sliced onion and 3 halved garlic cloves, and cook for 3 to 5 minutes, or until translucent. Add the water, bring to a simmer, and simmer for 1 hour, skimming any foam that rises to the top. Strain the stock and reserve; you should have at least 3 cups.

Place a heavy-bottomed casserole over high heat and add 2 tablespoons of the canola oil. Season the rabbit with salt, pepper, and a pinch of the curry powder. Dust the rabbit with flour. When the oil is hot, add the rabbit pieces and sear, turning once, until golden brown, about 4 minutes on each side. Transfer to a platter. Add the diced onion and sliced garlic and sweat until they are traslucent but not colored.

Add the reserved stock to the pot, stirring to scrape up any browned bits on the bottom. Return the rabbit pieces to the pot, add the ginger and the remaining curry powder, and bring to a boil. Lower the heat to a simmer and cook for 1 hour.

Add the coconut milk and continue to simmer for 45 minutes to 1 hour, until the rabbit is tender. Stir in the lime zest.

Meanwhile, just before serving, place the pineapple, mango, banana, tomato, almonds, coconut, and cooked rice in serving bowls.

Divide the rabbit pieces among six plates. Spoon the sauce over all. Pass the garnishes and rice at the table for your guests to add as they wish.

Eric makes a simple rabbit stew, with curry powder. The dish takes some time—first to butcher the rabbit, then to brown the bones and use them to make a stock, or braising liquid. But it's standard stewing technique—seasoning the meat, browning it, adding the liquid. It's not a surprise when Eric throws in more coconut milk. And lime zest. The rest is a Caribbean flourish of raw fruits and almonds. It's served with rice— Alfredo cooks it Puerto Rican style, simmering it uncovered till the liquid is gone, then allowing the rice to stick to the bottom of the pan and cook into a crust. He'll scrape this off and put the crunchy rice in a separate bowl to share, a delicacy.

"Alfredo," Eric calls out as he butchers the rabbit, "in the Hamptons, we had a rabbit. It cooked in five minutes and tasted like the flour they fed the poor creature."

It's customary in Puerto Rico to throw the meat in the pot with the stock and seasonings, to simply boil it. But I do it the more traditional way: browning the meat, then adding the curry and toasting it before adding the liquid. You can add more curry at the end if you want more powerful flavors, but it's always a good idea to toast your seasonings first. The tougher the rabbit, the longer you need to cook it—and in this case, the longer the better, because the meat and the bones enrich the stew.

Black Bean and Coconut Milk Soup

½ **pound dried black beans, soaked**
    overnight in water to cover generously

3 **ounces prosciutto, in one piece**

1 **carrot, peeled and halved**

1 **onion, peeled and halved**

6 **garlic cloves, peeled**

1 **thyme sprig**

8 **cups water**

Fine sea salt and freshly ground
    white pepper

¾ **cup coconut milk, fresh (page 98)**
    or canned

4 **tablespoons unsalted butter**

3 **tablespoons Pique (page 96)**

1 **lime, halved**

3 **tablespoons sour cream**

1 **tablespoon cilantro julienne**

PREP: 20 minutes — **COOK:** 1 hour and 15 minutes

Black bean soup with coco milk—this is interesting. The coco milk keeps surprising me. It works like butter but gives a light Caribbean flavor. Also, it smooths out the tannic and starchy sensations of the beans. In the South of France, we finish black beans with sherry vinegar to make the flavors sparkle. But here we finish with lime. Don't forget to eat the prosciutto that cooked in the bean water—that one bite by itself is almost worth cooking the whole pot of beans.

Drain the beans. In a large pot, combine the beans, prosciutto, carrot, onion, garlic, and thyme. Cover with the water and bring to a boil, then lower the heat and simmer until the beans are tender, about 1 hour. Halfway through the cooking time, season with salt and pepper.

Remove the prosciutto, carrot, onion, garlic, and thyme. (Save the prosciutto for a cook's treat.) Drain the beans, reserving the cooking liquid. Transfer the beans to a blender in batches and puree, adding 2 cups of the reserved cooking liquid as necessary.

Return the soup to the pot and bring to a simmer. Add the coconut milk, butter, and pique and stir to incorporate. If the soup is too thick, add additional cooking liquid.

Just before serving, squeeze the lime juice into the soup and stir to incorporate. Ladle into bowls and garnish with a dollop of sour cream in the center of each bowl and a sprinkling of cilantro.

Citrus Gelatin with Guanabana Sauce

SERVES 6

3 cups chardonnay

2 cups fresh grapefruit juice

2 cups fresh orange juice

1 vanilla bean, halved lengthwise

One 2-inch piece of ginger, peeled

¼ cup sugar

4 gelatin sheets

**¾ cup fresh or thawed frozen
guanabana puree**

**¼ cup coconut milk, fresh (page 98)
or canned**

**2 teaspoons anisette
(or any licorice-flavored liqueur)**

3 oranges, sectioned

1 tablespoon basil julienne

PREP: 10 minutes, plus 3 hours chilling time — COOK: 30 minutes

I like this dessert because it's such an easy concept that can be reproduced in countless forms. Vary the fruit, the wine, the puree on top, and you've got any kind of flavor combination the occasion or place calls for. The key is the consistency of those flavors. You don't want a Jell-O and Cool Whip effect. What makes this a lovely and deceptively simple dessert is the light texture of the gelled citrus.

In a small pot, bring the chardonnay to a boil. Reduce to 1 cup.

Combine the grapefruit and orange juice in another pot, add the vanilla bean, ginger, and 2 tablespoons of the sugar, and bring to a boil. Lower the heat and reduce to 2 cups. Strain.

Combine the two reductions. Add the gelatin sheets and stir until dissolved. Transfer to a bowl and refrigerate until set, at least 3 hours.

Meanwhile, for the sauce, combine the guanabana puree, the remaining 2 tablespoons sugar, the coconut milk, and anisette.

With a sharp knife, slice the top and bottom of each orange. Stand each orange on a cutting board and slice off the peel and bitter white pith. Working over a bowl, slice between the membranes to release the segments.

To serve, divide the orange sections among six chilled martini glasses. Spoon the gelatin over the orange sections. Drizzle the sauce over and sprinkle with the basil julienne.

Citrus gelatin with guanabana puree—a very refreshing dessert: chardonnay, and orange and grapefruit juice, cooked down and gelled. We made a puree of this enormous prickly-skinned fruit which was bursting with sweetness. If you can't find it fresh, it is available frozen, and it's surprisingly good.

This kind of cooking, it's like a car turning on ice—you have to find a way to make sure you don't crash into a tree. I'm glad I was no good in school and became a cook. I get to do *this*. But I'm nervous, too.

"I'm going to do a dessert!" Eric proclaims, padding to the balcony with a morning coffee in the cool tropical air. Eric struggles with desserts, and here the oven is broken, complicating the situation. He loves to eat desserts, but he could never be a pastry chef. He has no sense of dough, of sugar. "I don't feel it."

"I'm going to do a crêpe," he says, "and then I don't know. There's a lot of recipes for today. My notes say shrimp, chicken, crêpes with pineapple, pique. I want Alfredo to do more pique. Shepherd's pie with blood sausage, black bean cake, and then we'll do the tostones with caviar."

We won't do half that, but Eric is a list maker, and many things are possible in list form.

Discussion of lunch moves to escabeche, which Eric has had in his head all along. Traditionally, the term refers to a vinegar marinade poured over fried fish. Eric uses the term as a kind of all-purpose description of sweet and hot peppers cooked in vinegar and oil, then poured over whatever it is you're serving.

He asks Alfredo, "Do you ever do an escabeche like this with starch?"

"*Sí, sí,*" says Alfredo, who notes it's simply served over boiled root vegetables with herbs. "And we serve it with bacalao."

"*Con bacalao?*" asks Eric.

"*Sí.*"

"*Ah, con bacalao,*" Eric says, smiling. "That's a good idea, man."

"Sometimes a hard-boiled egg," Alfredo says, "some avocado, that's a typical—"

"Maybe an egg yolk, raw?"

"*Sí.*"

Eric is immediately productive and dispatches the shrimp in a simple pleasing dish, similar to the snapper (see page 101) in technique. He makes a broth, then seasons the shrimp with cilantro, scallion, ginger, and cayenne and cooks them just until rare. They finish cooking in warmed soup plates with the hot broth poured over them, with a garnish of calabaza squash and avocado.

The first of the day's escabeche preparations is one with tuna. Olive oil and sherry vinegar, with onion, garlic, thyme, bay leaves, and hot pepper, are brought to a simmer, pear tomatoes are added and cooked briefly, and it is removed from the heat to cool. This becomes the sauce for seared tuna, an easy, bright dish. The simplicity with which Eric's pulling this stuff off, and the strength and balance of the flavors, is thrilling.

Plates are cleared and Eric moves into the bacalao and root vegetable escabeche. He first boils the salt cod and root vegetables, then cooks the escabeche—onion, garlic, hot pepper, bay leaf, and thyme sweated, then simmered briefly in sherry vinegar and oil. Alfredo tells Eric to cut the root vegetables into big chunks—Eric had wanted to cut them into a smaller dice, but he says, "Okay, if you say so." The salt cod is broken up and marinated in a pepper, scallion, tomato, and pique combination, and the cooked vegetables are marinated in the warm escabeche.

Eric and Andrea plate the simple dish. The salt cod, finished with lemon juice, is placed on top of the vegetable escabeche. But the vegetables are too big, and that dilutes the impact of the escabeche, making each bite taste more starchy than it ought to be. The julienned pineapple, cooked in brown sugar and butter and served in rum-scented crêpes with crème fraîche, is a good idea but it's too sweet. Both will be fixed, but for now disappointment lingers in the air.

Bacalao and (too chunky) Tropical Root Vegetable Escabeche, page 114

Shrimp with Fresh Coconut Milk, Calabaza, and Avocado

SERVES 6

THE BROTH

1 tablespoon unsalted butter

2 shallots, thinly sliced

3 garlic cloves, thinly sliced

1 lemongrass stalk, thinly sliced

One 1-inch piece of ginger, thinly sliced

1 kaffir lime leaf

3 cups chicken stock

¾ cup coconut milk, fresh (page 98)
   or canned

4 cilantro sprigs

Fine sea salt and freshly ground
   white pepper

THE SHRIMP

2 tablespoons chopped cilantro

2 tablespoons chopped scallion

2 tablespoons chopped ginger

2 tablespoons canola oil

36 large shrimp, peeled and deveined

⅛ teaspoon cayenne pepper

1 medium calabaza squash
   (found in Latino markets; you can
   substitute butternut squash)

1 tablespoon unsalted butter

1 avocado

1 lime, halved

PREP: 35 minutes — COOK: 35 minutes

To make the broth, melt the butter in a small sauté pan over medium heat. Add the shallots, garlic, lemongrass, ginger, and kaffir lime leaf and cook until tender; do not allow them to color. Add the chicken stock and bring to a boil. Lower the heat and simmer for 15 minutes.

Add the coconut milk and cilantro and simmer for 5 minutes. Season to taste with salt and pepper. Strain through a fine-mesh sieve and set aside.

For the shrimp, combine the cilantro, scallion, ginger, and oil in a large bowl. Season the shrimp generously with salt, pepper, and the cayenne pepper and add to the bowl, tossing to coat the shrimp with the cilantro mixture. Place the shrimp on a baking sheet, making sure they are not touching one another, cover with plastic wrap, and refrigerate.

Peel the squash with a chef's knife. Cut the squash into ½-inch cubes; you will need at least 60 cubes.

Combine the butter and ½ cup water in a small saucepan and place over medium heat. When the butter has melted, add the squash dice, season with salt and pepper, and cook at a simmer until the squash is tender, about 10 minutes. Let cool to room temperature.

Divide the squash cubes among six ovenproof soup bowls, leaving space to alternate with the avocado dice (which you will prepare just before serving). Set aside. *(You can cover the bowls with plastic wrap and refrigerate until you are ready to serve the shrimp, up to 3 hours.)*

Preheat the oven to 350°F. Remove the bowls from the refrigerator.

Shortly before serving (to prevent the avocado from browning), halve, pit, and peel the avocado. Cut into ½-inch cubes and place 10 pieces in each of the prepared soup plates, alternating with the squash.

Place the shrimp in the oven for 4 minutes, or until just barely cooked. During the last minute of cooking, put the prepared soup bowls in the oven to heat.

Meanwhile, reheat the reserved sauce over medium heat.

To serve, place 6 shrimp in each bowl, to form a pinwheel. Spoon about ¼ cup of the sauce over the shrimp and squeeze the lime juice over all the bowls. Serve immediately.

Seared Tuna with Escabeche of Pear Tomatoes

SERVES 6

THE ESCABECHE

½ cup extra virgin olive oil

1 onion, thinly sliced

1 head garlic, cloves separated, peeled,
   and thinly sliced

1 thyme sprig

1 bay leaf

One ¼-inch slice of Scotch Bonnet or
   similar hot pepper

Fine sea salt and freshly ground
   white pepper

½ cup sherry vinegar

1 pint yellow pear tomatoes, halved

1 pint red pear tomatoes, halved

THE TUNA

Four 8-ounce tuna steaks, 1 inch thick

Fine sea salt and freshly ground
   white pepper

1½ tablespoons thyme leaves

2 tablespoons extra virgin olive oil

PREP: 20 minutes — **COOK:** 30 minutes, plus 1 hour marinating time

For the escabeche, heat ¼ cup of the olive oil in a sauté pan over medium heat. When the oil is warm, add the onion, garlic, thyme, bay leaf, and hot pepper, season with salt and pepper, and cook until the onion slices are softened and nicely browned, about 10 minutes.

Deglaze the pan with the sherry vinegar, scraping up any browned bits on the bottom, raise the heat, and bring to a boil. Add the remaining ¼ cup olive oil and return to a boil. Add the tomatoes and return to a boil. Take off the heat and let cool for 10 minutes, then season to taste with salt and pepper. Let stand at room temperature for at least an hour, or overnight in the refrigerator.

For the tuna, place two large nonstick sauté pans over high heat. Season each tuna steak on both sides with salt and pepper, sprinkle with about 1 teaspoon of the thyme leaves, drizzle with 1½ teaspoons of the olive oil. When the pans are hot, place 2 steaks in each pan and sear, turning once, until golden brown, about 2 minutes per side. The tuna should still be rare in the center.

To serve, remove the thyme, bay leaf, and hot pepper and divide the escabeche equally among six plates. Slice the tuna steaks into ½-inch-thick slices and fan 4 or 5 slices in the center of each plate. Serve immediately.

Bacalao and Tropical Root Vegetable Escabeche pictured on page 111

SERVES 6

THE ROOT VEGETABLES

1 yuca, peeled and cut into ½-inch dice
  (you can substitute a potato)

1 yautia, peeled and cut into ½-inch dice
  (you can substitute turnip)

1 apio (taro root), peeled and cut into
  ½-inch dice (you can substitute
  celery root)

1 batata, peeled and cut into ½-inch dice
  (you can substitute sweet potato)

1 cup extra virgin olive oil

1 onion, thinly sliced

1 head garlic, cloves separated, peeled,
  and thinly sliced

1 hot pepper, such as Scotch Bonnet,
  halved

1 bay leaf

1 thyme sprig

Fine sea salt and freshly ground
  white pepper

½ cup aged sherry vinegar

THE BACALAO

1 pound salt cod, soaked in cold water
  to cover for at least 24 hours in the
  refrigerator; change the water at least
  3 times

¼ cup extra virgin olive oil

1 Italian frying pepper, halved lengthwise,
  seeded, and cut into thin strips

3 tablespoons sliced scallions
  (white part only)

1 tomato, seeded and cut into ¼-inch dice

½ teaspoon Pique (page 96), or to taste

1 avocado

1 lemon, halved

PREP: 20 minutes, plus 24 hours soaking time — COOK: 30 minutes, plus 30 minutes marinating time

Place all the root vegetables in a pot of cold water with 2 tablespoons salt. Bring to a boil, then lower the heat to a simmer and cook until the vegetables are tender, 20 to 25 minutes. Drain and transfer to a platter.

While the vegetables are cooking, place ¼ cup of the olive oil in a medium sauté pan over medium heat. Add the onions, garlic, hot pepper, bay leaf, and thyme, season with salt and pepper, and sauté until golden, about 10 minutes. Deglaze the pan with the sherry vinegar and bring to a boil, scraping up any browned bits on the bottom. Add the remaining ¼ cup olive oil and bring to a boil. Take off the heat and let cool for 10 minutes.

Pour the sherry vinegar mixture over the vegetables and marinate for at least 30 minutes at room temperature.

Meanwhile, drain the salt cod, place in a pot, and cover with water. Bring to a boil, lower the heat, and simmer until the cod is tender but not falling apart, about 30 minutes; drain.

Break the cod into medallions and place in a large bowl. Add the olive oil, frying pepper, scallions, tomato, and pique and toss well. Marinate at room temperature for at least 30 minutes.

To serve, halve, pit, and peel the avocado. Cut into ½-inch dice and add to the vegetable escabeche. Divide the escabeche among six bowls. Squeeze the lemon juice over the salt cod and gently stir to incorporate. Top the escabeche with the salt cod.

Caramelized Pineapple Crêpes with Crème Fraîche

SERVES 6

THE CRÊPES

6 tablespoons unsalted butter

¾ cup all-purpose flour

2 tablespoons sugar

½ teaspoon fine sea salt

3 large eggs

1½ cups milk

2 tablespoons dark rum

THE SAUCE

1 cup crème fraîche

1 tablespoon sugar

1 vanilla bean, halved lengthwise

About 2 tablespoons unsalted butter

THE FILLING

½ cup sugar

4 tablespoons unsalted butter

2 tablespoons dark rum

1 pineapple, peeled, cored, and cut into julienne

PREP: 30 minutes — **COOK:** 35 minutes, plus 1 hour resting time

For the crêpes, melt the 6 tablespoons of butter in a small pot over medium heat. Simmer the butter until the milk solids turn brown. Set aside.

Sift the flour, sugar, and salt together into a bowl. Make a well in the dry ingredients, add the eggs, and whisk until incorporated. Whisk in the milk. Whisk in the browned butter and rum. Cover the batter and let rest in the refrigerator for at least an hour.

Meanwhile, for the sauce, whisk the crème fraîche lightly with the sugar until it becomes liquid. Scrape the beans from the vanilla pod and stir them gently into the crème fraîche. Cover and refrigerate until ready to serve.

To cook the crêpes, melt ½ teaspoon butter in an 8-inch nonstick sauté pan over medium-high heat. Ladle in ¼ cup of the crêpe batter and swirl to distribute it evenly. Cook for 1 minute, or until it is golden on the bottom. Flip the crêpe and cook for another minute, or until golden on the second side. Transfer to a plate and repeat with the remaining batter, adding more butter to the pan as necessary and stacking the cooked crêpes. You will need a total of 12 crêpes. Wrap the crêpes in plastic film until ready to serve.

For the filling, melt the sugar in a medium pot over medium-high heat, then simmer gently until the sugar has caramelized and is deep brown. Add the butter and rum and whisk to incorporate. Add the pineapple and cook until it is well coated and tender. Remove from the heat.

To assemble the dessert, place a crêpe on a work surface and spread ¼ cup of the pineapple down the center. Roll up the crêpe and place on a plate with the seam down. Continue with the remaining crêpes, placing 2 crêpes on each plate. Drizzle the crème fraîche over the crepes. Serve immediately.

el chillo

Eric awakes from an uncustomary nap after lunch. He is worried. He doesn't have the variety of ingredients he's used to. He calls the restaurant—What do they have that can be overnighted to us? He paces in the gathering dusk, cell phone to his ear, and when he hangs up, he speaks to Andrea and me. "Should we struggle with what we can find at the market," he asks, "or should I get a shipment from New York?" He is tired, that's all. Andrea and I think it would be better to work with what we have, and Eric agrees.

He has been cooking goat all day long and it retains its tree-bark toughness—"It's still the same, the *$@@!" Eric says after stewing the meat for six hours. But he tends it, meditating on other matters, while adding nutmeg to the developing stew—arrestingly fresh nutmeg, straight from its shell—and thinks what he wants to do for dinner tonight. That chicken stuffed with vermicelli, like he'd had in Morocco. Let's get that going, he thinks. Use those anchovies, somehow. He opens the fridge, studies it for a minute, and says, "And we'll do something with the snapper."

Alfredo had gone to see some fisherman this morning and he returned with beautiful snapper. Red snapper, called *chillo,* is perhaps the most popular fish in Puerto Rico. When a married man or woman has a lover, the lover is called a *chillo,* or *chilla.* In the afternoon, Alfredo and I took the fish down to the creek and scaled it.

Eric decides to fillet the snapper so that it's ready when he needs it. It's dark now, and the fatigue and discouragement that set in at lunch linger. Eric ties an apron around his waist and stands in the kitchen with feet spread, back arched, as he steels his long thin slicing knife.

"We take the knives in the kitchen for granted," he says, "but really they are beautiful objects." He loves most his slicing knife—its proportions, its design, the weight of it, the flexibility of the stiff blade, which he continues to steel. "It really pisses me off when people in the kitchen don't take care of their knives, don't keep them sharp."

He draws his knife down the back of the first snapper to remove the top fillet, then lays the fillet skin side down on his cutting board. The flesh is pink and translucent. He runs his fingers over it and says, "Wow." He cuts off a small slice and eats it. It is beautiful. He had had no plan for what he would do with it, but he knows immediately upon tasting. "We'll do a ceviche like they do in Peru," he says.

And he doesn't mean later—this fish is so beautiful, he must do it immediately. He butchers quickly and efficiently. He cleans his board, places two skinned fillets on it, thinly slices them on the bias, and sets the fish aside in a bowl. He quickly slices an onion, then grabs some cilantro and juliennes it. He adds these to the snapper, slices some limes, and squeezes a slice in each hand high over the bowl. Salt and white pepper. A few drops of pique. He tosses the ceviche and asks, "Alfredo, we have martini glasses?" Alfredo grabs the glasses, we shine them, and set them on the counter. Eric spoons the snapper, which the lime has "cooked" to milky white, into each glass and, suddenly, we are eating: The fish is miraculous.

Everyone is eating and smiling and tasting and talking about this dish. The failure of the lunch has been surmounted. The air feels suddenly charged with energy and we are alert. Eric is not given to overly praising his own food, but here he says, "This may be the masterpiece of the trip." But I think he is just happy again. Good food makes you happy. The evening has changed.

Snapper Ceviche

Serves 6

1¼ pounds snapper fillets, skinned
¼ cup thinly sliced red onion
3 tablespoons cilantro julienne
Fine sea salt and freshly ground
  white pepper
3 limes, halved
Pique (page 96) to taste

PREP: 15 minutes, plus 2 minutes marinating time

Slice the snapper as thin as possible on the bias (you want slices about 2 inches long by 1 inch wide). Cover and refrigerate until just before serving.

When ready to serve, place the snapper in a large bowl, add the onion and cilantro, and toss to combine. Season generously with salt and pepper. Squeeze the limes over the snapper and toss well. Add pique to taste and toss again. Marinate the ceviche for 2 minutes, to allow juices to be released from the snapper.

To serve, divide the snapper evenly among six martini glasses. Serve with warm toasts.

Marinated Anchovies and Baby Romaine "Caesar" Salad pictured on page 120

Serves 6

31 good-quality anchovies packed
  in extra virgin olive oil
2 teaspoons fresh lemon juice
3 garlic cloves
Fine sea salt and freshly ground
  white pepper
1 large egg yolk
¾ cup extra virgin olive oil
¼ cup canola oil
1 loaf Italian bread, crusts removed,
  cut into ½-inch cubes
3 heads baby romaine or
  1 large romaine head

PREP: 15 minutes

For the dressing, place 1 anchovy, the lemon juice, 1 garlic clove, ¼ teaspoon salt, and ⅛ teaspoon pepper in a blender and process to a smooth paste. Add the yolk and process until combined. With the blender on medium speed, slowly drizzle in ½ cup of the olive oil and all of the canola oil. Adjust the seasoning. If the dressing is too thick, thin it with water. Refrigerate.

For the croutons, heat the remaining ¼ cup extra virgin olive oil and the remaining 2 garlic cloves in a large sauté pan over medium heat until just shimmering. Add the bread cubes and toss to coat with the garlic oil. Remove the garlic cloves as they turn brown, or they will give an unpleasant bitter flavor to the oil. Fry the bread cubes until golden brown. Drain on paper towels. Season lightly with salt, and set aside.

To serve, place the romaine leaves in the center of six chilled plates. Brush the dressing over the lettuce. Season with salt and pepper. Lay 5 anchovies across the leaves on each plate. Sprinkle the croutons over the salad and serve immediately.

Chicken Pot-au-Feu with Ginger-Cilantro Vermicelli pictured on page 121

SERVES 6

½ pound bean thread vermicelli
   (found in Asian supermarkets)
¼ cup chopped cilantro
3 garlic cloves, minced
2 tablespoons minced shallots
2 tablespoons chopped ginger
Fine sea salt and freshly ground
   white pepper
Three 2½- to 3-pound free-range chickens
8 cups chicken stock
1 onion, peeled and halved
3 carrots, peeled
3 celery ribs
3 leeks
1 lemongrass stalk, bottom 4 inches only,
   bruised with the back of a knife
One 2-inch piece of ginger, peeled
2 beldi lemons (tiny, cured Moroccan
   lemons, found in specialty stores),
   halved, or 4 Lemon Confit quarters
   (page 21)
2 star anise
2 kaffir lime leaves
1 small head cabbage, cut into 6 wedges
1 tablespoon bottled lemon oil
SPECIAL EQUIPMENT
Cheesecloth, kitchen string, and
   a trussing needle

PREP: 40 minutes — COOK: 1 hour and 15 minutes

Soak the vermicelli in warm water until softened, about 10 minutes.

Drain the vermicelli and cut into 4-inch lengths. Place in a bowl and add the cilantro, garlic, shallots, and ginger. Season with salt and pepper.

Rinse the chickens with cold water and pat dry with paper towels. Season the cavities with salt and pepper. Divide the vermicelli mixture and stuff it into the cavities. Using a trussing needle and kitchen string, sew the opening closed; tie the legs together.

In a large pot, combine the chicken stock, onion, 1 carrot, 1 celery rib, 1 leek, the lemongrass, ginger, lemons, star anise, and lime leaves and bring to a boil over medium heat. Season with salt and pepper. Lower the heat to medium, just over a simmer, and add the chickens. Cook for 45 minutes.

Meanwhile, cut the remaining 2 carrots, 2 celery ribs, and 2 leeks into 3-inch by ½-inch strips. Wrap the carrots, celery, leeks, and cabbage in cheesecloth and tie with kitchen string.

Add the vegetables to the chicken pot and cook until the vegetables are tender, 10 to 15 minutes.

To serve, remove the vegetable bundle and the chickens from the pot. Strain the cooking liquid. Carve each chicken into four pieces: 2 breast halves and 2 leg-thigh pieces. Place about ½ cup of the vermicelli on each plate and top with 1 breast half and 1 leg-thigh portion. Arrange the vegetables around the chicken. Spoon the broth over each plate and drizzle ½ teaspoon of the lemon oil over the broth.

Ginger-Scented Hot Chocolate

SERVES 6

3 cups milk
1 cup heavy cream
½ cup sugar
One 2-inch piece of ginger, peeled and
   thinly sliced
2 cardamom pods, crushed
6 ounces bittersweet chocolate, chopped
¼ cup dark rum

PREP: 10 minutes — COOK: 10 minutes

Place the milk, heavy cream, sugar, ginger, and cardamom in a pot and bring to a boil. Lower the heat to a bare simmer to infuse the milk, about 10 minutes.

Add the chocolate and stir until melted. Add the rum. Strain and serve hot.

With beautiful anchovies, all kinds of possibilities
present themselves, simply because good
anchovies don't need anything done to them.
But Eric, now at ease, again returned to a
classic American invention, the Caesar salad,
using the dressed romaine as a garnish for the
anchovies themselves.

Eric has stuffed three chickens with cellophane noodles, or bean thread vermicelli (soaked and tossed with cilantro, garlic, shallots, and ginger), and is poaching them in a broth seasoned with lemongrass, ginger, lemon, anise, and kaffir lime leaves (see page 119). The technique is classic French, but the seasonings are Asian, and its origin for Eric was the city of Fez, Morocco. He ordered a similar dish there several years ago at a restaurant, and when the server brought it, Eric said, "I didn't know this vermicelli was Moroccan." The server replied, "It isn't."

It's not Puerto Rican either, but there we were, very happy to eat this concoction that Eric had been wanting to try ever since.

Traveling, Eric says, can be inspirational but not always the way you think. When he returned from Morocco, he immediately tried to do some things with Moroccan seasoning, but, he says, not until two years after the trip did he really begin to understand the Moroccan seasoning properly, authentically.

"Those inspirational trips," he says, "the ideas don't come right away. They take time to mature."

When the meal was done and contentedness lingered, Alfredo disappeared into the kitchen. He returned with one of the most comforting elixirs I've tasted—real hot chocolate, seasoned with cardamom and ginger and spiked with rum.

jazz

Eric doesn't know where he's going or why or how—he knows only that he has two spiny lobsters that will turn black if he doesn't cook them immediately. But how?

With this question, the real cooking begins.

"It's jazz," Eric says.

He starts with an idea, a note: court-bouillon. Court-bouillon is a quick stock—water, an acid, herbs, spices—most often used for cooking shellfish. Eric will poach the lobster tails in it—but the decision raises more questions. What kind of acid? He chooses sherry vinegar. He could use a wine for a more refined note, but he wants a wine flavor with the strength of a vinegar. Onion and carrot, sweet vegetables, always a good idea in stock. Garlic too. Salt, of course. Get that going, taste it—what seasonings? Ginger. Another note, cumin, another, coriander. Fennel seeds. Some heat—a fresh hot pepper. It's a melody Eric's developing. He's tasting—it's good. It could be a sauce. Aha—this *is* the sauce. Reduced, perhaps mounted with some butter, but kept light—not a traditional sauce. A lobster *à la nage,* but more seasoning. Tarragon, a classic pairing with lobster, but also lime zest and lime juice to make it sparkle, and scallion. Served with some vegetables in a mustard vinaigrette. Mustard and tarragon and lobster, classic, but now *à la nage.* A beautiful harmony, a new song.

We used spiny lobster because it's local, but you could use Maine lobster. Spiny lobster is a little more difficult because if you don't cook it right away, or if you undercook it, it turns black. With spiny lobster, you kill, you cook, you serve, all right away. I find spiny lobster richer and more dense than Maine lobster, which generally I like better because it's more refined.

When you do a classical lobster *à la nage* in France, you cook it in the court-bouillon, or nage, and then you take some of the nage and *beurre monté,* and you serve it with the vegetables of the nage: carrots, onions, and celery. Very traditional. But here we add Caribbean seasoning to give some *cojones* to the broth. And then instead of serving a whole lobster split open with the vegetables and broth on top and the buttery sauce on the side, I wanted to make it more in keeping with a classical nage. And I wanted fresh vegetables, not ones from the nage, but fresh ones with a little crunch, tossed with a vinaigrette.

Poached Spiny Lobster with Tarragon Nage pictured on page 124

SERVES 6

THE LOBSTER

4 quarts water

1 cup sherry vinegar

1 onion, peeled and halved

1 carrot, peeled and halved

6 garlic cloves, peeled

3 tablespoons salt

One 2-inch piece of ginger,
  peeled and halved

1 small hot pepper, seeded and halved

2 tablespoons fennel seeds

1 tablespoon coriander seeds

1 tablespoon cumin seeds

Three 1½-pound spiny lobsters
  (you can substitute Maine lobsters)

THE VEGETABLES

1 cucumber, peeled, seeded,
  and cut into ¼-inch slices

¾ cup Napa cabbage julienne

1 tomato, seeded and cut into
  ¼-inch julienne

THE VINAIGRETTE

1 teaspoon coarse-grain mustard

1 tablespoon sherry vinegar

Fine sea salt and freshly ground
  white pepper

1 tablespoon bottled lemon oil

2 tablespoons canola oil

THE SAUCE

2 cups reserved strained lobster
  cooking liquid

8 tablespoons (1 stick) unsalted butter

1 tablespoon chopped tarragon

1 scallion, thinly sliced

Finely chopped zest and juice of 1 lime

SPECIAL EQUIPMENT

6 wooden skewers

Six 3-inch by 2-inch-high ring molds

PREP: 30 minutes — **COOK:** 1 hour

For the lobster, place all the ingredients except the lobster in a large pot and bring to a boil. Lower the heat and simmer for 30 minutes.

Meanwhile, kill the lobsters by plunging a chef's knife between the eyes of each one and bringing the knife down through the head. Separate the tails from the bodies. (Reserve the claws and bodies for another use, such as Lobster Consommé, page 312.) One at a time, flatten each tail on a cutting board back side down and slip two wooden skewers between the meat and the bottom shell. This will keep the tails straight while they cook.

Add the tails to the simmering broth and cook for 5 minutes. Remove the pot from the heat and let the lobster stand in the cooking liquid for about 20 minutes. You need to take extra care when cooking spiny lobsters: If they are undercooked, they will turn black once cooled; if they are overcooked, they will be very dry. Keep a close eye on the lobster tails while they continue to cook in the hot liquid. Just as they lose their translucency, remove them from the cooking liquid. Strain and reserve the cooking liquid.

When they are cool enough to handle, remove the skewers from the tails. Remove the shell from each tail by squeezing it lengthwise until it cracks. Then force the shell outward until it breaks open and remove the meat. Slice each tail into ¼-inch slices. Lay the slices on a baking sheet, cover with plastic wrap, and refrigerate.

Preheat the oven to 350°F.

Place 2 quarts of the lobster poaching liquid in a pot and bring to a boil. Quickly blanch the cucumbers, then the cabbage, until crisp-tender, about 1 minute per vegetable. Remove with a wire skimmer, draining well, and add to the baking sheet with the lobster meat. Add the tomato julienne to the baking sheet, cover again, and refrigerate until ready to serve.

For the vinaigrette, in a small bowl, whisk together the mustard, sherry vinegar, and a pinch each of salt and pepper. Whisking constantly, slowly add the lemon oil and canola oil. Set aside.

For the sauce, bring the reserved lobster cooking liquid to a boil in a small saucepan. Whisk in the butter 1 tablespoon at a time. Remove from the heat.

To serve, warm the vegetables and lobster in the oven for 2 minutes. Gently reheat the sauce—do not boil, or the sauce will separate. Add the tarragon, scallion and lime zest and juice.

In a medium bowl, toss the vegetables with the vinaigrette.

Place a ring mold in the center of each plate. Divide the lobster meat evenly among the molds. Place a medley of the vegetables on top of the lobster in each the mold. Spoon the sauce around. Remove the molds and serve immediately.

MONTER AU BEURRE

Monter au beurre, "to mount with butter," means adding butter, or emulsifying butter into a sauce, often the final step in a sauce preparation. Whisking or swirling butter into a sauce or other liquid just before it will be served enriches its flavor, gives it a velvety texture and a tantalizing sheen. It finishes a sauce, gives it polish.

To mount a sauce with butter, you must remember two key steps: The sauce must be hot, and when you add the pieces of butter, you must keep them moving until they are thoroughly incorporated. So the sauce should be over a medium flame and you must swirl the butter vigorously or whisk it until it's completely incorporated.

Monter au beurre is such a common technique that some restaurant kitchens make a batch of *beurre monté*—butter that is already melted but kept emulsified over gentle but consistent heat—because it allows a cook to finish a sauce in a snap with a quick ladleful.

COURT-BOUILLON

Court-bouillon means "short" or "quick" stock and can be as simple as salted water and vinegar. It grows complex as you add onions and carrots and herbs and peppercorns, and it can be used to cook a whole fish or a variety of shellfish—lobster, shrimp, crayfish, snails—which absorb the flavors of the cooking liquid. The bouquet garni or sachet is an important ingredient—I like bay leaves, thyme, and parsley stems. Peppercorns are often added. The wine is typically red wine vinegar, but you can vary this. You can add garlic or add other seasonings and acids, but as it grows more sophisticated, it becomes less a court-bouillon and more a nage. You wouldn't want to drink a simple court-bouillon or put it in a sauce, but it can be refined into sauce, a light broth in which the food is served.

Always the intensity of the poaching liquid depends on what you are cooking. For snails, you want a very basic strong court-bouillon; for delicate halibut, a court-bouillon that suits it.

Poached Spiny Lobster with Tarragon Nage, page 123

Court-Bouillon

Makes about 4 cups

4 cups water

½ cup red wine vinegar

1 thyme sprig

2 flat-leaf parsley sprigs

1 bay leaf

3 garlic cloves

½ carrot, peeled

½ onion

1 tablespoon peppercorns

Fine sea salt

PREP: 10 minutes — **COOK:** 10 minutes

This is a basic court-bouillon that can be used to poach any kind of shellfish and most firm meaty fish.

Place all the ingredients except the salt in a pot and bring to a boil. Lower the heat and simmer for 10 minutes. Strain and season to taste with salt.

Tropical Fruit en Papillote

Serves 6

6 banana leaves (found in Latino markets),
  cut into 6-inch by 3-inch rectangles

1 mango, peeled, halved, pitted,
  and sliced ¼ inch thick

1 pineapple, peeled, cored, and cut into
  ¼-inch-thick 1-inch squares,

2 oranges, cut into segments

3 star fruit, cut crosswise into
  ½-inch slices

6 baby bananas (or 3 regular bananas,
  halved crosswise)

½ cup grated fresh coconut
  (you can substitute grated
  unsweetened dried coconut)

6 tablespoons unsalted butter,
  cut into ¼-inch dice

2 tablespoons brown sugar

2 tablespoons dark rum

1 pint good-quality store-bought
  vanilla ice cream

PREP: 20 minutes — **COOK:** 7 minutes

Preheat the oven to 400°F. Cut six 8-inch by 12-inch sheets of aluminum foil.

Place the banana leaves on a cutting board. Arrange 3 slices of mango, 5 pieces of pineapple, 3 orange segments, 3 slices of star fruit, and 1 banana on each leaf.

Sprinkle the coconut, butter, and brown sugar evenly over the fruit. Drizzle 1 teaspoon of the rum over each portion.

Place each leaf on an aluminum foil sheet. Pull the long sides to the center and fold over to close. Fold the ends over to seal tightly. Place on a baking sheet and bake until the packages puff with steam, 5 to 7 minutes.

Set each bundle on a plate, carefully open (avoiding the steam), and top with a scoop of ice cream.

Here is another jazz-like improvisation, one inspired by the sea—and leftover chicken. I wanted everyone to be near the sea for part of the trip. Puerto Rico is a big island, so the sea in many ways defines the place, determines its character. Alfredo found us beautiful accommodations on a beach in Guanica, on the southern coast of the island, and we packed up the van and our cooking gear and got on the road. But the move took all day, and so once we'd arrived, set the table, and lighted candles, I'd decided to do a simple meal, and also use up the chicken we'd cooked the other night. (Make a meal with leftovers that no one could ever call leftovers, and you've done something very special.)

Shredded chicken is not a beautiful sight, but a bright green bundle of something is. Wrapping food in a leaf, especially a tasty one such as savoy or Napa cabbage, is a great strategy for leftovers. I seasoned the chicken with Thai curry elements—ginger, lemongrass, coriander, coco milk—because I love the dramatic flavors.

I'd been wanting Alfredo to make the tostones—the essence of street food—and now was a good time. Tostones are simply twice-fried plantains and they are delicious all by themselves, sprinkled with salt and a few drops of pique. Cut a plantain into thick disks, blanch them in medium-hot oil, then lightly smash them to double their circumference and fry in hot oil until golden brown and crispy. In

Puerto Rico, they can accompany a meal the way French fries do in America. They can be topped with any number of garnishes as a canapé (smoked salmon and sour cream, for instance). I wanted to do tostones because they're so Puerto Rican, and representative of the street food that I love. I don't like to deep-fry but I love to eat deep-fried food, and street food here, deep-fried in big iron vats in beach shacks, is about people and music and being alive— and this is what tostones bring to me.

With this preparation, I love the idea of pairing an unrefined street food with something very, very elegant. It's amazing what we discover in Puerto Rico—tostones and caviar were made to go together. The lime juice entwines these two opposites, a beautiful combination of salt and acid with fried food—the best, most unusual fish and chips you'll ever eat.

For dessert—again, we needed something quick and easy, using ingredients we had on hand. Steam-roasting fruits (see page 125) is an easy way to draw out their flavors, which are further enriched with brown sugar, butter, and rum and served with vanilla ice cream.

Tostones and Caviar pictured on page 131

pictured on page 131

SERVES 6

4 green plantains

2 cups canola oil

1 tablespoon kosher salt

6 ounces osetra caviar

2 limes, quartered

PREP: 10 minutes, plus 30 minutes soaking time — **COOK:** 5 minutes

To prepare the plantains, cut off both ends. Peel the plantains by scoring each side lengthwise. Slip your fingers under the skin and peel it off. Place the plantains in a bowl of salted water for 30 minutes. Drain and pat dry.

Heat the oil in a large deep skillet to 275°F. Cut the plantains into 1½-inch slices. Blanch the plantain slices in the oil for 2 to 3 minutes; they should not color. Transfer them to paper towels to drain. Set the pan aside.

When they are cool enough to handle, wrap each slice in a towel dampened with salted water and mash gently, using a meat pounder or heavy pan, to a flat oval with a thickness of ¼ inch. (At this point, the tostones can sit for up to 2 hours at room temperature.)

Reheat the oil to 375°F. Blanch the tostones in the hot oil, turning once, for about 2 minutes per side, until golden in color, not brown. Transfer the tostones to paper towels to drain. Sprinkle with the kosher salt.

To serve, place a teaspoon of caviar on each tostone and squeeze lime juice over each.

Curried Napa Cabbage Bundles with Soy-Orange Vinaigrette

SERVES 6

2 blood oranges

1 orange

2 limes

¼ cup soy sauce

1 shallot, minced

½ garlic clove, minced

⅛ teaspoon ground star anise

½ teaspoon ground coriander

¼ cup canola oil

4 cups shredded cooked chicken

2 tablespoons chopped peanuts

1 tablespoon chopped ginger

1 teaspoon finely chopped lemongrass
   (tender inner stalks only)

2 teaspoons curry powder

1 cup coconut milk, fresh (page 98)
   or canned

Fine sea salt and freshly ground
   white pepper

12 savoy cabbage leaves

PREP: 25 minutes, plus 30 minutes marinating — **COOK:** 5 minutes

Using a sharp knife, slice off the top and bottom of the oranges, stand each one on a cutting board, and slice off the peel and bitter white pith. Working over a bowl, slice between the membranes to release the segments. Repeat with the limes. Cut the oranges and limes into ¼-inch dice.

In a large bowl, combine the soy sauce, shallot, garlic, star anise, coriander, and canola oil and whisk to blend. Add the citrus dice and the accumulated juice, and stir to combine. Marinate at room temperature for up to an hour to marry the flavors.

Meanwhile, in a large bowl, combine the chicken, peanuts, ginger, lemongrass, curry powder, and coconut milk. Season to taste with salt and pepper. Cover and marinate in the refrigerator for at least 30 minutes.

Bring a large pot of water to a boil and add salt. A few at a time, briefly blanch the cabbage leaves being careful to not overcook—then plunge the leaves into a large bowl of ice water to stop the cooking. Drain on paper towels and set aside.

To serve, place a medium skillet over medium heat, add the chicken mixture, and heat until warmed through.

Place about ⅓ cup of the chicken mixture on each leaf. Fold the bottom of the leaf up over the filling, fold over the sides, and roll up. *(The cabbage bundles can be prepared up to 3 hours in advance. Reheat them in a 350°F oven before serving.)*

To serve, place 2 cabbage bundles seam side down on each plate and drizzle the sauce over the bundles.

ON CAVIAR

Ever since I turned eighteen, I've been eating caviar. It's one of the perks of my job. Caviar is my favorite thing to eat, period. It's the essence of the sea. And it's buttery, and at the end it's nutty. Simply to see beautiful caviar in the can makes me happy.

Most people will find it difficult to buy great caviar in the United States, and even the best purveyors don't always have the best quality because of the volatility of the product. At Le Bernardin, I have to send back half of what we get. The main ways to evaluate caviar are sight and taste. The eggs should be uniform in shape and in color. They should be intact, not bruised or broken. You should check for oil at the bottom of the tin, which can indicate that the caviar is old and has been improperly stored. (Don't buy caviar stored in a jar; jarred caviar is typically pasteurized.) The eggs should taste fresh and clean, like the sea. The texture of the eggs is critical—they should not be mush or as hard as Ping-Pong balls. I always use osetra caviar, which is the perfect size. The smaller sevruga eggs I find too salty, and the big beluga eggs I find bland, generally, and usually overpriced.

Tostones and Caviar, page 128

tropical comfort

As on most tropical islands, tubers—root vegetables—grow in abundance here, as do rhizomes such as ginger, and gourds such as calabaza. Many varieties of bananas grow all over. And groupers swim in these waters.

These items appear almost out of nowhere—they would grow if this island were deserted. They are part of its natural bounty, and so we cook with them. This satisfies the palate because we use ingredients at their freshest. And it satisfies the soul because when you cook what the earth gives you, it can connect you to the natural order that we are a part of.

Apio and Black Truffle Soup

SERVES 6

6 tablespoons unsalted butter

1 leek, white part only, cut into small dice

2½ cups roughly chopped peeled apio
(taro root; you can substitute
celery root)

Fine sea salt and freshly ground
white pepper

6 cups chicken stock

1 cup heavy cream

3 ounces black truffles

PREP: 10 minutes — COOK: 35 minutes

Yes, I throw truffles in the soup—because I love them and I love their luxury, especially when paired with a lowly tuber. They make this a very special soup, though this recipe will work with or without truffles, with virtually any kind of root: celery root, taro, and tubers such as potatoes.

In a medium pot, melt 2 tablespoons of the butter. Add the leek and cook until tender, about 5 minutes.

Add the apio, stir to combine, and season with salt and pepper. Cover with the chicken stock and bring to a boil, then lower the heat to a simmer. Cook until the apio is tender when pierced with a knife, about 30 minutes.

Process the soup in a blender, in batches, blending until the soup is smooth. Return to the pot and set over low heat. Add the remaining 4 tablespoons butter and the cream and stir to incorporate. Adjust the seasoning.

Meanwhile, cut 2 ounces of the black truffles into julienne.

To serve, grate the remaining truffles into the soup and stir to combine. Divide the soup among six warmed soup bowls, sprinkle the truffle julienne over each bowl, and serve immediately.

Sautéed Grouper with Glazed Onions and Bacon-Butter Sauce

SERVES 6

1 pound thick-cut bacon

2 tablespoons canola oil

3 onions, thinly sliced

Fine sea salt and freshly ground white pepper

¼ cup aged sherry vinegar

1 teaspoon Pique (page 96), or to taste

1 cup chicken stock

8 tablespoons (1 stick) very cold unsalted butter, cut into 1-inch chunks

Six 6-ounce grouper fillets

¼ cup chives cut into 1-inch bâtonnets

PREP: 10 minutes — COOK: 25 minutes

Sautéed fillets of grouper with caramelized onions and a quick butter sauce—a very simple dish to make. Grouper is a hearty, meaty fish that can handle the rich, salty garnish of bacon and butter. The fish needs a little firmer hand in cooking than others do—if it's medium-rare, it will be tough. The sweetness of the onions, and the richness of the sauce, is offset by a solid dose of sherry vinegar. The sauce is simply chicken stock mounted with butter and flavored with bacon, so you must use very good stock.

Slice 3 pieces of bacon in half and cook in a large skillet until crisp, about 5 minutes. Drain on paper towels. Cut the remaining bacon into 1-inch pieces and cook until crisp, then drain again on paper towels. Reserve 2 tablespoons of the rendered bacon fat.

Preheat the oven to 450°F.

Heat the canola oil in a large sauté pan over medium heat. When the oil is hot, add the onions and cook until they are golden brown, about 10 minutes. Season with salt and pepper. Deglaze the pan with the sherry vinegar, scraping up any browned bits on the bottom. Add the pique. Adjust the seasoning. Set aside.

Bring the chicken stock to a boil in a saucepan. Whisking constantly, slowly add the butter. When all the butter is incorporated, remove from the heat. Place the small pieces of bacon in a blender, add the chicken stock, and blend at high speed until the bacon is finely chopped.

Place two large ovenproof nonstick sauté pans over high heat. Add 1 tablespoon of the reserved bacon fat to each pan. Generously season the grouper fillets with salt and pepper. When the fat is hot, place 3 fillets in each pan and cook until nicely browned on the first side, 3 to 4 minutes. Turn the fillets over, place the pans in the oven, and roast for about 3 minutes. To check for doneness, insert a metal skewer in the thickest part of a fillet; when removed, the skewer should be warm.

Meanwhile, reheat the onions over medium heat. Warm the sauce over low heat; do not allow it to boil, or it will separate.

To serve, spread about ¼ cup of the onions in the center of each plate. Top each with a grouper fillet. Drizzle the sauce around the plates and place a slice of cooked bacon on each fillet. Serve immediately.

Banana Mille-Feuille with Gingered Chocolate Sauce

SERVES 6

1 gelatin sheet

10 ounces peeled bananas (about 3 large)

2 tablespoons fresh lemon juice

1 tablespoon water

⅛ teaspoon freshly grated nutmeg

1½ cups heavy cream

7 tablespoons unsalted butter

5 sheets phyllo dough

5 tablespoons sugar

¾ cup milk

One 1-inch piece of ginger, peeled and
    cut into ¼-inch slices

4 ounces extra bittersweet chocolate,
    finely chopped

2 tablespoons dark rum

PREP: 30 minutes, plus 3 hours chilling time — **COOK:** 30 minutes

The bananas are so plentiful and delicious it would be a crime not to feature them in a dessert. In this dish, they are pureed, mixed with whipped cream, and dressed up in *mille-feuille*—French for "a thousand leaves." The term usually means flaky puff pastry; here we use layers of phyllo, an all-purpose structural dessert element. The sauce is chocolate melted in milk and cream, flavored with ginger and rum.

Place the gelatin sheet in cold water to soften.

Meanwhile, puree the bananas with the lemon juice in a blender.

Combine ¼ cup of the banana mixture and the water in a small pot and warm gently over low heat. Squeeze the softened gelatin sheet to extract the water and add to the banana mixture. Stir until the gelatin has dissolved. Combine with the remaining banana mixture in a small bowl, add the nutmeg, and stir to incorporate. Cover and refrigerate until well chilled.

In a medium bowl, whip 1 cup of the heavy cream to stiff peaks. Fold in ½ cup of the banana mixture to lighten, then gently fold in the remaining banana mixture. Cover with plastic wrap, placing it directly against the surface, and refrigerate for at least 3 hours, or overnight.

Preheat the oven to 400°F. Line a baking sheet with parchment paper.

Melt 6 tablespoons of the butter in a saucepan over low heat. Lay 1 sheet of phyllo dough on the baking sheet. Keep the remaining sheets covered with a damp towel to prevent them from drying. Brush the phyllo with melted butter and sprinkle with 1 tablespoon of the sugar. Place another sheet of phyllo over the first sheet, brush with butter, and sprinkle with sugar. Continue until you have used all 5 sheets. Cover with another piece of parchment, place another baking sheet over the parchment, and press down firmly.

Without removing the top sheet, bake for 20 minutes, or until the phyllo is golden brown. Remove from the oven and cool to room temperature. *(The phyllo can be baked several hours ahead; store in an airtight container.)*

For the chocolate sauce, combine the remaining ½ cup heavy cream, the milk, and ginger in a saucepan and bring to a boil. Take off the heat, add the chocolate, and stir to melt. Add the rum and the remaining 1 tablespoon butter and stir to incorporate. Set aside for 5 minutes to infuse the ginger into the sauce. Strain and set aside.

To serve, cut the phyllo dough into 18 triangles, 2 inches at the base and 4 inches long. Spoon 2 tablespoons of the banana mousse into the center of each plate and top with a phyllo triangle, then two more mousse-phyllo layers. Drizzle the chocolate sauce around. Serve immediately.

I'm telling you right now, these dishes are going to sound a little crazy. But they're not crazy at all. It's the whole reason for traveling to a place, to a culture—this is where the inspiration comes from, not from books or local restaurants. If we don't cook this way, we might as well stay in New York. Otherwise we don't learn anything.

First off, we had to make Sancocho because this rustic stew typifies Puerto Rican street food, along with all the deep-fried treats like the alcapurria found throughout the island.

Then, we had some nice beef tenderloin, and I was thinking beef stroganoff, which when it's done well is very, very good. And I thought about a goulash. But one, these preparations are too heavy to eat in hot Puerto Rico; and two, they are more or less stews, and our very expensive tenderloin would overcook. However, I kept the idea of a one-pot dish and the idea of the paprika. We had eggplant, and I figured that would work, and so we made paprika-spiked beef with eggplant.

Then we made shellfish and chorizo stew, which was straight out of the Portuguese and Spanish traditions. Their cuisines are not only suited to the land but make cultural sense, as Puerto Rico, along with Santo Domingo, remains among the few Spanish enclaves in the French-dominated Caribbean. The shepherd's pie is definitely French cooking, but with Caribbean flavors. In France, we would do a shepherd's pie with ground meat and mashed potatoes. Here we do the same thing, but we take the sausage that is made here, blood sausage, and use that for the ground meat, season it with cilantro, and serve it under mashed yuca, a local root vegetable. And it works beautifully.

Paprika-Spiked Beef Tenderloin and Eggplant, page 141

Sancocho pictured on page 89

SERVES 6

2 Italian frying peppers or sweet banana
   peppers, seeded and roughly chopped

5 small sweet red peppers, such as
   pimientos, seeded and roughly chopped,
   or 1 red bell pepper, cored, seeded,
   and roughly chopped

½ red bell pepper, seeded and roughly
   chopped

1 onion, roughly chopped

5 garlic cloves, peeled

1 bunch cilantro, leaves picked

2 pounds beef shank (bone in)

3 tablespoons canola oil

Fine sea salt and freshly ground
   white pepper

1½ pounds boneless pork leg,
   cut into 1-inch cubes

½ pound chorizo, sliced

4 cups water

1 green plantain

½ cup 1-inch dice peeled yautia,
   (you can substitute potato)

½ cup 1-inch dice peeled ñame,
   (you can substitute celery root)

1 avocado

Pique (page 96) for serving

PREP: 20 minutes — COOK: 2 hours and 40 minutes

Eric begins this as a traditional stew, seasoning and then browning the meat. He then adds sofrito—a mix of finely chopped peppers, onion, garlic, and cilantro used in many preparations, the dominant flavoring ingredient. Water is added, and the meat is simmered until it's nearly fork-tender. Plantains and root vegetables, added at the end, help to thicken the sauce and give it some bulk.

Place all the peppers and the onion, garlic, and cilantro in a blender or food processor, cover, and process for about 20 seconds, or until coarsely chopped. Set aside.

Slice the beef off the bones and cut the meat into 1-inch cubes; reserve the bones. Heat 1 tablespoon of the canola oil in a large heavy-bottomed pot over medium-high heat. Season the beef with salt and pepper, add the beef and bones to the pot, and brown on all sides. Transfer to a platter. Season the pork with salt and pepper, add to the pot in batches, and brown on all sides. Return all the beef and bones to the pot, add the pepper mixture, and cook for 2 minutes, or until softened. Add the chorizo and cook for 3 to 5 minutes. Add the water, bring to a simmer, and simmer for 2 hours. Add more water if the stew becomes too thick.

Meanwhile, prepare the plantain: Cut off both ends. Peel the plantain by scoring each side lengthwise. Slip your fingers under the skin and peel it off. Cut the plantain into 1-inch lengths.

Add the plantain, yautia, and ñame to the pot and cook until tender, about 25 minutes; add water as necessary to thin the stew. Remove and discard the bones. Adjust the seasoning.

Just before serving (to prevent the avocado from darkening), halve, pit, and peel the avocado. Cut into thin slices.

To serve, divide the stew among six bowls. Garnish with the avocado slices and pass pique at the table.

Eric breaks from the traditional recipe slightly: "I put chorizo in the Sancocho. The Puerto Ricans don't do that, but so what." This is a time to throw away "supposed to's" and cook as you feel, cook by instinct. And Eric's instinct almost always tells him this: Given a chance to eat chorizo, eat chorizo. The stew is garnished with smooth avocado and finished at the table with fiery pique.

Shellfish and Chorizo in Broth

SERVES 6

¼ cup extra virgin olive oil

½ onion, thinly sliced

6 garlic cloves, thinly sliced

1 lemongrass stalk, tender inner leaves
   only, finely chopped

½ teaspoon curry powder

2 links dried chorizo (not fresh),
   thinly sliced

2 cups chicken stock

2 pounds mussels, scrubbed and
   beards removed

24 littleneck clams, scrubbed

1 tablespoon cilantro julienne

1 tablespoon bottled lemon oil

PREP: 15 minutes — **COOK:** 15 minutes

When I am in a home kitchen and allowed to cook however I like, my true self seems revealed to me, and that true self is Spanish. Fish and shellfish stews are common to Portugal and Spain, and they are often flavored by spicy chorizo, as they are in this quick peasant stew.

Place two medium heavy-bottomed pots over medium heat and add 2 tablespoons of the olive oil to each pot. Divide the onion, garlic, lemongrass, and curry powder between the pots and cook slowly until the onions are softened, about 3 minutes. Add half the chorizo to each pot and cook for another 4 minutes.

Add 1 cup of the chicken stock to each pot and bring to a boil. Add the mussels to one pot and the clams to the other. Cover and cook until they steam open, then remove from the heat; be careful not to overcook the shellfish. Remove the clams and mussels and combine the broths in one pot. Remove the meat from the mussels and clams and discard the shells.

To serve, divide the clams, mussels, and chorizo equally among six soup bowls. Ladle the broth into the bowls, being careful to leave any sand in the bottom of the pot. Sprinkle the cilantro over the stew and drizzle ½ teaspoon of the lemon oil over each bowl. Serve with crusty bread.

Paprika-Spiked Beef Tenderloin and Eggplant pictured on page 139

SERVES 6

¼ cup canola oil

1 onion, cut into ¼-inch dice

4 garlic cloves, minced

1 tablespoon minced ginger

Fine sea salt and freshly ground
   white pepper

1 eggplant, cut into 1-inch cubes

3 tablespoons paprika

1 tablespoon ground cumin

1 star anise, finely ground

1 tomato, seeded and cut into ½-inch dice

¼ cup dry white wine

¾ cup coconut milk, fresh (page 98)
   or canned

4 cups chicken stock

2½ pounds beef tenderloin, trimmed and
   cut into 1-inch cubes

1 lime, halved

6 basil leaves, cut into julienne

1 tablespoon chopped peanuts

3 cups hot cooked white rice

PREP: 25 minutes — **COOK:** 30 minutes

We sautéed the eggplant with onions, garlic, paprika, and cumin and added stock. And then we added elements of the landscape, the staples: coco milk, lime, basil, peanuts. Sounds crazy, but I really love this dish, and it's the best kind of home cooking there is.

Heat 2 tablespoons of the canola oil in a medium pot over medium heat. Add the onion, garlic, and ginger and cook until translucent, about 5 minutes. Season with salt and pepper. Add the eggplant, paprika, cumin, and star anise and cook for another 5 minutes, or until the eggplant is softened. Add the tomato and cook for another 5 minutes. Add the wine and simmer until almost evaporated. Add the coconut milk and chicken stock and adjust the seasoning with salt and pepper. Simmer until the vegetables are tender, another 10 minutes.

Meanwhile, heat the remaining 2 tablespoons canola oil in a large sauté pan over high heat until hot. Generously season the beef with salt and pepper. Add the meat to the pan in batches and sear on all sides, about 2 minutes; the meat should still be rare.

Add the meat to the vegetable pot and stir well.

To serve, divide the meat and vegetables among six bowls. Squeeze some lime juice into each bowl and sprinkle with the basil and peanuts. Serve with the cooked rice on the side.

Blood Sausage and Yuca Shepherd's Pie

SERVES 6

THE SHEPHERD'S PIE

2 yucas (about 1½ pounds), peeled

½ cup milk

4 tablespoons unsalted butter

Fine sea salt and freshly ground
    white pepper

1 tablespoon canola oil

1½ pounds blood sausage

1 onion, chopped

1 tomato, seeded and cut into ¼-inch dice

1 tablespoon Pique (page 96), or to taste

2 tablespoons chopped cilantro

THE SAUCE

½ cup sour cream

1 cup tightly packed cilantro leaves

Fine sea salt and freshly ground
    white pepper

1 avocado

1 lime, halved

SPECIAL EQUIPMENT

Six 2½-inch by 2-inch-high ring molds

PREP: 20 minutes — **COOK:** 25 minutes

This shepherd's pie is me being playful with a very traditional peasant dish that is part of my French heritage. We dressed it up and used the spices and products of the Caribbean. The look is fancy, a restaurant presentation, because that's the mood I was in, but the flavors are rustic.

Yuca, also called cassava, is available in Latino markets. If necessary, however, you can use potatoes instead.

Place the yucas in a pot and cover with cold water. Add 2 tablespoons salt, bring to a boil, and cook until tender, 20 to 25 minutes. Drain, reserving ¼ cup of the cooking liquid.

Split the yuca down the center and remove the tough inner core. Mash the yuca with a fork.

In a medium saucepan, heat the milk and butter to a simmer. Add the yuca and stir to incorporate. Season with salt if necessary and pepper. Set aside.

Meanwhile, heat the canola oil in a large sauté pan over medium heat. Add the sausage and cook for 7 to 10 minutes, or until it is cooked through. Remove from the heat and let cool until you are able to handle the sausage.

Remove the casings and crumble the sausage. Return the sausage to the pan and add the onion and tomato. Cook until the onion is tender, about 5 minutes. Season to taste with salt and pepper. Add the reserved ¼ cup yuca cooking liquid, the pique, and cilantro and cook until heated through, about 3 minutes.

Meanwhile, for the sauce, place the sour cream and cilantro in a blender and process until pureed. Season to taste with salt and pepper. Set aside.

Just before serving, gently reheat the yuca. Halve, peel, and pit the avocado, and cut each half into 3 wedges.

To serve, place a ring mold on each plate, slightly off center. Fill each mold three-quarters full with the sausage mixture, then top them with the mashed yuca. Place an avocado wedge on each plate. Squeeze the juice of the lime into the sauce and stir to incorporate. Drizzle the sauce over the avocado. Remove the molds and serve immediately.

Paella

SERVES 6

2 tablespoons canola oil

36 large shrimp, peeled and deveined, shells reserved

1 shallot, thinly sliced

9 garlic cloves, 3 halved, 6 chopped

1 tablespoon tomato paste

8 cups chicken stock

¼ cup extra virgin olive oil

1 onion, chopped

½ teaspoon saffron threads, minced

1 teaspoon turmeric

2 cups medium-grain white rice

Fine sea salt and freshly ground white pepper

2 links chorizo, cut into ¼-inch slices

½ cup peas

1 red bell pepper, roasted, peeled, seeded, and cut into 2-inch by ¼-inch strips (see Note)

1 green bell pepper, roasted, peeled, seeded, and cut into 2-inch by ¼-inch strips (see Note)

Three 6-ounce grouper or red snapper fillets, cut into 2-inch medallions

2 tablespoons sliced scallions

PREP: 30 minutes — **COOK:** 1 hour

Heat the canola oil in a heavy-bottomed pot over medium heat. Add the shrimp shells and cook until they are bright orange, about 3 minutes. Add the shallot, halved garlic cloves, and tomato paste and cook until the shallots and garlic are tender, about 5 minutes. Cover with the chicken stock, reduce the heat to a simmer, and simmer for 30 minutes.

Strain the shrimp stock through a fine-mesh sieve, pressing on the vegetables and shells to extract all the liquid. Pour the stock into a pan and keep warm over low heat.

For the paella, heat the olive oil in a large (at least 12-inch) paella pan or flameproof casserole over medium heat. Add the onion and the chopped garlic and sauté until translucent and limp, but not browned, 5 to 7 minutes. Add the saffron and turmeric and cook for another 3 to 5 minutes. Add the rice and stir to coat with the oil.

Add 3 cups of the warm stock and stir to incorporate. Season with salt and pepper. Add the chorizo and stir to incorporate. Cook until the stock has almost been absorbed, 5 to 7 minutes. Add a ladleful of stock and cook until it has almost been absorbed. Continue adding stock a ladleful at a time, only adding more once the previous stock has been absorbed; you may not need to use it all. Be careful not to add too much stock, or the rice will be soupy and soft. It should be just cooked through and moist.

Immediately after the last addition of stock, stir in the peas. Adjust the seasoning. Arrange the strips of peppers around the pan, alternating colors, like spokes of a bicycle wheel. Place the shrimp and fish medallions between the peppers. Cover with foil and cook for 4 to 5 minutes, or until the shrimp are bright orange.

Uncover and sprinkle with the sliced scallions. Serve immediately.

NOTE: To roast bell peppers, place each pepper directly on the flame of a gas burner, turning the pepper occasionally, until it is nicely charred on all sides. You can also roast peppers in a 400°F oven, for about 20 minutes. Place the roasted peppers in a bowl, cover with plastic wrap, and let steam for 10 minutes. The skin should slip easily off the peppers. Discard the cores and seeds.

What is a real paella? A rice dish in a paella pan, that's all. A technique, a pan. You can add what you want—chicken, fish, whatever—it's up to you. This is an outdoor paella; you don't cook it in an oven as it's usually done. You can do it on the beach, or anywhere you have an open flame; you could cook a paella on top of the barbecue, which would give you really a great flavor. We should have done that in Sag Harbor.

Shrimp is nice in paella because it gives color and flavor to the liquid. Monkfish would work well. It would almost become like chicken. For paella, you can do snapper, you can do grouper, which has a tough consistency, like monk. To do snapper in paella, you must be careful, put it in at the end, or it will be dry and fall apart. Again, the Spanish origins of the dish make it perfectly suited to Puerto Rico.

Rice Pudding with Sautéed Bananas and Chocolate Sauce

SERVES 6

4 cups milk, or more as needed

2 cups heavy cream

1 vanilla bean, halved lengthwise

½ cinnamon stick

½ cup sugar

Finely chopped zest of 2 limes

1½ cups medium-grain white rice

4 ounces extra bittersweet chocolate, finely chopped

2 tablespoons unsalted butter

2 bananas

1 tablespoon brown sugar

1 tablespoon dark rum

PREP: 15 minutes, plus 20 minutes chilling time — **COOK:** 35 minutes

In a medium pot, combine the milk, 1½ cups of the heavy cream, the vanilla bean, cinnamon stick, and sugar and bring to a simmer. Add the lime zest and rice and stir to incorporate. Continue to simmer until the rice is tender, about 30 minutes. Stir occasionally, so the rice does not stick to the bottom; if all of the liquid evaporates, add more milk to moisten. Remove from the heat.

Remove the vanilla bean and cinnamon stick. Divide the rice pudding among six martini glasses (or similar glasses) and refrigerate until well chilled, 30 to 40 minutes.

Meanwhile, for the chocolate sauce, bring the remaining ½ cup heavy cream to a boil in a small suacepan. Add the chocolate, take off the heat, and stir until melted. Add 1 tablespoon of the butter and stir to incorporate. Set aside.

Melt the remaining 1 tablespoon butter in a large nonstick sauté pan over medium-high heat. Thinly slice the bananas and add them to the pan. Add the brown sugar and sauté until the sugar melts and the bananas are caramelized, about 2 minutes. Add the rum and bring to a boil. Take off the heat and set aside.

To serve, spoon the bananas evenly over the rice pudding. Drizzle the chocolate sauce over all and serve immediately.

We had rice, and I was looking for another dessert idea. Initially, I wanted to try a rice and beans dessert because rice and beans are so much a part of this culture. But after I'd cooked the beans in a sweet liquid, I didn't like them. The rice was good, so on my next effort, I skipped the beans. I used local bananas and chocolate, which in my mind are very Latino/South American ingredients. The critical point is to make sure the rice is very moist. If it's dry, mix in some whipped cream at the end.

No matter where he is, Eric cooks fish with an ease that seems almost thoughtless. The grace of his cooking and the delicate nature of the product seem to go hand in hand. How did this work, though, in the West Indies, where the ingredients are so bright, the seasoning so vivid? Eric's tropical fish cookery turns out to be an exciting example in contrasts because the delicate meat handles very well the acidity and spice the landscape demands. Here he puts such lively ingredients as ginger and various hot peppers to excellent effect.

Sautéed Monkfish with "Sofrito" in Dende Oil

SERVES 6

¼ cup dende oil (palm oil from Brazil;
   available in Latino markets)
1 onion, cut into tiny dice
2 red bell peppers, cored, seeded,
   and cut into tiny dice
1 yellow bell pepper, cored, seeded,
   and cut into tiny dice
2 sweet banana peppers, seeded and
   cut into tiny dice
1 jalapeño pepper, cut into tiny dice
2 tomatoes, seeded and chopped
5 garlic cloves, minced
2 tablespoons minced ginger
1 cup coconut milk, fresh (page 98)
   or canned
1 cup water
2 tablespoons canola oil
Six 6-ounce monkfish fillets
Fine sea salt and freshly ground
   white pepper
2 limes, halved
2 tablespoons cilantro julienne
4 cups hot cooked white rice

PREP: 35 minutes — COOK: 30 minutes

Heat the dende oil in a large pan over medium heat. Add the onion, peppers, jalapeño, and tomatoes and cook for about 5 minutes, until they have softened. Add the garlic and ginger and cook for another 5 minutes. Add the coconut milk and water and simmer until the vegetables are tender, another 10 minutes. Set aside.

Heat two large nonstick sauté pans over high heat, then add 1 tablespoon of the canola oil to each. Generously season the monkfish with salt and pepper. When the oil is almost smoking, add 3 monkfish fillets to each pan. Cook until nicely browned on the first side, about 6 minutes. Turn the fish over and cook for another 3 minutes, until cooked through.

Meanwhile, gently reheat the pepper mixture. Squeeze the lime juice and sprinkle the cilantro over and stir to combine.

To serve, spoon the pepper mixture into the center of each plate and top with the monkfish fillets. Serve with the cooked rice.

Warmed Snapper with Ginger Oil

<small>SERVES 6</small>

Three 6-ounce snapper fillets, skinned

3 tablespoons Ginger Oil (page 96)

**Fine sea salt and freshly ground
   white pepper**

1 tablespoon thinly sliced chives

1 lime, halved

PREP: 20 minutes — **COOK:** 2 minutes

Preheat the oven to 350°F.

Slice the snapper ¼ inch thick on the bias. Brush each plate with ginger oil and season with salt and pepper. Arrange the snapper slices to form a square on each plate. Brush with the remaining ginger oil. Season with salt and pepper.

Just before serving, warm the snapper in the oven for 1 to 2 minutes; be careful not to overcook. Sprinkle the chives and squeeze the lime juice over each plate. Serve immediately.

Marinated Conch

<small>SERVES 6</small>

4 conches

¼ cup cilantro julienne

3 tablespoons Ginger Oil (page 96)

2 tablespoons minced ginger

2 tablespoons prepared wasabi paste

1 tablespoon minced jalapeño pepper

1 tablespoon minced shallot

3 tablespoons fresh lime juice

2 tablespoons organic soy sauce

PREP: 30 minutes — **COOK:** 5 minutes

Trim the ends off each conch and peel away the thick outer skin. Slice the conches as thin as possible. Place in a bowl and refrigerate until chilled.

No more than 5 minutes before serving, add the cilantro, ginger oil, ginger, wasabi, jalapeño, shallot, and 2 tablespoons of the lime juice to the conch. Gently mix to combine.

To serve, divide the conch among six chilled bowls, mounding it in the center. Drizzle the remaining 1 tablespoon lime juice and the soy sauce around the conch. Serve with warm toasts.

THE NATURE OF SNAPPER

Snapper is a refined fish, very lean and without fat, so you don't get any fishiness. It reminds me of the *dorade* in France, same shape, similar texture. The texture and the delicate flavor make snapper special. It's very good as a ceviche, and it's very good poached as we did with coconut milk (see page 98). You can also sauté red snapper, but you must sauté very carefully because it can dry out and lose all its flavor—it becomes like cardboard. At the restaurant, if we cook a fillet four minutes total, the first three and a half are on one side and then it's very briefly cooked on the other. Raw to rare maintains its flavor and almost creamy texture.

When you buy whole snapper, you must make sure it's very, very fresh. In Puerto Rico, it is beautiful. The problem with snapper in the United States is that there is a lot of garbage, so when you buy it you must be careful if you intend to serve it raw or rare. The blood has to be very red, bright red, and there must be no smell in the belly. This is the best test for snapper and many fish. If the belly smells fishy or smells like the guts, then it is no good. If the belly smells like the ocean, then it's good, the rest of the flesh will be pure. Ask the fishmonger to let you smell it—you should not be ashamed to ask. Look for firm, bright, elastic flesh, good color, clear eyes. Fishmongers have tricks—they can brush an old dull snapper with baking soda to make the skin look very bright red for a couple of hours, the eyes look good again—but with the smell of the belly, there's nothing they can do.

The snapper here is merely warmed snapper, super-rare, what chefs call "black and blue." Again, it must be sushi-quality. Once you have good-quality snapper, you do almost nothing to it other than flavor it, here with ginger oil, chives, and lime juice. The lime is especially important, both for its flavor and its acidity. When snapper is raw or just warm, its very, very smooth texture gives you the impression of richness, so it's nice to have an acidic component to balance that experience of richness as well as to boost what could otherwise seem a bland flavor.

THE NATURE OF CONCH

Conch is a giant sea snail native to the Caribbean and the waters off southern Florida, but it's now being farm-raised and therefore can be found in other locales as well. It's a very interesting product that is like the geoduck—the giant clam—and the razor clam because the tough, muscular flesh almost has a crunch to it. In the United States, it's usually cooked, in fritters or in chowder. But it makes a great ceviche. I enjoy it raw because, like the geoduck, like abalone, it has a very delicate flavor that cooking kills. It is much better raw, more interesting to have in your mouth, to chew, and this recipe couldn't be simpler: sliced conch seasoned with sushi flavors—ginger, wasabi, soy.

THE NATURE OF MONKFISH

Monk is the most meaty fish, and you can treat it almost as if it were meat. When you have fillets, the best sauté method is a pan-roast: Get good color on one side in a hot pan, then flip it and pop it in the oven to finish it. (We would have done it here but our oven didn't work!) You can roast it whole, just like a pork loin, but you should remove the bone. I always recommend that you cook fish at the last minute because if it sits, it dries out—every fish, that is, except for monkfish. Monkfish has to rest, like meat. It becomes more tender. Generally speaking, the bigger, the better, so buy big pieces.

Monkfish has a great bite, like lobster, and is sometimes called poor man's lobster. In the South of France, it's a Christmas dish, with *sauce américaine*. When I was a kid, my aunts and uncles would make believe it was lobster. I was a spoiled little brat, and I would never have wanted monkfish. They said to me it was lobster.

This recipe is like a South American version of a Basque dish. In Basque cuisine, they use a lot of peppers, garlic, onions, called a *piperade*. In our "sofrito," we also use tropical flavors—coco milk and dende oil, which is oil from palm flowers. So it's really a Basque dish converted to the Caribbean.

THE NATURE OF MAHI MAHI

Mahi mahi is a fish that becomes very dry if overcooked, so you must cook it carefully. It has a very delicate flesh, and it's somewhat fatty. I don't use mahi mahi at the restaurant—I think a lot of people don't like it—but I like it a lot. It reminds me of hamachi, a completely different fish, but very similar. Mahi mahi is a tropical fish. It's best sautéed, but very quickly. Try to get a very thin crust. If your pan is too hot, the crust will be dry and thick, so the temperature of your pan is important, as is the cut of the fillet. If it's too thick, the inside will still be raw when the crust is perfect. If it's too thin, it will be overcooked before the crust develops. I don't eat mahi mahi raw; when I'm not intimately familiar with a fish and it's from the tropics, I'm careful. And I wouldn't poach it, because it's fatty. Would you like steamed tuna? Think about it: Does steamed mackerel or poached sardines sound appealing? Salmon is probably the best of the fatty fishes to steam or poach.

In the dish on page 153, the mahi mahi is sautéed with okra. I had never cooked with okra before. When I'd eaten it, it was terrible, because it gets slimy as you cook it. But we had okra on hand, and I thought if it was very quickly cooked, then it might be okay. And it worked. Okra, seasoned with curry, and sautéed mahi mahi.

THE NATURE OF TUNA

Tuna is one of the most popular fish available in sushi quality to the home cook. Generally, the less done to excellent tuna, the better. Never cook it through; don't even cook it to medium rare. French culinary books from a few decades ago, such as *Larousse Gastronomique,* advise cooking tuna to death. If you do, that's what it will taste like. Tuna is special in its raw state because it has a mild fresh taste that carries the flavors of oils and herbs and seasonings exceptionally well. This neutral flavor allows a cook countless directions to take the tuna in—whether with coriander and wasabi or with olives or simply with fresh herbs, salt, and a neutral oil. A cook should treat tuna like a canvas, a vehicle for flavors. Its flesh is soft, has an almost buttery feel to it, and conveys this kind of richness as well. To take advantage of these qualities, it's important always to serve tuna rare or raw.

Rare-Seared Tuna with Ratatouille, page 152

Rare-Seared Tuna with Ratatouille pictured on page 151

SERVES 6

½ cup extra virgin olive oil

2 red bell peppers, cored, seeded,
and cut into ½-inch dice

2 banana peppers, seeded and
cut into ½-inch dice

1 large onion, cut into ½-inch dice

2 small zucchini, cut into ½-inch dice

3 tomatoes, seeded and cut into
½-inch dice

1 head garlic, cloves separated,
peeled, and thinly sliced

2 tablespoons chopped oregano

2 medium eggplants, peeled and
cut into ½-inch dice

Fine sea salt and freshly ground
white pepper

1 cup chicken stock

2 tablespoons fresh lime juice

2 tablespoons canola oil

Six 6-ounce tuna steaks

1 tablespoon basil julienne

6 large organic eggs

Gray sea salt for garnish

2 tablespoons soy sauce

PREP: 35 minutes — COOK: 25 minutes

For the ratatouille, heat ¼ cup of the olive oil in a large sauté pan over medium-high heat. Add the red peppers, banana peppers, and onions and cook until tender, 5 to 7 minutes. Then add the zucchini, tomatoes, garlic, and 1 tablespoon of the oregano and cook until the vegetables are tender, 5 to 7 minutes.

Add the eggplant and season with salt and pepper. Cook for another 5 minutes. Add the chicken stock and cook until it has been almost completely absorbed, about 5 minutes. Add the lime juice and stir to combine.

Meanwhile, for the tuna, heat 1 tablespoon of the canola oil in each of two large nonstick sauté pans over high heat. Season the tuna generously on both sides with salt and pepper and drizzle 1 teaspoon of the olive oil over each. Sprinkle each tuna with ½ teaspoon oregano leaves. When the oil is hot, sear the tuna steaks, turning once, until golden on both sides, about 2 minutes per side. The tuna should be warm in the center but still quite rare.

To serve, spoon about ½ cup of the warmed ratatouille onto each plate. Sprinkle the basil julienne over the ratatouille. Top each portion with a tuna steak. Separate the eggs and place an egg yolk on top of each tuna steak (discard the whites or reserve for another use). Place a pinch of gray salt on each egg yolk. Drizzle 1 teaspoon each of the soy sauce and the remaining extra virgin olive oil over the ratatouille on each plate. Serve immediately.

Why ratatouille with the tuna and an egg yolk? In the Basque country and in the South of France, we do a ratatouille with eggs. When the ratatouille is burning-hot, we put eggs on top and put it in the oven, and it's very good. Tuna also goes well with the piperade; piperade and ratatouille have similar flavors. Tuna is neutral and carries strong flavors well. Also, I think of tuna very much as a steak, and I love a raw egg yolk on a steak or on a hamburger. You draw on such material when you're cooking.

Sautéed Mahi Mahi with Okra and Citrus Vinaigrette

SERVES 6

THE VINAIGRETTE

1 tablespoon Dijon mustard

Finely grated zest of 1 lime

Finely grated zest of 1 blood orange
(you can substitute the zest of a
regular orange)

Finely grated zest of 1 lemon

2 tablespoons fresh lime juice

2 tablespoons sherry vinegar

Fine sea salt and freshly ground
white pepper

½ cup canola oil

1 shallot, minced

1 teaspoon minced ginger

3 tablespoons (¼-inch) diced seeded
tomatoes

THE OKRA AND MAHI MAHI

6 tablespoons canola oil

1 pound okra, ends trimmed,
cut into ½-inch slices

Six 6-ounce mahi mahi fillets

Fine sea salt and freshly ground
white pepper

¼ teaspoon curry powder

PREP: 25 minutes — **COOK:** 15 minutes

For the vinaigrette, place the mustard in a bowl and whisk in the lime zest, orange zest, lemon zest, lime juice, and sherry vinegar. Season with salt and pepper. Whisking constantly, slowly add the canola oil. Add the shallot and ginger and whisk to combine. Add the tomatoes and gently stir to combine. Set aside at room temperature.

For the okra, heat 2 tablespoons of the canola oil in a large sauté pan over medium-high heat. Add the okra, season with salt and pepper, and sauté until the okra is crisp-tender, 2 to 3 minutes.

Meanwhile, pour 2 tablespoons of the remaining canola oil into each of two large nonstick pans and heat over medium-high heat. Season the mahi mahi fillets with salt and pepper and lightly dust with the curry powder. When the oil is hot, add 3 fillets to each pan and cook until nicely browned on one side, about 5 minutes. Turn the fillets over and cook for an additional minute, or until heated through.

To serve, place a fillet in the center of each plate and arrange the okra evenly around the fillets. Drizzle 2 to 3 tablespoons citrus vinaigrette over each. Serve immediately.

TOWARD THE CENTER OF THE COOK

We're so used to seeing chefs performing before a camera, preparing one of their signature dishes with deceptive ease, that few realize that much about being a great chef depends on repetition. I was once invited to a dinner party where one of the guests, a chef at one of the best French restaurants in town, helped to prepare the meal—and overcooked a beautiful leg of lamb. He was furious and embarrassed, but it underscored the fact that chefs can be just as fallible as any cook in a home kitchen.

Eric had deliberately placed himself in such a situation, but with even higher expectations: new recipes that were not only pleasing for our group, but that were also reproducible. Furthermore, he'd done so here in Puerto Rico—which doesn't have the variety of products available to him in New York. To increase the difficulty by one more level, the kitchen where he'd be cooking didn't have a working oven. He was openly nervous at one point, a little panicky, but ultimately he decided not to play his trump card—to call his restaurant purveyors and have the best of anything he wanted overnighted straight to the house.

Our decisions describe us, and this decision, I think, helped to mark who Eric is. A good cook likes a challenge. A good cook chooses the most difficult road. I was always watching for clues to the kind of cook he is, and this was a clear one. Smaller physical clues continued to deepen my initial impressions as I watched him. His movements and gestures remained efficient and definitive—whether he was boning a fish, pan-roasting a pork loin, or removing the green germs from cloves of garlic with the tip of a paring knife. His knives were always very, very sharp—more so than in even the best kitchens I'd been in. He sharpened them himself, and each time he picked up a clean one, he steeled it in exactly the same way.

And he was always tasting. He always had a spoon to dip into the pot, or a paring knife to cut off a loose scrap of meat to taste. Before adding a powerful ingredient to a batch of something—say, sherry vinegar to a sauce—he'd always lift up a spoon of sauce and let a drop of the vinegar or other ingredient fall into it, then taste and consider it before either adding the ingredient to the sauce or not. When he couldn't imagine how arugula would taste with the lobster, or beets with a raw fish, he'd put a little of each on a spoon and eat it.

You expect a chef to be a good taster, and it was instructive to listen to Eric taste, which he had to do continually because Andrea needed to write everything down. For instance, when we sat down to leftover chicken, cleverly enhanced with Thai seasonings—lemongrass, ginger, coconut milk—and presented in bright green bundles, sauced with a soy-citrus vinaigrette with finely diced pineapple (see page 129), we all tasted and nodded. Something was not right, but I couldn't figure out what it was. After a couple of bites, Eric said to Andrea, who took notes, "I want to take the pineapple off. The pineapple confuses everything." He was absolutely right. "And add peanuts. And the gray salt does nothing, we take that off."

Returning to my notes, I found something I'd written midway through the trip, still trying to figure Eric out, to understand what it was we were all doing in Puerto Rico, of all places: He's trained to cook for many, many people every night, his job, his work. This is a good thing. And yet cooking the way he's cooking here is better food, more graceful food. It's the best way of cooking, and you couldn't possibly cook this way in a restaurant.

He was definitely getting somewhere—moving toward himself. I'd been happy to go along for the ride, but I'd been skeptical. It was one thing to cook the same dishes night after night at Le Bernardin with your purveyors dropping the very best products from across the globe at your doorstep, and quite another to make astonishing meals out of what is at hand. Eric had returned to the kind of powerful flavors and seasonings he loved—sharp escabeche, fiery peppers, exotic ginger and coconut milk, pique—the sorts of flavors he'd become accustomed to growing up so close to Spain. This was at his core. After the night of the snapper ceviche he seemed to find himself again, or to be returned to himself.

{ **spring** }

Napa—Bounty

Roasted Leg of Lamb and Garlic with Goat Cheese Mashed Potatoes, page 222

Our first trip to the market is exciting—baby artichokes, favas, snap peas, English peas, very sweet English cucumbers, dried lavender (for the house), purple asparagus, bread, spinach, baby arugula, fresh herbs, cheeses, salami, chorizo (of course), olives, baby turnips, handfuls of fresh morels, cèpes—it goes on. You'd have to work very hard to be a bad cook here. To cook in the Napa Valley will be a joy.

BOUNTY, BEAUTY, AND VASTNESS

Like most visitors to the Napa Valley, we arrive here after flying into San Francisco, then hopping on the main interstate heading north. As we pass through the outskirts of San Francisco, Oakland, and Berkeley, burbs on the way to Highway 29, the valley's main artery, the effect is a sloughing off, an unburdening, of city life, of one's daily work. The sky turns from nondescript cloud cover to a deep cobalt. The land, changing to a dry green and gold, spreads out and begins to roll. Huge bushes of wild fennel and rosemary dot the roadside, and then the vineyards appear. This is about the only coastal land in America that's more valuable as tillable soil than paved over for a mall or office complex.

The Indians who lived in the Napa Valley called it by their word for plenty, because food grew all year round. The growing, gathering, and making of food—everything from artisanal breads and cheeses to heirloom vegetables to hand-raised livestock to true wild mushrooms—as well as wine and some of the country's most famous restaurants, make this one of the food meccas of the United States.

Eric has been here before, but he has never cooked from within its landscape, and I'm eager to see his response to *la terroir*. We've just come from a hot winter landscape that had him, for a moment, considering whether to ship ingredients in from New York. Eric in the Napa Valley will be like Scrooge waking to find the ghost of Christmas Present in his living room.

After pulling into an unmarked drive that takes us up a nearly verticle winding path and back down an equally steep driveway, I see that Andrea has rented a House with a View. We are still within the limits of the city of Napa, one of a handful of towns that dot the Napa Valley, but the whole of the valley is ours from the rear deck. It's an extraordinary vista of mountains and vineyards, birds, and flowers, a nineteenth-century landscape painting in vibrant heat-hazy oils. After a trip to the local markets and a quick meditation, Eric is eager to begin.

I've never encountered a place where the gesture of cooking and the instinct are so complementary —gesture meaning the physical acts of cooking, including picking food (whether fennel by the roadside or morels out of a basket in the produce section), cleaning it, cutting it, sautéing it, roasting it, marinating it, and instinct meaning your soul as cook. No matter who you are, here the gesture and the instinct can be one because the products are so elemental and so bountiful. Puerto Rico all but demanded that you use flavors that dazzle—ginger and lime and pique. Napa can be almost anything you wish. For me, it takes me back to my youth.

Here I see the freshest, most beautiful ingredients I've encountered since I left Europe. I hold a tomato, a fresh yellow tomato from the market, and I'm thinking how to cook it, until I realize that it is perfect the way it is, that to cook it in any way would be to diminish it. And so we make it part of a salad and simply let salt and olive oil bring out its complete tomato-ness. The artichokes—in Provence, I used to find them so young and fresh I ate them raw. Baby beets, oh my God, they're amazing, so sweet and so plentiful. Even the turnip here is beautiful. And then a poached egg. You say, "A poached egg? On a spring salad? What are you doing?" But this is true cooking, seeing what you have and following your instinct. And in Napa, instinct spurs results that are amazing in their simplicity and their deliciousness.

I wasn't planning to cook veal chops for lunch, but we saw some at a market that were so beautiful I felt *obligated* to buy them. Morels and veal are a classic pairing, and we'll do this without the customary cream sauce. We'll try something edgier—crème fraîche and mustard, I think—and we'll add the richness and bright pale green of a parsley butter sauce. A fresh vegetable salad followed by this veal with morels—this is cooking from the landscape, letting place determine the menu.

Spring Vegetable Salad with Poached Egg and Herb Vinaigrette pictured on page 168

SERVES 6

12 baby yellow beets

12 baby red beets

12 baby turnips, peeled

12 baby Yukon Gold potatoes

12 baby carrots, peeled

3 baby fennel bulbs, tops removed

6 baby leeks, white and tender
   green parts only

12 asparagus spears, tips only
   (stalks reserved for another use)

¼ pound haricots verts, ends trimmed

1 tablespoon Dijon mustard

6 tablespoons aged sherry vinegar

2 tablespoons balsamic vinegar

1 tablespoon chopped shallots

Fine sea salt and freshly ground
   white pepper

6 tablespoons canola oil

6 tablespoons extra virgin olive oil

6 extra-large eggs

1 tablespoon chopped basil

1 tablespoon chopped tarragon

1 tablespoon thinly sliced chives

1 tablespoon chopped flat-leaf parsley

Gray sea salt and coarsely ground
   black pepper

¼ pound aged goat cheese

PREP: 35 minutes — COOK: 30 minutes

This is a quintessential spring dish and it's beautiful for its simplicity, but you needn't use all the vegetables we used for it to be great. The salad is all about freshness; use vegetables that are beautiful, that are exciting because they are so fine. The egg adds a rich tasty element, and if the yolk is runny, as it ought to be, it will enrich the dressing as you eat. It's also a great dish to make ahead of time. Even the eggs can be poached and transferred to ice water, where they can be kept for a day, then reheated in simmering water before serving.

Bring three small pots of salted water to a boil. Add the yellow beets to one, the red beets to the second, and turnips to the third and cook until tender, 7 to 9 minutes. Drain and immediately plunge into an ice water bath to cool; then drain again. Peel the beets. Cut all the vegetables in half. Set aside.

Fill four pots with fresh water, bring to a boil, and salt generously. Cook the potatoes, carrots, fennel, and leeks separately until tender: the potatoes will cook in about 10 minutes, the carrots, fennel, and leeks in about 5 minutes. Drain and immediately plunge into an ice water bath to cool; then drain again. Slice the potatoes in half and the fennel into quarters. Cut the leeks lengthwise in half if large. Set aside.

Fill two of the pots with fresh water, bring to a boil and salt generously. Cook the asparagus and haricots verts separately until crisp-tender, 3 to 4 minutes. Drain and immediately plunge into an ice water bath to cool. Drain and set aside.

Meanwhile, prepare the vinaigrette. In a medium bowl, combine the Dijon mustard, 2 tablespoons of the sherry vinegar, the balsamic vinegar, the shallots, ¼ teaspoon salt, and a pinch of white pepper. Whisk to incorporate. Whisking constantly, slowly add the canola and olive oils until fully incorporated. Adjust the seasoning. Set aside. *(The vegetables and vinaigrette can be prepared early in the day and refrigerated; keep the beets separate from the other vegetables.)*

Just before serving, bring 3 quarts of salted water to a simmer in a large deep skillet and add the remaining ¼ cup sherry vinegar. Crack an egg into a small bowl. Create a small whirlpool in the simmering water by stirring it in a circular manner, gently drop the egg into the whirlpool, and allow the edges of the white to curl around the yolk. Repeat with the remaining eggs, creating a whirlpool for each egg and waiting each time to make sure the last one has come together before you add the next egg. Cook until the whites have solidified but the yolks are still soft, about 1½ minutes per egg. Remove the eggs with a slotted spoon and trim the edges. *(If necessary, cook only 2 or 3 eggs at a time and transfer the first batch[es] to a platter; they can be rewarmed in the hot water just before serving.)*

To serve, divide the vegetables among six plates and place a warm poached egg in the center of each. Add the herbs to the vinaigrette and mix to combine. Drizzle over the vegetables. Season the poached eggs with gray salt and coarsely ground black pepper. Using a vegetable peeler, shave the goat cheese over each plate. Serve immediately.

Veal Chops with Morels and Herb Butter Sauce pictured on page 169

THE MUSHROOMS

2 tablespoons canola oil

1 pound morel mushrooms, cleaned,
   halved if large

2 tablespoons minced shallots

1 tablespoon minced garlic

1 tablespoon chopped flat-leaf parsley

THE SAUCE

2 cups packed flat-leaf parsley leaves

½ cup packed chervil leaves

½ cup packed tarragon leaves

¼ cup water

½ pound (2 sticks) cold unsalted butter,
   cut into small dice

THE VEAL

¼ cup canola oil

6 thick-cut veal chops (from the first ribs)

Fine sea salt and freshly ground
   white pepper

½ cup Cognac

1 tablespoon Dijon mustard

½ cup crème fraîche

PREP: 25 minutes — **COOK:** 30 minutes

For the mushrooms, heat the canola oil in a large sauté pan over medium-high heat. Add the morels and sauté until they are tender and have given up their liquid, about 5 minutes. Add the shallots, garlic, and parsley and sauté until softened, about 3 minutes. Set aside.

For the sauce, bring three pots of salted water to a boil. Blanch the parsley, chervil, and tarragon separately until tender, 1 to 2 minutes each. Drain in a strainer and run cold water over them until cool, then place all the herbs in a blender and puree, adding a little water if necessary. Set aside.

Preheat the oven to 400°F.

Bring the ¼ cup water to a boil in a small saucepan. Lower the heat to a simmer and slowly add the butter, whisking constantly until all the butter has been absorbed. Set aside at room temperature.

For the veal, heat 2 tablespoons canola oil in each of two large ovenproof sauté pans over high heat. Generously season the veal chops on both sides with salt and pepper and add 3 chops to each pan. Sear until golden brown on the first side, about 4 minutes, then turn and sear the other side until golden brown, about 4 minutes.

Place the pans in the oven to finish cooking the veal, about 6 minutes, or until desired doneness. Transfer the chops to a warm platter while you prepare the sauce.

Deglaze the pans with the Cognac, scraping up any browned bits on the bottom, then combine the liquid in one pan. Add the Dijon mustard and stir to incorporate. Add the crème fraîche and mushrooms and bring to a boil. Adjust the seasoning.

Meanwhile, gently rewarm the butter sauce, add the pureed herbs, and just heat through. Adjust the seasoning.

To serve, place one veal chop on each plate and spoon the mushrooms evenly over the chops. Drizzle each plate with herb sauce around the veal. Serve immediately.

Spring Vegetable Salad with Poached Egg and Herb Vinaigrette, page 166, before being dressed

Eric took an old standard, veal with a morel cream sauce, and made it feel new with the acidic flavorful elements of crème fraîche and mustard. He enriched the dish further with gorgeous herb butter. He made what are essentially two sauces for the veal, but either would suffice on its own, especially the morel mixture. The two together are over the top. The veal is treated like a steak—seasoned well with salt and pepper shortly before cooking.

GREEN HERB BUTTER SAUCE

This may be one of the simplest sauces of all to make—butter, liquid but remaining emulsified, has all the attributes of a sauce, and all you need to do is add flavor and color via the herbs. If you make it with olive oil, the oil will overpower the flavor of the herbs. If you do it with a neutral oil, you will have a puree or an herb oil, not a sauce. Doing it with butter, you have a sauce immediately, and the butter doesn't interfere with the flavor of the herb; in fact, it captures its essence. This can be done with any soft herb or leaf: basil, tarragon, arugula, mint, watercress, what have you. As with all basic preparations, there are a couple of critical points. You must cook the herbs very briefly in vigorously boiling water, shock them immediately in cold water, and then gently drain and squeeze them dry. They can be stored in the refrigerator until you're ready to use them (though the sooner you use the herbs to complete the sauce the better), and the butter emulsion can be made in advance and held at room temperature. The second critical point is that the sauce must be finished at the last minute, or the volatile flavors of the herbs will disappear. Other than that, it's as simple as it sounds: Cook the herbs, puree in a blender, and stir into your butter.

Veal Chops with Morels and Herb Butter Sauce, page 167

Mornings tend to get busy quickly—Andrea negotiating refrigerator space for the live scallops, for the bag filled with baby eels, thousands of them, just a couple translucent squiggly inches each. Called *pibales*, these are a spring luxury. Tammar and Shimon are clicking away almost continuously. Eric lights the tall candles we have brought with us from Puerto Rico, ties on an apron, and begins to cook. Valentino appears out of nowhere, like the Cheshire cat, and tests some new pens he's brought with very fine black tips.

It's almost too beautiful here. We sit on the deck, having eaten an extraordinary lobster salad, and stare out at the rolling Mayacamas, gaze at intensely colored blooms and bright songbirds against the vastness of the landscape, sensing here a mixture of high style and wildness. The beauty is so astonishing that it's all but impossible not to talk about it. I'm grateful when darkness comes because we then can talk about something else; last night it was the New York restaurant world, then spirituality. As we get to know each other and spend more time together, conversation becomes more intimate. The food, too, is more relaxed, although it's also more sophisticated. "We're going to cook

a bit more fancy," Eric says. Tammar and Shimon have also developed a very clean style in their images in response to the environment. Valentino, however, isn't near refining anything; he has arrived with almost no materials or tools, and Eric is annoyed. "I wish he would be more focused."

Valentino shrugs at me and smiles. "I brought the most important things—my brushes and my hands."

Portobello and Eggplant Tart

Six 3½-inch-wide portobello mushrooms

10 garlic cloves, peeled

¾ cup extra virgin olive oil

3 rosemary sprigs

**Fine sea salt and freshly ground
   white pepper**

8 tablespoons (1 stick) unsalted butter

5 sheets phyllo dough

**5 Japanese eggplants, peeled and
   cut into ½-inch dice (about 3 cups)**

3 tablespoons diced (¼-inch) red onion

SPECIAL EQUIPMENT

3½-inch ring mold or round cookie cutter

PREP: 40 minutes — COOK: 35 minutes

I love the flavor of the roasted portobellos you find in Italian restaurants, but it is too much mushroom. This I think is a very elegant way to serve a portobello, sliced and served in a crunchy phyllo shell, with a spread of eggplant (eggplant and mushrooms is always a good combination). All the components can be prepared ahead of time and rewarmed, but you must assemble the dish at the last minute, or the phyllo will become soggy.

Preheat the oven to 400°F.

For the mushrooms, remove the stems. Peel the thin skin from the caps and discard. Place the mushrooms on a baking sheet. Roughly chop 8 of the garlic cloves. Drizzle ½ cup of the olive oil over the mushrooms, making sure they are thoroughly coated on top and bottom, then scatter the garlic over the mushrooms. Cut each rosemary sprig in half and place one on each mushroom. Season with salt and pepper.

Roast the mushrooms until they have released their liquid, about 15 minutes. Set aside to cool briefly. Leave the oven on.

Melt the butter in a small pan. Place one phyllo sheet on your cutting board and brush with melted butter. Top with another phyllo sheet and brush with butter. Continue in this manner until all the sheets are used. Using the ring mold or cookie cutter, cut out 6 circles of dough. Place the circles on a parchment paper–lined baking sheet.

Bake the phyllo until golden brown and flaky, about 15 minutes. Remove from the oven and let cool. Reduce the oven temperature to 350°F.

Meanwhile, when the mushrooms are cool enough to handle, discard the rosemary and garlic. Press on the mushrooms to release their liquid, then strain the juices that have collected on the baking sheet. Pour the mushroom jus into a small saucepan and set aside. Slice the mushrooms on the bias into ¼-inch-thick slices, but do not separate the slices. Cut 6 parchment rounds slightly larger than the whole mushroom caps and place the mushrooms gills down on the rounds. Set aside on a baking sheet.

Peel and chop the remaining garlic cloves. In a large sauté pan, heat the remaining ¼ cup olive oil over high heat. Add the eggplant and toss to coat. Add the garlic and red onion and season with salt and pepper. Cook until the vegetables are tender, 3 to 5 minutes. Remove from the heat.

Just before serving, place the mushrooms in the oven to warm. Warm the mushroom jus. Gently reheat the eggplant mixture if necessary.

To serve, place a phyllo round in the center of each plate. Top with the eggplant mixture. Remove the mushrooms from the oven and invert one onto each portion of phyllo. Remove the parchment paper. Drizzle the mushroom jus around the plates. Serve immediately.

Lobster Salad with Mango and Foie Gras, page 174

Panna cotta has the feel of a very modern dessert—it's very simple, very clean, and much lighter than its cousin, the bavarois, which is a crème anglaise (egg yolk, cream, vanilla) set with gelatin and mixed with whipped cream. This is simply cooked cream set with gelatin. You can flavor it in countless ways; we used fresh fennel, which is in season now.

Fennel-Scented Panna Cotta with Wild Strawberries, page 175

Lobster Salad with Mango and Foie Gras pictured on page 172

THE LOBSTER

4 quarts water

1 cup sherry vinegar

1 onion, peeled and halved

1 carrot, peeled and halved

6 garlic cloves, peeled

3 tablespoons kosher salt

2 tablespoons fennel seeds

1 tablespoon coriander seeds

1 tablespoon cumin seeds

Three 1½-pound lobsters

4 tablespoons unsalted butter, melted

THE SALAD

1 tablespoon Dijon mustard

2 tablespoons sherry vinegar

1 tablespoon mango puree
   (mashed with a fork)

Fine sea salt and freshly ground
   white pepper

3 tablespoons canola oil

3 tablespoons extra virgin olive oil

1 shallot, diced

2 slices fresh duck foie gras
   (about 4 ounces) or one 4-ounce
   foie gras terrine

3 cups mesclun greens

½ cup diced (¼-inch) mango

PREP: 40 minutes — **COOK:** 45 minutes

A simple salad can suddenly become very elegant simply by adding lobster. We make this one a little more so with foie gras, which adds a meaty flavor to the dish. When I serve lobster salad, I want the lobster to be warm. I hate cold lobster—it loses its flavor, it becomes tough. Note that the tail of the lobster is skewered before cooking to keep it straight as it cooks; this makes it easier to slice and more elegant to present.

For the lobster, place all the first ingredients except the lobsters and butter in a large pot and bring to a boil. Lower the heat and simmer for 30 minutes.

Meanwhile, kill the lobsters by plunging a chef's knife between the eyes of each lobster and bringing the knife down through the head. Separate the tails and claws from the body. Reserve the bodies for another use (such as Lobster Consommé, page 312). Insert a wooden skewer lengthwise into each lobster tail. Add the tails and claws to the pot and cook for 5 minutes. Remove the pot from the heat and let the lobster continue to cook in the hot liquid. Remove the claws after 10 minutes and the tails after 20 minutes. Discard the cooking liquid.

Once the lobster is cool enough to handle, remove the skewers, crack the shells, and carefully remove the meat. Cut the tail on the bias into thin slices. Cut the claws into julienne strips and the meat from the "knuckles" into small dice. Lay the tail meat, claw meat, and lobster dice on a baking sheet, keeping them separate, cover with plastic wrap, and refrigerate.

For the vinaigrette, whisk together the mustard, sherry vinegar, mango puree, a pinch of salt, and pepper to taste in a small bowl. Whisking constantly, slowly add the vegetable and olive oils. Add the diced shallot. Adjust the seasoning. Set aside.

Preheat the oven to 350°F.

Cut the foie gras into small dice. Heat a 12-inch nonstick pan over medium-high heat and quickly sauté the foie gras dice just until nicely browned. Remove from the heat and drain off the excess fat.

Meanwhile, brush the lobster with the melted butter. Place in the oven until warmed.

To serve, combine the salad greens, foie gras, mango dice, and lobster dice in a bowl and season with salt and pepper. Toss with enough vinaigrette to coat. Mound the salad in the center of each plate. Top with the lobster julienne and place 4 tail slices around each salad. Drizzle the remaining vinaigrette around the plates. Serve immediately.

Fennel-Scented Panna Cotta with Wild Strawberries pictured on page 173

pictured on page 173

SERVES 6

THE PANNA COTTA

3 gelatin sheets

½ cup cold water

1 fennel bulb

2½ cups heavy cream

½ cup milk

⅓ cup sugar

2 tablespoons anisette
** (or any licorice-flavored liqueur)**

Vegetable cooking spray

THE GARNISH

¾ cup heavy cream

2 tablespoons sugar

2 cups (about 1 pint) wild strawberries or
** quartered regular strawberries**

SPECIAL EQUIPMENT

Six 6-ounce ramekins

PREP: 15 minutes, plus 4 hours chilling time — **COOK:** 15 minutes

Place the gelatin in the cold water to soften.

Meanwhile, trim the fennel bulb, reserving the fronds, and slice it. Chop enough of the fronds to make ½ cup. In a large saucepan, bring the cream, milk, sugar, sliced fennel, and fennel fronds to a boil, stirring until the sugar is dissolved. Lower the heat to a simmer and infuse the fennel into the cream for 10 minutes.

Drain the cream in a colander (the fennel fronds should not be strained out, only the large slices of fennel. Set over a bowl. Add the anisette and stir to incorporate. Squeeze the excess water from the gelatin sheets, add to the hot cream mixture, and stir until the gelatin has melted.

Spray the ramekins with vegetable cooking spray. Divide the gelatin-cream mixture among them and let cool to room temperature. Cover with plastic wrap and chill until set, at least 4 hours, or overnight.

To serve, dip the ramekins in hot water for 3 seconds. Run a thin knife around the sides of each ramekin and invert the panna cotta onto the center of a plate.

Combine the heavy cream and sugar in a bowl and whisk until the cream is foamy. Add the strawberries and mix gently. Spoon the strawberry cream around the panna cotta. Serve immediately.

Fish whose texture or flavor would be ruined by the caramelizing effect of a sauté should be poached. Halibut can be sautéed, as I sometimes do, but it is best poached because its flavors and textures are so delicate. I generally don't like sautéed scallops. They sauté beautifully, develop a pretty golden crust, and this is how they seem most often served, but to me the already sweet scallop becomes too sweet. A crust on these or other delicate fish destroys their flavor.

Gilbert was a purist; for years, he wouldn't sauté a piece of fish. A fish lived in water: This was its natural medium and this was the environment in which it should be cooked. This may sound extreme, but it reflects the passion and purity he brought to cooking fish.

More and more, I find I like cooking fish in salted water, not in a nage or a court-bouillon or a fumet. At Le Bernardin, all the fish is cooked this way now. I feel that a flavored cooking medium sometimes adds too much flavor, interfering with that of the fish itself. Such would be the case with the salmon on page 178. The scallops, on the other hand, are very mild, and the court-bouillon works as a seasoning device. The third recipe (page 180) uses a fumet, a liquid that both cooks the fish (a combination of salmon, scallops, and crab) and works as the soup broth.

Because the temperature of a liquid never goes above 212°F, as opposed to oil in a sauté pan, which can be 400°F or higher, the fish is cooked gently and so can take a longer cooking time. It holds well in liquid, which is important for chowders, and fish cooked submerged in liquid is less likely to become dry.

We've included one poached meat dish here, which originates from the pot-au-feu technique—in effect, poached meat and vegetables. Typically meat is poached for the same reason it's braised—to transform a big tough piece of meat into one that is tender. It's possible to poach tender cuts of meat with good results, but this is less common. The only real difference between braised meat and poached meat is that braised meat is first seared to develop a flavorful crust, and then poached on top of the stove or in the oven. In America, poached meat has a bad reputation, but there are some very interesting uses for the technique—beef tenderloin poached in stock with root vegetables, for instance, or chicken breast poached in spicy tomato water.

Eric chose to leave the salmon almost raw
(see page 178), not only because it was a
beautiful fish, but also because it was wild.
"Is there a difference between wild and
farm-raised salmon?" I asked.

Yes, a big difference. Wild salmon has a natural
flavor that reflects where it was living: If it was
eating shrimp all its life on the bottom of the
ocean, it may have a sweeter taste. If there was
a lot of seaweed in the area, maybe it will have a
slight herby flavor. It's almost like a wine—it gets
flavor from where it comes from.

Barely Cooked Salmon with Parmesan Polenta and Mushroom Consommé, page 178

Barely Cooked Salmon with Parmesan Polenta and Mushroom Consommé pictured on page 177

SERVES 6

1 pound button mushrooms

10 cups water

Fine sea salt and freshly ground white pepper

1 pound gyromitre or morel mushrooms (see Note)

1 tablespoon canola oil

1 tablespoon chopped shallots

1 tablespoon chopped garlic

7 to 8 tablespoons (1 stick) butter

1 tablespoon chopped flat-leaf parsley

2 cups milk

⅓ cup instant polenta

½ cup freshly grated Parmesan

One 2½-pound salmon fillet

PREP: 30 minutes — **COOK:** 3 hours and 25 minutes

Here salmon is poached simply in salt water and served very rare with mushrooms and a mushroom broth, along with creamy polenta. The polenta adds a starch that the salmon needs, but it is also delicate and won't overwhelm the flavors of the fish. Mushrooms and polenta are a great classical pair, and a sturdy, satisfying match for the meaty salmon.

Place the button mushrooms in a pan, cover with 8 cups of the water, and bring to a boil. Lower the heat to a simmer and cook for 3 hours.

Strain the stock through a fine-mesh strainer, pressing on the mushrooms to release the liquid. You should have at least 2 cups mushroom stock. Season to taste with salt and pepper. Pour into a saucepan and set aside. *(The stock can be made in advance and refrigerated for up to 3 days or frozen for up to a month.)*

Trim the gyromitre or morel mushrooms, discarding the stems, and halve them. Because these mushrooms can be particularly sandy, soak them in cold water to remove any dirt. Lift out of the water, rinse, and repeat two more times.

Heat the canola oil in a large sauté pan over high heat. Add the mushrooms, shallots, and garlic, season with salt and pepper, and sauté until the mushrooms are tender and have given up their liquid, but are not dry, 10 to 15 minutes. Add 3 tablespoons of the butter and the parsley and toss to incorporate. Set the pan aside.

Bring the milk, the remaining 2 cups water, and 4 tablespoons of the butter to a boil in a medium saucepan. Lower the heat to a simmer. Whisking constantly, slowly add the polenta, continuing to whisk until the polenta is completely incorporated. Cook for 5 minutes. The polenta will be very thin. Add the Parmesan and stir to incorporate. Set the pan aside.

Cut the salmon crosswise into 1-inch slices. Pull the ends of each side together, as if you were closing a book, and secure with a toothpick. In a flameproof shallow casserole large enough to accommodate all the salmon fillets, bring ¼ inch of generously salted water to a simmer. Season each fillet on both sides with salt and pepper and add to the casserole. Gently poach for 3 to 5 minutes, until the salmon is warm to the touch on top, but still quite rare on top and inside.

Meanwhile, gently reheat the mushroom broth, the wild mushrooms, and polenta. If the mushrooms are dry, add another tablespoon of butter and a bit of water to moisten.

To serve, spoon a circle of polenta into the center of each plate. Spoon ¼ cup of the mushroom broth around each polenta circle. Place 2 salmon fillets on each bed of polenta and spoon the mushrooms over the salmon. Serve immediately

NOTE: We used the very earthy gyromitre mushrooms for this recipe, but as some types are toxic if uncooked, and all are difficult to find, we offer morels as a substitute.

Poached Scallops with Caviar Sauce

SERVES 6

1 cup clam juice

½ cup heavy cream

1 tablespoon cold unsalted butter

3 cups Court-Bouillon (page 125)

18 large sea scallops or 6 jumbo live scallops in the shell

Fine sea salt and freshly ground white pepper

3 ounces osetra caviar

½ lemon, seeds removed

2 tablespoons thinly sliced chives

SPECIAL EQUIPMENT

Rock salt (if using scallop shells)

6 jumbo scallop shells (reserved from the live scallops or purchased at a gourmet shop) (optional)

PREP: 5 minutes — **COOK:** 10 minutes

This is a hugely luxurious dish, with the sweet flesh of the scallops enhanced by a sauce flavored and thickened with caviar. The dish is rich and creamy, sweet and salty. And it's very easy to make. The sauce base is clam juice, cream, and butter. The scallops are poached for just a minute or two, and caviar is added to the sauce just before serving. That is the only tricky and critical part of this dish: You must be careful to heat the sauce gently once the caviar has been added, bringing it just up to heat without letting it boil. It is, after all, an egg-thickened sauce, and you must be careful of overcooking eggs in this sauce or the caviar will turn hard and white. Treat it as the delicate product it is. Or, as Eric would put it, "Don't whisk it like an idiot. You must be extremely gentle."

Bring the clam juice and heavy cream to a simmer in a small saucepan. Add the butter and whisk to incorporate. Set aside.

Bring the court-bouillon to a simmer in a pan large enough to accommodate the scallops. Season the scallops on both sides with salt and pepper. Add the scallops to the simmering court-bouillon and poach gently until they are cooked just to rare, about 1½ minutes for large scallops, 2 to 2½ minutes for jumbo scallops.

To serve, place a bed of rock salt on each plate and rest a scallop shell on it (if you do not have scallop shells, serve the scallops in shallow bowls). Place 3 large scallops or 1 jumbo in each shell.

Meanwhile, gently reheat the sauce. Remove from the heat, add the caviar, and stir until the caviar is just heated through, about 45 seconds. Squeeze the juice of the lemon into the sauce, add the chives, and season with pepper. Spoon the sauce over the scallops, making sure the caviar is evenly distributed. Serve immediately.

Salmon, Crab, and Scallop Chowder

SERVES 6

2 slices double-smoked bacon, sliced
   crosswise into julienne strips

¾ cup sliced leeks (white and tender
   green parts only)

½ cup dry white wine

3 cups fish fumet (see below)

1 cup water

1 pound baby Yukon Gold potatoes,
   peeled and halved

Fine sea salt and freshly ground
   white pepper

½ cup heavy cream

1 tablespoon canola oil

One 6-ounce salmon fillet,
   cut into ¾-inch cubes

4 ounces crabmeat, picked over
   for shells and cartilage

6 large sea scallops, cut horizontally
   in half

1 tablespoon chopped dill

Grated zest of 1 lemon

PREP: 20 minutes — **COOK:** 40 minutes

Cook the bacon julienne in a large pot over medium heat, until it has rendered its fat and is crisp. Remove the bacon with a slotted spoon and drain on a paper towel. Remove all but 1 tablespoon of the fat from the pot. Add the leeks and sauté until limp and lightly caramelized, about 4 minutes.

Deglaze the pot with the white wine, stirring to incorporate the browned bits in the bottom of the pot. Return the bacon to the pot, cover with the fumet and water, and bring to a simmer. Add the potatoes and season with salt and pepper. Raise the heat and boil gently until the potatoes are tender, 10 to 15 minutes.

Meanwhile, preheat the oven to 400°F.

Add the cream to the fumet and bring to a simmer. Remove from the heat until ready to serve.

Line a baking sheet with parchment and brush it with the canola oil. Place the salmon, crab, and scallops on the sheet and season on both sides with salt and pepper. Place in the oven for 2 to 3 minutes, until just barely heated through. The salmon and scallops should still be quite rare.

Meanwhile, gently reheat the soup. Add the dill and lemon zest and stir to incorporate. Adjust the seasoning.

To serve, divide the warmed salmon, crab, and scallops among warmed bowls. Ladle the soup over and serve immediately.

Eric wanted to do a chowder because we had extra fish, and because the last chowder he had had, made by his friend Alan Richman, had so intrigued him. He's always enjoyed flour-thickened chowders, but he felt like making a light brothy chowder. We used the leftover salmon and scallop and crab from the refrigerator, but they make such a great combination, they are worth buying just for this. On the other hand, just about any variety of fish that poaches well will work here, because the secret to this dish is the fumet, a concentrated, very flavorful stock.

Fumet is very easy to make once you have good bones. The bones of the turbot are the best for fumet because of their high gelatin content, but generally any white bones from a nonoily fish can be used. To make a fumet, you sweat sliced onion and fennel until they're tender, add the bones and cook them gently, then add water just to cover and a bouquet garni and simmer very gently for 10 or 15 minutes. Let the fumet sit off the heat for another 15 minutes, then strain it through cheesecloth. That's all there is to it— just be sure not to cook the fumet too hard or too long.

A classical chowder begins with pork, traditionally salt pork; here Eric rendered bacon, sautéed the leeks with the bacon, and added the fumet to this. To serve, the fish is warmed, then placed in heated soup bowls, and the hot fumet, mounted with a little cream, is poured over it to finish the cooking. This is a beautiful soup if you take care to make a good fumet.

Poached Beef and Veal Shank with Herbed Vinaigrette and Celeriac Salad

SERVES 6

THE SHANKS

One 4-pound beef shank (bone in)

One 3-pound veal shank (bone in)

Fine sea salt and freshly ground
  white pepper

1 onion

1 carrot

1 bay leaf

Gray sea salt

Cracked black pepper

THE CELERIAC SALAD

3 tablespoons Dijon mustard

3 tablespoons crème fraîche

1 tablespoon fresh lemon juice

Fine sea salt and freshly ground
  white pepper

1½ cups peeled celeriac julienne

½ cup peeled Granny Smith apple julienne

1 teaspoon thinly sliced chives

THE VEGETABLES

6 baby golden beets

6 baby red beets

2 heads young garlic, cloves separated
  and peeled

6 spring onions (scallions), trimmed

1 bunch watercress, tough stems trimmed

PREP: 35 minutes — **COOK:** 3 hours

An old idea, revised for the spring. People think pot-au-feu is a heavy, rich dish for wintertime, but it's really a light dish because there is no heavy sauce or stock, only meat, vegetables, and water. The meat is served warm so that its natural gelatin is melted and the meat is moist, then the vegetables are served with a vinaigrette—it's a perfect spring salad.

Tie each shank at the top and bottom with kitchen string and place in a large pot. Cover with water and bring to a boil; drain.

In the rinsed-out pot, cover the shanks with water and add the onion, carrot, and bay leaf. Generously season with salt and pepper. Bring to a boil, then lower the heat to a simmer. Cook for 2 hours, skimming the foam as it rises to the top. Check the veal shank by inserting a paring knife down the shank, near the bone. When it can be easily inserted, remove the veal shank.

Continue to cook the beef shank for another hour, or until a paring knife is easily inserted in the meat. Remove the vegetables and bay leaf from the pot and discard. Return the veal shank to the pot. *(The recipe can be completed to this point early in the day and reserved in the refrigerator. Gently reheat the shanks in the cooking liquid just before serving.)* If serving immediately, simmer gently to rewarm the veal shank.

Meanwhile, prepare the celeriac salad: Place the Dijon mustard, crème fraîche, and lemon juice in a medium bowl and stir to incorporate. Season to taste with salt and pepper. Add the celeriac and apple julienne and toss to coat. Adjust the seasoning. Cover and refrigerate.

For the vegetables, bring three small pots of salted water to a boil. Add the golden and red beets to two of the pots and cook until tender, about 5 minutes. Drain and set aside until cool enough to handle, then peel the beets and cut them in half if large. Meanwhile, blanch the garlic in the third pot until tender, about 3 minutes. Reserve in the refrigerator, keeping the red beets separate.

THE HERBED VINAIGRETTE

2 tablespoons Dijon mustard

3 tablespoons sherry vinegar

¼ teaspoon fine sea salt

Pinch of freshly ground white pepper

¼ cup extra virgin olive oil

5 tablespoons canola oil

¼ cup chopped shallots

3 tablespoons chopped cornichons

2 tablespoons chopped capers

1 tablespoon prepared horseradish

1 tablespoon chopped tarragon

1 tablespoon chopped flat-leaf parsley

1 tablespoon thinly sliced chives

SPECIAL EQUIPMENT

Kitchen string

For the vinaigrette, combine the Dijon mustard, vinegar, salt, and pepper in a small bowl and whisk to incorporate. Whisking constantly, slowly drizzle in the olive oil, then the canola oil. Add the shallots, cornichons, capers, and horseradish and stir to incorporate. Set aside.

To serve, gently rewarm the shanks in the cooking liquid. Cut the kitchen string from the veal and beef shanks. Remove the bones. (Reserve the stock for another use.) Thinly slice both shanks against the grain. Fan 3 slices of veal and 3 slices of beef in the center of each plate. Garnish the meat with gray salt and cracked black pepper. Arrange the beets, garlic, and spring onions around the meat. Spoon about ¼ cup of the celeriac salad onto each plate at the 5 o'clock position. Sprinkle the celeriac with the 1 teaspoon sliced chives.

To complete the vinaigrette, add the tarragon, parsley, and chives and stir to incorporate. Place the watercress in a bowl and toss with enough vinaigrette to coat. Divide the watercress among the plates, mounding it at 3 o'clock. Drizzle the remaining vinaigrette over the meat and vegetables. Serve immediately.

In France, pot-au-feu is a one-pot dish, but several courses are served out of the same pot. Short ribs and shank or other tough cuts of meat, or a chicken, or whatever you have is poached in water, and vegetables are added. When the meat is done, the broth is served separately, perhaps with some vermicelli. Then the meat and vegetables are served; sometimes the vegetables are served with a vinaigrette.

We tend to think of the exotic as being from far away, like the South Pacific perhaps, or the Far East, but exotic can be from your backyard. Snails are exotic. So are frogs' legs. So are pibales, live squirming baby eels. Squid in all its forms is exotic because of its shape and unusual flesh.

Exotic things are fun to cook and serve precisely because they're uncommon. Some, like the sepia, or cuttlefish, a cephalopod common in the Mediterranean, are exotic and a little freaky in their form rather than in their taste. They don't have a strong or distinctive flavor, but they carry flavors well, and so they are fun to cook because you must use your skills as a cook to multiply their qualities, to stretch their canvas well so that they may carry bold flavors. Small sepia can be very tender. You can almost eat them like sushi or barely cooked; don't overcook them.

The pibales—the babies of the long eels that swim to the Sargasso Sea to mate and then return home to the marshy inlets of Maine and France each spring to spawn—are a perfect example of the exotic. They're alive, they jump out of the bowl and try to escape, you throw the wriggling writhing mass into a pan—cooking with them is an adventure. But for them to become great, you have to play with the spices and the garlic—without that and plenty of flavorful fat, they are slimy and tasteless. In northern France, they poach pibales, but I prefer the Spanish sauté for its bright strong spiciness.

Frogs' legs are the same. Because there is nothing else shaped like a frog's leg, you can't help but picture the whole frog while you work with them. They are almost a cartoon or caricature. Frogs' legs from farm-raised frogs need plenty of garlic and butter and lemon juice and parsley; and we sauté them, of course, because this adds flavor as well.

Of all of these dishes, the pibales are the most important to me. They are a part of my childhood. Pibales are a great delicacy and, for me, they mean spring.

Sautéed Pibales with Pepper Oil

1 red bell pepper

½ cup extra virgin olive oil

½ red onion, cut into large dice
   (about ¼ cup)

8 garlic cloves, 5 roughly chopped,
   3 halved

⅛ teaspoon cayenne pepper, plus a pinch

1½ pounds live pibales
   (in seawater; see headnote)

Fine sea salt and freshly ground
   white pepper

2 tablespoons minced flat-leaf parsley

1 tablespoon unsalted butter

½ lemon, seeds removed

PREP: 10 minutes — **COOK:** 15 minutes

Finding live pibales will be the hardest part of this dish. Eric buys them from a Maine supplier (see Sources, page 320) for sixty-five dollars per pound; in Europe, where they are a popular delicacy, they cost twice as much. Once you have them, happily swimming in a plastic bag like your childhood goldfish, it's simply a matter of sautéing them in flavorful oil the same way you might reheat some pasta. A translucent gray when alive, they turn white when cooked, and you'd think they *were* pasta were it not for the fact that each strand has two teensy black eyes. This preparation, with its spicy peppery flavors— "Spanish all the way," Eric says—should be served immediately, on small plates with some crusty bread, or nothing at all.

Cut off the top and bottom of the pepper and reserve. Slice the pepper open down one side and lay it out flat. Cut out the white membranes and seeds and discard. With your knife held parallel to the work surface, slice off the skin and discard it. Cut enough of the pepper into tiny dice to make ⅓ cup. Roughly chop the remaining pepper, including the top and bottom.

Heat the olive oil in a small sauté pan over low heat. Add the roughly chopped pepper, the red onion, the 5 roughly chopped garlic cloves, and the ⅛ teaspoon cayenne and cook until the vegetables are lightly caramelized, about 10 minutes. Remove from the heat and let cool to room temperature. Strain the oil and discard the vegetables.

Heat 2 tablespoons of the pepper oil in each of two large sauté pans over medium heat. Divide the halved garlic cloves between the pans. Divide the pepper dice between the pans. Drain the pibales and divide between the pans, stirring so they cook evenly. Season with salt, white pepper, and the pinch of cayenne and cook until the pibales are opaque, 1 to 2 minutes. Add half the parsley and butter to each pan and toss to combine. Discard the garlic.

To serve, squeeze the lemon juice over the pans, and divide the pibales among six warmed plates. Serve immediately.

Frogs' Legs with Parsley Sauce and Sautéed Frisée pictured on page 188

SERVES 6

2 cups tightly packed flat-leaf
  parsley leaves
½ cup water
10 tablespoons unsalted butter
½ cup extra virgin olive oil
1 rosemary sprig
4 garlic cloves, 2 halved and 2 sliced,
  plus ¼ teaspoon finely minced garlic
30 frogs' legs
1 large head frisée
Fine sea salt and freshly ground
  white pepper
All-purpose flour for dusting

PREP: 20 minutes — COOK: 25 minutes

Eric loves the frisée, which adds a little crunch and a little bitterness that combines with the garlic and parsley and spiciness of the freshly ground white pepper for a very special, flavorful dish that is also very simple.

Bring a medium pot of salted water to a boil. Add the parsley and cook just until tender and bright green, about 2 minutes. Drain in a strainer and run cold water over the parsley to cool. Place in a blender, add ¼ cup of the water, and blend until pureed. Store the parsley puree in the refrigerator.

In a medium saucepan, bring the remaining ¼ cup water to a boil. Cut the butter into small chunks and slowly add them to the boiling water, whisking constantly to incorporate the butter. Set aside at room temperature.

Combine ¼ cup of the olive oil, rosemary sprig, and 2 halved garlic cloves on a large platter and stir to marry the flavors. Add the frogs' legs and toss to coat. Cover and marinate the frogs' legs while you cook the frisée.

Wash the frisée and remove the core, separating the frisée into individual stalks. Pat dry. Place two large nonstick sauté pans over high heat and add 1 tablespoon of the olive oil to each pan. When the oil is hot, divide the frisée between the pans and add 1 sliced garlic clove to each one. Season with salt and pepper. Sauté the frisée until lightly browned and limp. Combine all the frisée in one pan, add ¼ cup water, and cook until the water has evaporated and the frisée is tender. Set aside.

Place two sauté pans over high heat and add 1 tablespoon of the olive oil to each pan. Remove the frogs' legs from the marinade and shake to remove excess oil. Season the frogs' legs with salt and pepper (you can gently dust with cayenne if you wish). Dust each leg with flour and add to the pan. Sear, turning once, until golden brown and cooked through, 3 to 4 minutes per side; be careful not to overcook, or they will become tough.

Meanwhile, gently reheat the butter sauce, and add 2 tablespoons of the parsley puree and the minced garlic; do not boil or the parsley will lose its vibrant green color and the sauce will separate. Season to taste with salt and pepper.

To serve, arrange the frisée down the center of six warmed plates. Top each portion of frisée with 5 frogs' legs, with the legs, forming arrows upward. Spoon the parsley sauce over the legs. Serve immediately.

Sautéed Sepia with Chorizo Broth and Spaghetti pictured on page 189

SERVES 6

THE SAUCE

2 tablespoons canola oil

1 small onion, thinly sliced

6 garlic cloves, thinly sliced

Fine sea salt and freshly ground
   white pepper

½ teaspoon cayenne pepper

25 baby sepia (cuttlefish), beaks removed
   (you can substitute 1 pound calamari)

1 cup dry white wine

3 cups water

1 ounce chorizo, thinly sliced
   (about ¼ cup)

1 thyme sprig

THE GARNISH

6 chives

¼ pound spaghetti

1½ cups chicken stock

THE SEPIA

2 tablespoons canola oil

30 baby sepia (cuttlefish; the smallest
   you can find), beaks removed
   (you can substitute 1 pound calamari)

Fine sea salt and freshly ground
   white pepper

Cayenne pepper

1 tablespoon chopped flat-leaf parsley

1 lemon, halved

PREP: 20 minutes — **COOK:** 1 hour and 20 minutes

For the sauce, heat 1 tablespoon of the canola oil in a medium saucepan over medium heat. Add half of the sliced onion and all but one-sixth of the sliced garlic, season with salt, pepper, and the cayenne, and sauté until lightly caramelized, about 7 minutes. Add the sepia and sauté for another 3 minutes.

Deglaze the pan with the white wine, stirring to release any browned bits in the bottom of the pan. Add the water and bring to a boil, then lower the heat and simmer for an hour. Strain the stock and reserve. *(The stock can be made up to 1 day in advance, covered, and refrigerated.)*

To finish the sauce, heat the remaining 1 tablespoon canola oil in a medium saucepan over medium heat. Add the chorizo, the remaining sliced onion and garlic, and the thyme and cook until the onion and garlic are translucent, about 5 minutes. Add the reserved sepia stock and bring to a boil. Remove from the heat and let infuse for 10 minutes. Strain the sauce and pour into to a clean saucepan.

For the garnish, bring a large pot of salted water to a boil. Add the chives (in a strainer) and cook until limp, less than 10 seconds. Transfer the chives to an ice water bath to stop the cooking; drain. Add the spaghetti to the boiling water and cook until it is almost tender but still quite al dente. Drain and run cold water over the spaghetti to stop the cooking.

Divide the spaghetti into six piles, straighten them, and trim to the same size if necessary. Tie each bundle at the top with a chive, and trim the excess chive, to leave ½ inch. Set aside.

Heat two large nonstick pans over high heat. Add 1 tablespoon of the canola oil to each pan. Place the sepia in a single layer on your cutting board and season with salt, pepper, and a pinch of cayenne pepper on each side. Divide the sepia between the pans and sear, turning once, until golden, about 2 minutes per side. Sprinkle the parsley over the sepia and squeeze the lemon juice over them.

Meanwhile, bring the chicken stock to a simmer in a wide skillet over medium heat.

Reheat the spaghetti bundles in the chicken stock until warm and cooked through. Gently reheat the sauce.

To serve, place a spaghetti bundle in the center of each plate, slightly arced. Arrange 5 sepia around each spaghetti bundle and spoon about ¼ cup of the sauce around each plate. Serve immediately.

Frogs' Legs with Parsley Sauce and Sautéed Frisée, page 186

The flavors of this dish are great. Sepia are like calamari, but the flesh is thicker and tastier and they can be very, very tender. Be sure to sauté them only until barely medium-rare. They may be difficult to find fresh, but they are available, and of good quality, frozen. What makes the flavors so compelling here is the broth, which is in effect a sepia stock seasoned with spicy chorizo. The spaghetti is a quirky but effective addition. Eric wanted a starch to help pick up the loose broth, and he chose one that mirrored the tentacled creature it would accompany.

Sautéed Sepia with Chorizo Broth and Spaghetti, page 187

It's practically impossible to be a bad cook in
Napa. The only danger is overcomplicating
ingredients that are excellent by themselves:
fresh potatoes, leeks, and arugula for soup;
smoked salmon with crème fraîche, cucumber,
and red onion for a main course; and a crumble
made with fresh spring fruits for dessert. This
menu underscores again how much fun cooking
can be, how satisfying eating is when the
landscape and the ethos of a place tell you
what to serve.

Smoked Salmon on a Cucumber Crown with Créme Fraîche–Dill Sauce, page 192

Arugula Vichyssoise

Serves 6

2 tablespoons unsalted butter

2 cups diced leeks (white and tender green parts only)

1 Idaho potato, peeled and cut into 1-inch dice

2 cups chicken stock

2 cups water

Fine sea salt and freshly ground white pepper

2 cups arugula, thoroughly washed and dried

PREP: 10 minutes, plus 2 hours chilling time — **COOK:** 30 minutes

Valentino loves soup, so I wanted to make him one, but the weather was warm—thus a cold vichyssoise. Vichyssoise is nice, but I always think of it more as a base, a potato and leek base for other flavors. We had plenty of arugula, and I like the peppery, almost mineraly flavor it brings to the soup. It really acts as a seasoning component in the recipe.

In a medium pot over medium heat, melt the butter. Add the leeks and sweat until tender, about 4 minutes. Add the potato, chicken stock, and water and cook until the potato is tender, 15 to 20 minutes. Season with salt and pepper.

Drain the vegetables, reserving the cooking liquid. Measure out ¾ cup of the cooking liquid and place in the refrigerator to cool. Place the vegetables in a blender container, cover with the remaining cooking liquid, and process until pureed. Add more water if the soup is too thick. Pass the soup through a fine-mesh strainer into a bowl. Cover and refrigerate until chilled, at least 2 hours.

Immediately before serving, roughly chop 1¾ cups of the arugula. Place the reserved cooking liquid in the blender with ⅓ cup of the potato-leek soup, add the chopped arugula, and blend until pureed. Season to taste with salt and pepper.

To serve, adjust the seasoning of the soup. Ladle ½ cup of the soup into each chilled bowl. Ladle about ¼ cup of the arugula puree into the center of each serving. Drag a toothpick or the tip of a paring knife through the arugula puree a few times, from the center outward, to create an interesting design. Slice the remaining arugula and garnish the center of each bowl with it. Serve immediately.

Smoked Salmon on a Cucumber Crown with Crème Fraîche–Dill Sauce pictured on page 190

SERVES 6

1½ pounds smoked salmon,
   in one piece, skin removed

1 tablespoon canola oil

1 hothouse (seedless) cucumber,
   thinly sliced

½ red onion, thinly sliced

Fine sea salt and freshly ground
   white pepper

2 tablespoons chopped dill

1 cup crème fraîche

2 tablespoons thinly sliced chives

1 lemon, halved

PREP: 15 minutes — COOK: 10 minutes

This dish is so deceptive. At first it seems like an elaborate and very difficult preparation from a white-tablecloth restaurant, but in fact it is ridiculously easy. With the salmon and the cream, it's really very rich, and yet it feels light and refreshing. One of its main components is cucumber—cooked cucumber—something we almost never do. It works well here, though, along with red onion. And the sauce is an interesting way to use crème fraîche.

Slice the salmon crosswise into ¼-inch-thick slices. You should have about 30 slices. Place the slices in one layer on a parchment-lined baking sheet. Cover with plastic wrap and refrigerate.

For the cucumber, heat a sauté pan over medium-high heat and add the canola oil. Add the cucumber and red onion, season with salt and pepper, and cook until limp, about 1 minute. Add 1 tablespoon of the dill and adjust the seasoning. Transfer the cucumbers to a bowl to cool.

Once they are cool enough to handle, arrange the cucumbers in an overlapping circle on each of six plates. Place 2 or 3 red onion slices each over the cucumbers.

Preheat the oven to 350°F.

For the sauce, bring the crème fraîche to a boil. Boil until reduced and thickened, about 5 minutes. Remove from the heat and let cool slightly. Add the chives and the remaining 1 tablespoon dill. Squeeze the lemon juice into the sauce and stir to incorporate. Set aside.

To serve, uncover the salmon and gently warm it in the oven—be careful not to overcook; it should just be barely warmed. Top each cucumber crown with 5 slices of salmon, overlapping them slightly in the center of the plate. Drizzle the warm sauce over the salmon and serve immediately.

Apricot and Peach Crumble with Rhubarb Puree

Serves 6

THE FILLING

4 tablespoons unsalted butter

¼ cup packed dark brown sugar

15 apricots, halved and pitted

3 cups peeled and sliced peaches
   (about 6)

1 cup fresh almonds, shelled
   (you can substitute ½ cup toasted
   sliced almonds)

THE TOPPING

⅓ cup almond flour
   (available in specialty stores)

¾ cup all-purpose flour

½ cup packed dark brown sugar

6 tablespoons cold unsalted butter

THE SAUCE

1 tablespoon unsalted butter

2 cups sliced rhubarb (3 large stalks)

⅓ cup sugar

½ cup water

SPECIAL EQUIPMENT

Six 3-inch ring molds

PREP: 30 minutes — **COOK:** 45 minutes

When I was young, I ate crumbles all the time, usually apple. I loved the crunch and the almond flour used to make them. I hadn't had peaches like this before in America. And the fresh apricots were amazing. So we made this easy preparation using the fruits of the area and the season.

For the filling, melt 1 tablespoon of the butter with 1 tablespoon of the dark brown sugar in a large sauté pan over medium heat. Add half the apricots to the pan in a single layer skin side down and cook until lightly caramelized, 1 to 2 minutes. Turn the apricots over and cook for another minute. Transfer to a plate and repeat with the remaining apricots, adding another 1 tablespoon each butter and sugar to the pan.

In another large sauté pan, melt 1 tablespoon of butter with 1 tablespoon of the dark brown sugar over medium heat. Add half the peaches to the pan in a single layer and cook until lightly caramelized, about 1 minute. Be careful not to overcook, or they will fall apart. Transfer to a plate and cook the remaining peaches, adding the remaining 1 tablespoon each butter and sugar to the pan.

Preheat the oven to 350°F.

Place the ring molds on a Silpat- or parchment-lined baking sheet. Fill the bottoms of the molds with the peaches, patting them down to pack evenly. Sprinkle the almonds over the peaches. Top each with 5 apricot halves, arranging them skin side up in an overlapping circle.

For the topping, in a mixing bowl, combine the almond flour, all-purpose flour, and brown sugar and stir to combine. Using a pastry blender or fork, add the butter and blend it in until the mixture resembles coarse sand. Divide the topping among the ring molds.

Bake the crumbles until the topping is golden and the inside is bubbling, 25 to 30 minutes.

Meanwhile, for the sauce, melt the butter over medium heat in a medium saucepan. Add the rhubarb and sugar and cook until the rhubarb breaks down to a puree, about 15 minutes, adding water as necessary. Set aside.

To serve, let the crumbles cool slightly, then remove the molds. Place each crumble in the center of a dessert plate and drizzle about 3 tablespoons of the rhubarb sauce around it. Serve warm or at room temperature.

Valentino Costazar 7-10-2001

The sauté, one of the basic cooking techniques, can refer to a range of temperatures, but the basic principles are the same: hot pan and tender pieces of meat. You want the oil in the pan to smoke, and you want meat that doesn't need to be cooked much, meat that is juicy by nature, meat that you want to put a crust on. When you put steak or duck breast, for instance, in the pan, try to leave it alone at first. It needs time to develop the crust, and each time you lift it, you cool the pan a little. Don't look at it every two seconds to see how it's doing. After it has cooked for a few minutes or so and you sense that it has good color, check it, turn it, and finish cooking either on the stovetop or in a hot oven. Which method you choose depends on the cut itself: If the meat is very thin, pounded chicken or veal, you won't need a hot oven. If you have a thick cut of monkfish or other meaty fish, sauté it with the intense direct heat of the sauté pan, and then finish it in the hot ambient heat of the oven.

Be sure to consider each item you will be sautéing separately. Each piece requires the same heat, but you have to keep in mind that if you put four fillets in a pan, the pan will be much cooler by the time the fourth fillet goes in. If you try to squeeze six in, it can be a disaster, because instead of searing, your fillets will steam in the not-quite-hot-enough pan, and then you'll have a mess.

I like sautéing fish. If it's nicely done, sautéing adds crunch to something juicy. I like the flavor of the caramelization that results. And certainly there is no better way to crisp the skin of a fish, which is filled with flavor. Once you have sautéed codfish, you will never want to eat it any other way. I like sautéed scallops only when they are very big and very young; when they are smaller, they release too much sugar and overcaramelize.

Sautéed Turbot with Creamy Jasmine Rice and Coriander Broth, page 198

Sautéed Turbot with Creamy Jasmine Rice and Coriander Broth pictured on page 197

SERVES 6

3½ cups chicken stock

1 tablespoon coriander seeds

1½ teaspoons fennel seeds

½ star anise

Pinch of cayenne pepper

Fine sea salt and freshly ground
   white pepper

3 cups water

1½ cups jasmine rice

2 tablespoons canola oil

Six 6-ounce turbot fillets

¾ cup heavy cream

Grated zest of 2 lemons
   (about 3 tablespoons)

2 tablespoons cilantro julienne

PREP: 20 minutes — **COOK:** 30 minutes

Turbot is great for sautéing because it is a big, muscular, flavorful fish. But it's also lean, so we need a rich element on the plate. What I like about this dish is that it reverses the rich and lean components. Typically the sauce is rich and the garnish is light. Here the sauce is a light but powerfully flavorful broth and the jasmine rice is enriched with the cream.

For the sauce, place the chicken stock in a medium pot and bring to a simmer over medium heat. Add the coriander, fennel, star anise, and cayenne pepper and simmer for 20 minutes. Season to taste with salt and pepper, strain, and set aside.

Meanwhile, place 2¾ cups of the water in a medium saucepan and bring to a boil over high heat. Add 1 teaspoon salt and ⅛ teaspoon pepper, then add the rice and lower to a simmer. Cook until underdone, still with a bit of crunch, 6 to 8 minutes. Drain and set aside.

Place two large nonstick sauté pans over high heat and add 1 tablespoon of the canola oil to each pan. Season the turbot on both sides with salt and pepper. When the oil is hot, add 3 turbot fillets to each pan. Cook until nicely browned on the first side, 4 to 6 minutes. Turn the fillets over and cook until done, about another 2 minutes.

Meanwhile, combine the remaining ¼ cup water and the heavy cream in a pan and bring to a simmer. Add the rice and stir to incorporate. Adjust the seasoning. Add about 2 tablespoons of the lemon zest and the cilantro julienne and stir to incorporate.

Gently reheat the sauce and add the remaining lemon zest.

To serve, place about ½ cup rice in the center of each of six warmed plates. Top each with a turbot fillet. Spoon the sauce around the plates. Serve immediately.

Pan-Seared Skirt Steak with Herbed-Butter Frites and Bitter Greens

SERVES 6

THE HERBED BUTTER

12 tablespoons (1½ sticks)
   unsalted butter, at room temperature

4 teaspoons minced garlic

4 teaspoons minced shallots

4 teaspoons chopped flat-leaf parsley

2 tablespoons chopped tarragon

1 teaspoon chopped fennel fronds
   (optional)

Fine sea salt

THE FRITES

4 large Idaho potatoes

8 cups canola oil

THE STEAK

1 tablespoon chopped shallots

2 teaspoons chopped garlic

¼ cup soy sauce

1 tablespoon fresh lemon juice

Pinch of cayenne pepper

¼ cup canola oil

2½ pounds skirt steak, trimmed and
   cut into 6 steaks

Fine sea salt and freshly ground
   white pepper

THE SALAD

2 teaspoons soy sauce

1 teaspoon sherry vinegar

1 teaspoon Dijon mustard

1 teaspoon minced garlic

Fine sea salt and freshly ground
   white pepper

3 tablespoons canola oil

2 bunches watercress,
   thick stems trimmed

PREP: 25 minutes — **COOK:** 30 minutes

I love brasserie food when I feel like something simple, but often it is prepared badly: The cut of meat is no good, it's not properly cooked, the fries are like McDonald's—no, worse; McDonald's fries are good. One of the keys to the success of this dish is timing; it's not difficult, but it's the critical factor. The steak must be very hot, and the fries must be finished just before you serve them so that they remain crispy.

I add a twist to each item. The steak gets a little flash marinade of soy, shallot, and lemon. The frites are incredible because when they're finished deep-frying, we toss them in a garlic-herb butter. And the bitter greens are a welcome contrast to all the delicious richness.

For the herbed butter, combine the butter, garlic, shallots, parsley, tarragon, fennel fronds, if using, and salt to taste in a bowl and stir with a wooden spoon to combine. Shape into a log and wrap in plastic film. Store in the refrigerator.

For the fries, peel the potatoes, placing them in a large bowl of water as you go to prevent discoloration. Cut the potatoes into ½-inch-thick bâtonnets and return them to the water. Heat the oil in a large deep pot over high heat until it reaches a temperature of 250°F. Drain the potatoes and pat dry. In batches, blanch the fries in the oil until cooked through, about 5 minutes and drain on paper towels. Bring the oil back up to 250°F between batches. When all the fries are cooked, set the oil aside.

For the steak, 30 minutes before serving, combine the shallots, garlic, soy sauce, lemon juice, cayenne pepper, and canola oil in a shallow baking dish and stir to blend. Add the steaks and turn them to coat. Marinate at room temperature.

For the vinaigrette, whisk together the soy sauce, sherry vinegar, Dijon, garlic, ¼ teaspoon salt, and a pinch of pepper in a small bowl. Whisking constantly, slowly add the canola oil until it is emulsified.

To finish the fries, bring the canola oil to 450°F. In batches, add the potatoes and cook until golden brown. Drain on paper towels. These are best if served right out of the oil, while still crisp, but you can hold them in a low oven for a couple of minutes.

Meanwhile, heat two large sauté pans over high heat until they are almost smoking. Remove the steaks from the marinade and shake to remove the excess liquid. Season with salt and pepper and place 3 steaks in each pan. Sear for 3 to 4 minutes on each side.

To serve, place a steak on each warmed plate. Cut six ¼-inch-thick slices (about 1 tablespoon each) of the herbed butter and place one on top of each steak. Cut the remaining herbed butter into small chunks and place in a large bowl. Add the fries and toss until well coated. Season with salt and divide among the plates. Toss the watercress with enough dressing to coat, season with salt and pepper, and mound on the plates. Serve immediately.

Pan-Seared Muscovy Duck Breast with Cherries and Rhubarb Puree

Three 4- to 5-pound Muscovy ducks

¼ cup canola oil

2 shallots, thinly sliced

5 garlic cloves, thinly sliced

2 tablespoons all-purpose flour

½ cup Cognac

4¼ cups water

Fine sea salt and freshly ground
   white pepper

2 tablespoons unsalted butter

1 tablespoon brown sugar

3 cups sliced rhubarb
   (about 5 large stalks)

1 pound Bing cherries, pitted

¼ cup Banyuls vinegar

PREP: 35 minutes — **COOK:** 50 minutes

Duck with fruit is a classic combination, though dishes like duck à l'orange—a cliché with its overcooked fruit reduced until it becomes almost a marmalade—have fallen out of favor. But the sweet-sour elements of fruit can work well with rich, meaty duck. With this basic duck breast (sautéed and finished in the oven), the main fruit—cherries—is cooked only briefly, and then a light stock quickly made from the duck bones is added so that the cherries are as much a savory element as a sweet one. The rhubarb—in season and plentiful as well—adds a nice sour component. The vinegar is a sharp fruity one made from Banyuls wine, the special fortified wine produced in southwest france.

Wash the ducks and pat dry. Cut off the legs and wings; reserve the legs for another use. Remove the whole double breast, on the bone, from each duck. Cover the breasts with plastic wrap and refrigerate. Roughly chop the bones and wings and set aside.

Preheat the oven to 400°F.

Heat 2 tablespoons of the canola oil in a roasting pan over medium-high heat. Add the reserved bones and wings and sear until golden brown on all sides, about 5 minutes. Add the shallots and garlic and place in the oven until the bones are golden brown and caramelized, about 10 minutes.

Remove all but 2 tablespoons of fat from the roasting pan. Sprinkle the flour over the bones and stir to incorporate. Set the roasting pan on the stovetop over medium-high heat, add the Cognac, and stir to release any browned bits in the bottom of the pan. Bring the Cognac to a boil and cook until reduced by half. Add 4 cups of the water. Lower the heat to medium and cook until the sauce coats the back of a spoon. Season with salt and pepper. Strain the sauce through a fine-mesh sieve, pressing on the bones to extract the maximum liquid. You should have at least 2 cups sauce; set aside.

Melt 1 tablespoon of the butter with the brown sugar in a small saucepan over medium heat. Add the rhubarb and cook until softened. Add the remaining ¼ cup water and cook until the rhubarb has broken down to a puree but is still a bit chunky, 8 to 10 minutes. Set aside.

In a large sauté pan, melt the remaining 1 tablespoon butter over medium heat. Add the cherries and sauté for 2 minutes. Deglaze the pan with the Banyuls vinegar and bring to a boil. Reduce the vinegar by half. Add the reserved duck sauce and bring to a simmer. Set aside.

For the duck, heat 1 tablespoon of the canola oil in each of two large ovenproof sauté pans over high heat. Generously season the double breasts with salt and pepper and place two in one pan and one in the other skin side down. Sear until golden brown, moving the breasts in the pans as necesary so that each breast is evenly seared, 4 to 6 minutes. Turn the breasts over and place in the oven for 7 minutes, or until medium-rare. Transfer to a platter to rest for 5 to 10 minutes.

Meanwhile, gently reheat the rhubarb puree and cherry sauce.

To serve, carve the breasts off the bone and slice them crosswise on the bias. Arrange one sliced breast on each warm plate, just left of center. Spoon about ⅓ cup of the rhubarb puree onto each plate, just right of center. Spoon the cherry sauce over the duck breasts. Serve immediately.

FLOUR-THICKENED SAUCE VS. JUS

Flour is often looked down on as a sauce thickener because a lot of people were using it like crazy in their sauce bases and they wound up making gravy instead. From flour you can have a gravy or, if you use it delicately, you have a sauce. Flour doesn't hide flavor if it's used wisely. It just brings the little liaison at the end that you need. I almost always use a little flour for meat-based sauces. When you use a little bit, a tablespoon or two, your sauce remains alive; without it, you have to reduce and reduce to achieve good consistency, and in the process, you overcook your sauce. The more you reduce, the more you kill the freshness.

The technique is very straightforward. Sprinkle flour over the bones you are roasting—just dust them lightly—so that the flour toasts as well. A sense of how much flour to use relative to the amount of bones you have comes with time and experience.

A sauce you manipulate more than a jus—you cook it longer, reduce it, play with consistency. A jus has a lighter consistency and a more powerful flavor than a sauce because it's very very fresh, getting its consistency from fat rather than from flour.

The jus technique is simple: Deglaze, simmer, strain, and serve. Typically a jus is made in the same pan as the meat or poultry you are serving it with, pan-roasted chicken, for instance. The pan thus has developed a *fond*, a golden coating of proteins and sugars that helps to flavor the sauce. Remove the meat to rest and discard excess fat. While the pan is still very hot, add your liquid, typically stock. The liquid will help lift the *fond* off the bottom of the pan—the *fond* imparting its flavor to the liquid while the remaining fat emulsifies into the liquid. Herbs or meat scraps can be added to enhance the flavor, but a jus is a last-minute preparation.

We chose not to use veal stock on our outings. With flour to adjust the consistency and the careful use of good chicken stock, you can get amazing results. At home, you don't use veal stock because it's inconvenient. True, once you have it, you can get good results very easily, without thinking, almost. But you don't need it; in fact, what we're doing is better. It's cleaner, tastes like the meat. But it does take some care and continual tasting. It's like cooking a fish using cream and butter or using a fumet. Just by mixing cream and butter you have something good. But with a little more care, you can have something tastier, lighter, more refreshing.

raw (or almost raw)

I had planned a tuna tartare for lunch. I didn't know how it would be flavored, but I wanted a light opening course. When I unwrapped the block of tuna we'd bought, it was so amazing, I realized it would be a shame to chop it up. I thought, "This needs to be cut like a steak or a piece of meat." And there was the idea— I'd cut it like a paillard. I would sear it on one side only and leave the other side raw. You must always be flexible when cooking, ready to do what's appropriate with what you have if you're surprised by something special, not fit what you have into a preconceived form. The tuna paillard would show off the beautiful cut of meat, and in the evening or the next day, we would use the scraps for an elegant tartare.

When I see very beautiful fish, my inclination is to serve it raw or barely cooked. Extremely fresh fish carries amazing flavors, like the sea, but such flavors are very volatile. Cooking destroys them and so does too much acid or spice. You can use acid and spice, but the trick is to always taste to fine-tune each dish.

The texture of very, very fresh fish is also a great pleasure. Cooking destroys this. As America's sophistication increases regarding the quality of fish, the availability of sushi-quality fish increases as well. I encourage you, when you find such products, to treat them thoughtfully, which often means serving them raw or only barely touched by cooking, by either heat or acid.

Seared Tuna Paillard with Spring Vegetables

6 baby artichokes

3 baby turnips, peeled

½ pound haricots verts

½ fennel bulb, cut into 2-inch by ¼-inch
    julienne strips

12 baby carrots, peeled

6 stalks purple asparagus, tips only
    (reserve the stalks for another use),
    halved (you can substitute large
    green asparagus)

1 yellow bell pepper, cored, seeded, and
    cut into 2-inch by ¼-inch julienne strips

6 spring onions, trimmed and halved

6 green olives, pitted and halved

Fine sea salt and freshly ground
    white pepper

¼ cup Vinaigrette (recipe follows)

Two 8-ounce tuna steaks (about 4 inches
    by 3½ inches by 1 inch thick)

¼ cup extra virgin olive oil

1 tablespoon thyme leaves

2 tablespoons thinly sliced chives

½ lemon

6 small basil tops (optional)

PREP: 45 minutes — **COOK:** 15 minutes

This dish can be prepared well in advance and assembled last minute, just before the briefest of sautéing of the tuna on one side.

Prepare the artichokes by removing the outer tough green flesh from the stems and cutting away all the tough outer green leaves.

Bring three small pots of water to a boil and salt generously. Blanch the artichokes, turnips, and haricots verts separately until crisp-tender, about 7 minutes for the artichokes and turnips and 5 minutes for the haricots verts. Plunge the vegetables into an ice water bath to stop the cooking. Drain and cut the artichokes and turnips into quarters. Set the vegetables aside.

Fill two of the pots with fresh salted water and bring to a boil. Blanch the carrots and asparagus separately until crisp-tender, about 5 minutes for the carrots and 3 minutes for the asparagus. Plunge the vegetables into an ice water bath to stop the cooking. Drain and cut the asparagus tips lengthwise in half. *(All the vegetables can be blanched ahead and reserved in the refrigerator until ready to serve.)*

For the salad, place the blanched vegetables, the bell pepper, spring onions, and olives in a bowl and season with salt and pepper. Toss with enough vinaigrette to coat and divide evenly around the rim of the six plates.

For the tuna, cut each steak horizontally into 3 equal slices. Place two nonstick pans over high heat. When pans are hot, brush the tuna on one side with olive oil, using 1 teaspoon per slice. Season generously with salt and pepper. Sprinkle the oiled side with the thyme leaves. Add the tuna oiled side down to the pans and sear until nicely browned but still rare, about 30 seconds. Remove from the pans.

Brush the rare side of the tuna slices with the remaining 2 tablespoons olive oil, season with salt and pepper, and sprinkle with the chives. Place a tuna slice rare side up in the center of each plate. Squeeze the lemon juice over the tuna and garnish each slice with a basil top, if using. Serve immediately.

VINAIGRETTE

MAKES 1 CUP

2 teaspoons Dijon mustard

1 teaspoon fine sea salt

2 pinches freshly ground white pepper

¼ cup sherry vinegar

⅓ cup extra virgin olive oil

½ cup canola oil

PREP: 5 minutes

In a small bowl, whisk together the mustard, salt, pepper, and vinegar until the salt dissolves. Constantly whisking, slowly drizzle in the olive oil, then the canola oil. Store in the refrigerator for up to 1 week.

Tuna Tartare with Endive pictured on page 209

SERVES 6

¾ cup Vinaigrette (page 205)

3 tablespoons chopped cornichons

2 tablespoons chopped capers

2 tablespoons minced spring onions

1¼ pounds sushi-quality tuna,
   cut into small dice

½ teaspoon Tabasco sauce

2 tablespoons Dijon mustard

1 tablespoon cilantro julienne

2 tablespoons fresh lemon juice

Fine sea salt and freshly ground
   white pepper

18 endive leaves, trimmed

12 slices country bread,
   toasted and still warm

PREP: 30 minutes

Here's a straightforward tuna tartare preparation using the beef tartare elements of capers and cornichons. Tuna tartare is all about texture and the flavor of the seasonings, so you have to taste and adjust accordingly. The presentation of this appealing first course (see photograph) evokes a Buddhist temple. The dramatic visual appeal and its simplicity make this a great first course for company.

For the sauce, combine ½ cup of the vinaigrette, 1 tablespoon of the cornichons, 1 tablespoon of the capers, and 1 tablespoon of the spring onions. Set aside.

Just before serving, place the tuna in a large bowl. Top with the remaining 2 tablespoons cornichons, the remaining 1 tablespoon each capers and spring onions, the Tabasco, Dijon mustard, cilantro, and lemon juice. Season with salt and pepper. Gently toss with a fork to combine. Do not overmix, or you will incorporate too much air, causing the tuna to turn brown.

Toss the endive leaves with the remaining ¼ cup vinaigrette and season with salt and pepper.

To serve, place about 2 tablespoons of the tuna mixture in the center of each plate and top with an endive leaf. Cover each one with another tablespoon of tuna and another endive leaf. Place 1 more tablespoon of tuna on top of each and cover with an endive leaf. Top with the remaining tuna. Drizzle the sauce around the plates. Serve immediately, with the warm toast.

Barely Cooked Shrimp with Bok Choy and Coriander Broth pictured on page 208

SERVES 6

24 extra-large head-on spotted shrimp
    (about 2 pounds; see Note)
1 orange
1 tablespoon canola oil
One 2-inch piece of ginger,
    peeled and thinly sliced
4 garlic cloves, roughly chopped
½ white onion, roughly chopped
1 star anise
1 tablespoon cardamom pods
Pinch of cayenne pepper
2 tablespoons tomato paste
3 cups water
Fine sea salt and freshly ground
    white pepper
2 jalapeño peppers, cut in half and
    seeds removed
1 tablespoon ground coriander
½ pound (2 sticks) unsalted butter
9 baby bok choys, cut in half
    (or quartered if large)
3 heads baby garlic, cloves separated
    and peeled (optional)
Curry powder to taste
2 limes, halved

PREP: 25 minutes — COOK: 40 minutes

Laurent Manrique, chef at Campton Place in San Francisco and a friend of Eric's, brought us some spotted shrimp he had found in Chinatown. They were so sweet and delicate you could eat them raw, and that was Eric's first inclination—to savor their texture and delicacy. The dish is not much more complicated than that: Shrimp is just warmed in the oven and then in broth, a broth made with a standard shellfish-stock method and brightly seasoned with ginger, garlic, onion, orange peel, star anise, cardamom, and cayenne, served with bok choy.

Remove the heads from the shrimp and reserve. Peel the shrimp and reserve the shells with the heads. Devein each shrimp by running a paring knife down the back and removing the dark line. Refrigerate the shrimp while you prepare the sauce.

Remove a 2-inch-wide strip of zest from the orange; set aside. Grate the remaining zest, and juice the orange; set the grated zest and juice aside.

For the sauce, heat the canola oil in a large pot over high heat. Add the reserved shrimp heads and shells and sauté until bright orange. Add the ginger, garlic, onion, strip of orange zest, the star anise, cardamom, and cayenne, lower the heat, and cook until the garlic and onion are softened but have not colored, about 5 minutes. Add the tomato paste, stir to incorporate, and cook for 2 minutes. Add the water and bring to a boil, then lower the heat and simmer for 10 minutes. Turn off the heat and let infuse for 10 minutes. Strain the sauce and season to taste. You should have at least 2 cups sauce; set aside.

Preheat the oven to 350°F.

In a large pot, combine 4 quarts water, the jalapeños, grated orange zest and juice, ground coriander, and butter. Generously salt the water and bring to a boil over high heat. Add the bok choys and cook until crisp-tender, about 4 minutes. Remove with a slotted spoon, place on a baking sheet, and refrigerate to cool the bok choy quickly and preserve its bright green color.

If using the baby garlic, bring a small pot of salted water to a boil. Add the garlic and cook until crisp-tender, about 2 minutes. Drain and set aside.

Season the shrimp on both sides with salt, pepper, and curry powder and place them on a baking sheet (line them up in the same direction to make serving them easier).

Place the baking sheets of bok choy and shrimp in the oven for about 3 minutes; be careful not to overcook either. Meanwhile, reheat the sauce over medium heat.

To serve, place 3 pieces of bok choy (6 if you quartered them) around the edges on each of six warmed bowls, in a circular pattern. Spiral 4 shrimp in the center of each bowl. Spoon the sauce over each plate. Garnish with 4 or 5 garlic cloves, if you have them. Squeeze the lime juice over each plate. Serve immediately.

NOTE: You can find whole spotted shrimp in Asian fish markets. If necessary, substitute regular extra-large shrimp, and substitute 5 additional whole shrimp for the heads in the stock.

Barely Cooked Shrimp with Bok Choy and Coriander Broth, page 207

Tuna Tartare with Endive, page 206

At first it just seemed strange—the ever-present bottle of Tabasco sauce in Sag Harbor. Eric had it at the ready almost like salt. When I'd made fun of the idea of pasta salad in Sag Harbor, he made sure to give it plenty of kick with Tabasco. Odder still, he added it to the sherry-soy vinaigrette for the sautéed cod, then to the cucumber soup and cucumber sauce. Now in Napa, the Tabasco has become cayenne pepper. The thing is, I never *taste* the Tabasco or the cayenne. Eric seasons aggressively, but with such finesse that you are never conscious of it. Countless times, I would taste the food as he was cooking—like most chefs, he seasons throughout the cooking process—and then again when it was finished but still in the pot. I'd think, "Wow, that's really good." Why mess with something so good? But then Eric would finish it by seasoning it one last time—salt, a pinch of cayenne, a few drops of vinegar—and the dish would all but shimmer on the plate.

It can't be said enough: Seasoning is fundamental to cooking. It's hard to teach seasoning, but with patience, it can be done. At the restaurant, I stand with my chef, Chris, to make a sauce, for instance, and then season it the way I want it and have him taste. We have to taste it together until he understands it. Now you can't tell which sauces I've seasoned and which he has.

Some people have no instinct for seasoning, and I don't know if that can be changed. It may be something either you have or don't have. So much of it stems from your childhood, your background. Have you eaten spicy food, powerfully flavored food, all your life? That will make a difference in how you season a dish for other people.

I like spicy foods, but not when they burn your tongue. Great seasoning should have a tickling effect, a teasing, to give you the exciting sense of loving what you're eating without knowing what gives it the sparkle. Seasoning comes in many, many forms. Garlic, onion, ginger oil, coconut milk, curry powder, cayenne, truffle juice—all of these are seasonings, ways to fine-tune the various flavors in any given dish.

Lamb Tartare and Creamy Cucumber Salad, page 213

Curried Peekytoe Crab and Granny Smith Apple Napoleon

SERVES 6

THE TUILES

1 cup all-purpose flour

2 tablespoons rice flour

1 tablespoon sugar

½ teaspoon salt

¼ teaspoon freshly ground white pepper

¼ teaspoon freshly grated nutmeg

⅔ cup egg whites

½ cup heavy cream

8 tablespoons (1 stick)
   unsalted butter, melted

THE CRAB SALAD

3 tablespoons fresh lemon juice

3 tablespoons sour cream

3 tablespoons mayonnaise

1 teaspoon curry powder

12 ounces peekytoe crabmeat
   (you can substitute lump crabmeat),
   picked over for shells and cartilage

¼ cup small dice of peeled
   Granny Smith apple

¼ cup small dice of peeled and
   seeded tomato

1 tablespoon thinly sliced chives

Fine sea salt and freshly ground
   white pepper

THE SAUCE

3 tablespoons sour cream

3 tablespoons mayonnaise

2 tablespoons milk

1 tablespoon fresh lemon juice

1 tablespoon small dice of peeled
   Granny Smith apple

1 tablespoon small dice of peeled and
   seeded tomato

1 teaspoon thinly sliced chives

1 teaspoon curry powder

Fine sea salt and freshly ground
   white pepper

Curry powder for dusting

PREP: 30 minutes, plus 30 minutes resting time — **COOK:** 15 minutes

Crab is a great vehicle for flavors, and a crab salad is an easy preparation and a refreshing dish to serve. This one uses curry to give sweet Maine crabmeat some force, but gently, as a seasoning rather than a main component, as it can be in curried stews. It's served here with great tuiles, made with rice flour. The light, golden tuiles give the dish some nice crunch, but the tuiles can be used in many other ways, or even seasoned with salt and cayenne and served as a snack.

For the tuiles, whisk together all the dry ingredients in a medium bowl. Slowly whisk in the egg whites. Whisk in the heavy cream, then the melted butter. Let the batter rest for 30 minutes.

Preheat the oven to 350°F.

Using a pastry brush, spread the batter in slight arcs 1½ inches wide by 5 inches long on a baking sheet lined with a Silpat or a nonstick baking sheet. Bake until crisp and golden, about 4 minutes. Transfer to a rack to cool. Repeat with the remaining batter. You should have at least 20 tuiles (you need 18 plus a few extra to allow for breakage).

For the crab salad, whisk together the lemon juice, sour cream, mayonnaise, and curry powder in a large bowl. Add the crabmeat, apple, tomato, and chives and gently stir with a fork to combine. Season to taste with salt and pepper.

For the sauce, whisk together the sour cream, mayonnaise, milk, and lemon juice. Add the apple, tomato, and chives and stir to incorporate. Season to taste with the curry powder and salt and pepper.

To serve, place about 2 tablespoons of the crab salad in the center of each plate and place a tuile on top of the salad. Continue with two more layers, rotating the tuile 45 degrees for each layer. Drizzle the sauce around the salads and dust the edges with curry powder.

Lamb Tartare and Creamy Cucumber Salad pictured on page 211

THE CUCUMBER SALAD

6 kirby cucumbers (you can substitute
  1 large seedless cucumber),
  thinly sliced

1 tablespoon kosher salt

2 tablespoons mint julienne

1 teaspoon chopped shallot

¼ teaspoon chopped garlic

¼ teaspoon diced Lemon Confit (page 21)

3 tablespoons sour cream

2 tablespoons bottled lemon oil

Pinch of cayenne pepper

Pinch of ground cumin

Fine sea salt, if necessary, and freshly
  ground white pepper

1 baguette, thinly sliced

THE TARTARE

1 pound freshly ground lean lamb
  (see Note)

3 tablespoons minced shallots

2 tablespoons chopped cornichons

2 tablespoons chopped capers

¼ cup mint julienne

¼ cup Dijon mustard

2 tablespoons bottled lemon oil

1 tablespoon extra virgin olive oil

1 tablespoon fresh lemon juice

¼ teaspoon Tabasco sauce, or to taste

Fine sea salt and freshly ground
  white pepper

6 mint sprigs for garnish

SPECIAL EQUIPMENT

A 3-inch ring mold

PREP: 30 minutes

This dish—raw ground lamb spiked with cumin and mint—was inspired by Lebanese cuisine, which I love for its aggressive seasoning. I love tartares. I love raw meat and the raw egg yolks that often accompany beef tartare—these may be the two sexiest things to eat. But I don't serve this tartare with a yolk, only with toasted bread and a cucumber salad seasoned like the lamb.

For the salad, place the cucumbers in a bowl and sprinkle the kosher salt over all, tossing to coat evenly. Allow the cucumbers to rest for 10 minutes; drain.

In a large bowl, combine the remaining salad ingredients except the salt and pepper and stir to incorporate. Add the cucumbers and toss to combine. Season to taste with salt and pepper (it may not need additional salt). Cover and refrigerate.

Preheat the oven to 400°F.

Place the baguette slices on a baking sheet and toast until golden brown, about 5 minutes. Set aside.

No more than 5 minutes before serving, combine all the ingredients for the tartare except the salt and pepper and garnish in a large bowl and gently stir to incorporate. Try not to incorporate too much air, as this would cause the lamb to take on an unpleasant dark color. Season to taste with salt and pepper.

To serve, place the ring mold left of center on one plate and fill with the lamb tartare. Garnish with a mint sprig. Lift off the mold and repeat for the remaining plates. Place the cucumber salad right of center on each plate. Place 4 or 5 slices of toasted baguette on each plate. Serve immediately.

NOTE: It is best if the lamb is ground just before serving. If you must have it ground by your butcher, keep it tightly covered to prevent discoloration.

on roasting

We roast big things—whole birds, whole fish, thick pieces of fish, legs of animals, and other big muscular cuts. We roast them because they cook better in ambient heat than with the intense direct heat of the fat in a sauté pan. A sauté pan gets very, very hot. Oil heated to 400°F in a pan will cook protein faster than a 400°F oven because the oil is so much more dense than air. But you need to distinguish between roasting meat and roasting fish. The roasting technique differs for each. If you are roasting meat, you distinguish further—red meat or white meat. You must evaluate size, and the potential for

a golden crust—you always want a great crust when you roast, otherwise there's no point.

So we cook thin cuts and cuts to be served rare in a sauté pan, and we roast bigger items that require time for even cooking throughout.

The general rules are these: To roast fish, one typically wants a very hot oven and a short cooking time, four or five minutes, or the fish will dry out. For the same reason, let it rest only a minute a two, or, if the fish is lean, not at all. I consider a 500°F oven to be very hot. But in the home kitchen, be careful—if your oven isn't clean, you'll be rushing around to all the smoke alarms.

Shiitake-Stuffed Squab (page 224) with Coriander-Infused Jus, before being sauced

It's often helpful to finish the fish with a spoonful of butter, a last-minute baste that flavors it, ensures even cooking, and keeps it moist. This must be done at the end, or the butter will burn in the hot pan. Fish on the bone should roast a little longer, at a lower temperature. Cooking fish on the bone is always preferable. The bones give flavor, help to keep the flesh moist, and also prevent the fish from shrinking, which results in a much more tender piece of fish.

To roast poultry, you want a lower temperature and a longer cooking time. This is common sense. If the heat is high, you'll overcook the exterior and the inside will be raw. The bigger the bird, the lower the temperature. Low is 350° to 375°F. (Ovens are erratic—have yours calibrated periodically or buy an oven thermometer.) With birds, I like to baste them all the time, adding butter or some other kind of flavorful fat—I'm very generous, a ton of fat—to keep the meat moist and ensure even cooking. Also, I always put herbs and some bread in the cavity, even if the bread is not to be served. The bread collects the juices and fat and steams inside the cavity, helping to keep the meat moist from within— a country trick. Birds that are completely stuffed will take longer to cook than unstuffed poultry. Long roasting at a low temperature will also

ensure a golden brown, crispy crust. Let a chicken rest for about fifteen minutes after taking it from the oven. If you let it rest longer, the beautiful crispy skin will steam and become soggy.

For red meat that is to be served rare or medium-rare, refined cuts such as a tenderloin of beef or venison, or a veal chop, you want a high temperature. And quite often you will start this on top of the stove in a hot pan to get a good sear or crust, then finish quickly in a hot oven. (Small chickens you might also want to begin on the stovetop, searing all sides for a great crust.) These tender cuts of red meat should rest for ten minutes once out of the oven. This is loosely called pan roasting, starting the item in the pan, and it works well also with muscular fish such as monk, cod, and turbot. I like the way heat goes through a fish this way. It's gentler to finish the fish in the oven, and it clears your stovetop for other work.

Roasted Chicken with Poached Egg, Asparagus, and Truffle Jus pictured on page 218

Two 3-pound chickens

Fine sea salt and freshly ground
  white pepper

8 garlic cloves

4 oregano sprigs

6 tablespoons unsalted butter,
  cut into chunks

6 slices day-old French bread

3 cups chicken stock

¾ cup canned truffle juice (we recommend
  Pébeyre brand; see Sources, page 320)

18 jumbo asparagus spears,
  trimmed and peeled

¼ cup sherry vinegar

6 extra-large eggs

Gray sea salt and coarsely ground
  black pepper

¼ pound Parmesan cheese

PREP: 20 minutes — **COOK:** 1 hour

This sounds like a country dish, and the method is country, but in fact it's a very elegant way to serve a roast chicken, very fresh and spring-like, tasty, and light. The sauce is a broth—reduced chicken stock flavored with truffle juice. The stuffing is just day-old bread. The runny yolk from the poached egg enriches the sauce and enhances the chicken.

Preheat the oven to 400°F.

Rinse the chickens inside and out; drain well and pat dry. Season the cavities with salt and pepper and stuff with the garlic, oregano, butter, and bread. Make sure some of the bread covers the opening to prevent the juices from running out of the chickens during cooking. Season the outside of the chickens with salt and pepper and place on a rack in a roasting pan.

Roast for about 45 minutes, basting at least three times with the collected pan juices. To test for doneness, pierce the thigh of one chicken with a fork—when the juices run clear, remove the chickens from the oven and let rest for at least 10 minutes.

Meanwhile, for the broth, place the chicken stock in a saucepan over medium-high heat, bring to a boil, and reduce to 1½ cups. Stir in the truffle juice. Season to taste with salt and pepper. Set aside.

Bring a large pot of salted water to a boil. Add the asparagus and cook until crisp-tender, about 4 minutes. Immediately plunge into an ice water bath until cooled. Drain and set aside.

Just before serving, bring 3 quarts salted water to a simmer in a deep skillet and add the vinegar. Crack an egg into a small bowl. Create a small whirlpool in the simmering water by stirring it in a circular manner, gently drop the egg into the whirlpool, and allow the edges of the white to curl around the yolk. Repeat with the remaining eggs, with each egg coming together before you add the next one. Cook until the whites have solidified but the yolks are still soft, about 1½ minutes per egg. Remove each egg with a slotted spoon and trim the edges. *(If necessary, cook only 2 or 3 eggs at a time and transfer the first batch[es] to a platter; they can be rewarmed in the hot water just before serving.)*

To serve, gently reheat the truffle broth. Remove the bread from the chickens and reserve. Carve each chicken into 6 pieces, then remove the meat from the breasts, legs, and thighs and cut into ½-inch slices. Arrange 6 asparagus spears in a ring around each of six warmed plates. Place the chicken meat inside the asparagus circles, dividing the breast, leg, and thigh meat evenly. Top the chicken with a reserved bread slice, and place a poached egg on the bread. Season the eggs with gray salt and coarsely ground black pepper. Using a vegetable peeler, shave slices of Parmesan over each plate. Serve immediately.

Roasted Whole Turbot with Spring Vegetables and Truffle Sauce pictured on page 219

SERVES 6

3 tablespoons canola oil

1 ounce prosciutto, cut into
1-inch julienne strips

3 tablespoons finely diced red onion

1 cup chicken stock

2 large black truffles, chopped
(about ¼ cup)

One 6- to 8-pound turbot

Fine sea salt and freshly ground
white pepper

2½ cups shelled baby peas

½ cup shelled fava beans,
tough skins removed

5 tablespoons unsalted butter

½ cup shelled fresh almonds (optional)

1 lemon, halved

Gray sea salt

PREP: 30 minutes — **COOK:** 1 hour

Preheat the oven to 450°F.

Combine 1 tablespoon of the oil, the prosciutto, and red onion in a saucepan over medium heat, and cook until the onions are soft and translucent. Cover with the chicken stock and bring to a simmer. Add the truffles, and set aside.

Season both sides of the turbot with salt and pepper. Heat a roasting pan over medium heat and add the remaining 2 tablespoons canola oil. When the oil is hot, add the turbot and sear until golden brown on the first side, about 5 minutes. Turn over, place in the oven, and roast for 10 minutes. Turn the fish over and cook for another 15 minutes. Remove the turbot from the oven and let it rest for 10 minutes.

Meanwhile, bring two small pots of water to a boil and generously salt. Blanch the peas and fava beans separately until just tender, about 1 minute. Drain and immediately plunge the vegetables into an ice water bath to stop the cooking process. Drain, and set the fava beans and ½ cup of the peas aside.

Place the remaining 2 cups of peas in a blender and process until pureed. Force the puree through a fine-mesh sieve to remove any lumps. Set aside.

Just before serving, bring the sauce to a boil and gradually whisk in 4 tablespoons of the butter. Add the reserved ½ cup peas, the fava beans, and almonds and keep warm over low heat. Reheat the pea puree, add the remaining 1 tablespoon butter, and stir to incorporate.

To serve, slice the turbot off the bone and remove the skin. Cut the turbot into 6 individual pieces. Squeeze the lemon juice over the fish. Spoon ¼ cup of the pea puree down the center of each plate and top with a piece of the turbot. Spoon the sauce over each plate. Add a pinch of gray sea salt over the turbot and serve immediately.

Roasted Chicken with Poached Egg, Asparagus, and Truffle Jus, page 216

Roasted Whole Turbot with Spring Vegetables and Truffle Sauce, page 217

Turbot is one of the very best fish—it's flavorful, meaty, but delicate. You can sauté it, roast it, or poach it. Because the bones are loaded with gelatin, they make a rich fumet (always remove the gills and the eyes). It's such a hearty fish we can use a meat-based sauce for it—here, chicken stock flavored with prosciutto. The turbot is pan-roasted: seared on the stovetop and finished in the oven.

The fresh pea puree adds sweetness and a beautiful color to the dish, and the sauce is garnished with whole peas and favas, gifts of spring, along with fresh young almonds. These are soft and juicy, picked before they turn hard, not like a nut at all. They are not critical to this recipe, but if you find them at a farmers' market, buy them and experiment with them.

Guinea Hen with Artichokes, Foie Gras, and Sautéed Broccoli Rabe

SERVES 6

THE GUINEA HENS

Three 3-pound guinea hens

Fine sea salt and freshly ground
  white pepper

3 rosemary sprigs

3 sage sprigs

3 oregano sprigs

14 garlic cloves (1 large head), peeled

3 Lemon Confit quarters (page 21)

3 slices day-old French bread

½ onion, peeled

1 carrot, peeled

3 thyme sprigs

3 cups chicken stock

PREP: 35 minutes — **COOK:** 1 hour

Preheat the oven to 400°F.

For the hens, remove the necks and giblets and set aside. Rinse the birds inside and out and pat dry. Remove the wings from each bird and roughly chop. Season the cavities of the hens with salt and pepper and place 1 rosemary sprig, 1 sage sprig, 1 oregano sprig, and 3 garlic cloves in each one. Place 1 lemon confit quarter in each bird. Seal the opening of each bird with a slice of bread. Truss with kitchen string.

Season the outside of the birds with salt and pepper and place in a roasting pan. Add the chopped wings, the necks and giblets, onion, carrot, the remaining 5 garlic cloves, and the thyme to the roasting pan. Roast for 30 to 40 minutes, basting at least three times with the pan juices. To test for doneness, pierce the leg of a bird with a needle or small paring knife; the bird is done when the juice runs clear. Set the birds on a platter, tent with aluminum foil, and let rest for at least 10 minutes.

Place the roasting pan on the stovetop over high heat. Deglaze the pan with the chicken stock, stirring to loosen any browned bits in the bottom of the pan. Bring to a boil, then lower the heat to a simmer. Simmer until the sauce thickens slightly, about 20 minutes. Strain into a small saucepan and reserve.

Meanwhile, prepare the artichokes. Add the juice of the lemons, 2 tablespoons of the olive oil, 2 tablespoons salt, and 1 teaspoon pepper to a large pot of water. Cut the stem off each artichoke. One at a time, using a small knife, starting at the base of each artichoke and holding the knife blade parallel to the leaves, remove the leaves. Trim off all of the green parts from the base of the artichoke (if you leave any green parts, they will turn brown during cooking). Leave the choke in the artichoke. As you finish each artichoke, place it in the pot of lemon water (see Note for alternative cooking instruction).

When all the artichokes are finished, bring the pot to a boil, then lower the heat to a simmer, and cook until the artichokes are tender, 10 to 15 minutes. Cool in the cooking liquid until cool enough to handle, then remove the chokes and cut the artichokes into ¼-inch dice. Set aside in a bowl.

Heat the remaining 2 tablespoons olive oil with the sliced garlic in a large sauté pan. Add the broccoli rabe and cook until tender, 5 to 7 minutes. Season with salt and pepper. Set aside.

1 lemon, halved

¼ cup extra virgin olive oil

Fine sea salt and freshly ground
white pepper

4 large artichokes

2 garlic cloves, sliced

2 bunches broccoli rabe (about 1½ pounds)

1 cup diced (½-inch) fresh duck foie gras

1 tablespoon thinly sliced chives

¼ cup Vinaigrette (page 205)

SPECIAL EQUIPMENT

Kitchen string for trussing

Six 3-inch ring molds

Heat another large sauté pan over high heat until it is almost smoking. Add the foie gras and sauté just until golden brown. Using a slotted spoon, remove the foie gras, leaving the fat in the pan, and add to the artichoke dice. Discard all but 1 tablespoon fat.

Just before serving, gently reheat the broth. Gently reheat the artichokes and foie gras in the reserved foie gras fat. Strain the fat off and discard, add the chives and vinaigrette, and toss to combine. Season to taste with salt and pepper.

To serve, place a ring mold in the center of each plate and spread the artichoke–foie gras mixture in them. Remove the molds. Carve each hen into 4 pieces and place 1 breast and 1 leg over each bed of artichokes and foie gras. Place the broccoli rabe in a circle around the hens. Spoon the warmed broth over each plate. Serve immediately.

NOTE: If you find it too difficult to prepare the artichokes the recommended way, you can cook the artichokes whole (cut off the tips of the leaves and the stems before cooking), then pull off the leaves after cooking and scoop out the chokes.

GUINEA HEN

Guinea hen, or guinea fowl, originated in Africa and is now domesticated throughout the Americas, but it remains a curiosity in the poultry world. We found some sort of wild guinea fowl in Puerto Rico and cooked it for about thirty-seven hours, but it never became tender. (There its name is a nickname for a difficult woman.) Here, where it's farm-raised, it's very tender and much more flavorful than chicken. It has a very large breast relative to its legs, so it cooks quickly and evenly.

Eric paired it with an unusual garnish of foie gras and artichokes. The artichoke hearts, which act like a sponge for the flavors of this dish, are cooked and diced, sautéed in foie gras fat, and then tossed with the diced sautéed foie gras. He sautéed some broccoli rabe with garlic "to give some guts to the dish."

Roasted Leg of Lamb and Garlic with Goat Cheese Mashed Potatoes pictured on page 160

SERVES 6

THE SAUCE

2 tablespoons canola oil

Reserved lamb bones (see Note)

½ onion, roughly chopped

5 garlic cloves, roughly chopped

1 tomato, roughly chopped

½ cup dry white wine

3½ cups chicken stock

THE LAMB

2 tablespoons chopped flat-leaf parsley

1 tablespoon chopped garlic

1 teaspoon chopped oregano

1 tablespoon extra virgin olive oil

½ teaspoon ground cumin

One 5-pound leg of lamb, butterflied and bones reserved (see Note)

Fine sea salt and freshly ground white pepper

2 tablespoons canola oil

2 heads garlic, left whole

PREP: 25 minutes — **COOK:** 1 hour and 25 minutes

This classical-style leg of lamb is butterflied and stuffed with herbs and garlic, then pan-roasted with more garlic. Though it's great to roast on the bone, in large part because there are numerous different muscles that make up the leg and each one cooks differently from the others, so it's almost like a mixed grill on the platter, there are advantages to butterflying. While these different muscles become more intertwined and less distinct when the leg is butterflied, you get to season the meat from within, as it were; you can use the bones to make a jus; and it makes carving easier. Eric serves the lamb with potatoes enriched and flavored with goat cheese. If you wind up with an older leg of lamb, rub the meat with rosemary, which will disguise any rangy mutton flavor—an effect Eric suspects is the reason rosemary and lamb were paired traditionally.

For the sauce, heat the canola oil in a large pan over medium-high heat. Add the bones and sear until golden brown on all sides, 5 to 7 minutes. Add the onion and garlic and cook until caramelized, 3 to 5 minutes. Add the tomato and cook until it begins to soften, about 2 minutes.

Deglaze the pan with the white wine, scraping up any browned bits in the bottom of the pan, and bring to a boil. Add the chicken stock. Bring to a boil, lower the heat to a simmer, and simmer for 30 minutes. Strain and reserve. You should have at least 2 cups sauce.

Preheat the oven to 400°F.

For the lamb, combine the parsley, chopped garlic, oregano, olive oil, and cumin in a bowl and stir to mix. If there is a thick layer of fat on the lamb, trim it to ¼ inch thick (the fat will help keep the lamb moist while cooking). Open out the lamb on a cutting board skin side down and season the inside of the lamb with salt and pepper. Spread the garlic-oregano mixture over the lamb. Roll up the lamb and use 5 pieces of kitchen string to secure it.

Place a roasting pan on your stovetop over medium-high heat and add the canola oil. Season the outside of the lamb with salt and pepper. Sear the lamb on all sides until golden brown, 5 to 7 minutes. Add the garlic heads, place in the oven, and roast for 25 minutes.

Remove the garlic heads and transfer to a platter. Continue to cook the lamb for another 20 to 25 minutes, or until an instant-read thermometer reads 130°F.

2 pounds Yukon Gold potatoes

4 tablespoons unsalted butter

½ cup milk, or as necessary

¾ cup fresh goat cheese

**Fine sea salt and freshly ground
white pepper**

6 tablespoons extra virgin olive oil

2 round summer squash or zucchini

3 garlic cloves, halved

3 thyme springs

3 rosemary sprigs

2 medium yellow tomatoes

2 medium red tomatoes

SPECIAL EQUIPMENT

Kitchen string

Potato ricer or food mill

Meanwhile, peel the potatoes and place them in a large pot of salted water. Bring to a boil and cook until the potatoes are tender. Drain. Pass the potatoes through a ricer or food mill.

Melt the butter with the milk in a large saucepan over medium heat. Add the mashed potatoes and stir to incorporate. Add the goat cheese and stir to incorporate. Season to taste with salt and pepper. Set aside.

When the lamb is done, transfer it to a platter and let the lamb rest for at least 10 minutes before carving. Remove all but 1 tablespoon of the fat from the pan and place the pan on the stovetop over medium heat. Deglaze the pan with the sauce, stirring up the browned bits in the bottom of the pan, and simmer for 10 minutes. Season to taste with salt and pepper. Strain into a small saucepan and reserve.

For the vegetables, heat 2 tablespoons of the olive oil in a large sauté pan over medium heat. Slice the tops and bottoms off the squash and cut each one into 3 equal slices. Season on both sides with salt and pepper and add to the pan. Add 1 halved garlic clove and 1 sprig each of the thyme and rosemary. Cook, turning once, until the zucchini is tender and golden brown on both sides, 2 to 3 minutes per side. Remove the garlic if it begins to burn. Transfer the squash to a platter.

Cut the tops and bottoms off the yellow and red tomatoes and slice each one into 3 equal slices. Heat 2 tablespoons of the olive oil in a large nonstick pan over medium heat. Add 1 halved garlic clove and 1 sprig each of the thyme and rosemary. Add the yellow tomato slices and cook, turning once, until golden brown on both sides, about 1 minute per side. Transfer to the squash platter. Cook the red tomato slices in the same manner, with the remaining 2 tablespoons oil, garlic, and herb sprigs. Add to the platter.

Gently reheat the mashed potatoes, adding milk if necessary to thin them. Reheat the sauce.

To serve, carve the lamb into thin slices and place 2 (or more) slices on each of six warmed plates. Using a large spoon, drop two quenelles (oval shapes) of the mashed potatoes onto one side of each plate. Place a yellow tomato, red tomato, zucchini slice, and 2 garlic cloves on each plate. Spoon the sauce over the plates.

NOTE: Have your butcher butterfly the lamb and chop the lamb bones into several smaller pieces. Or debone the lamb yourself and chop the bones using a cleaver.

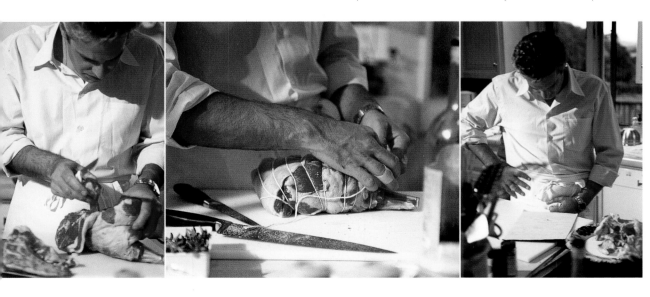

Shiitake-Stuffed Squab with Coriander-Infused Jus pictured on page 214

SERVES 6

THE SQUAB

1 pound caul fat

6 squabs

3 tablespoons canola oil

3 cups sliced shiitake mushrooms
   (about ¾ pound, stems discarded)

Fine sea salt and freshly ground
   white pepper

1 garlic clove, minced

1 teaspoon minced ginger

1 tablespoon minced shallots

1 tablespoon chopped flat-leaf parsley

1 teaspoon finely grated lemon zest

1 large egg

¼ teaspoon ground coriander

¼ teaspoon ground star anise

PREP: 45 minutes — **COOK:** 1 hour and 30 minutes

Squab is a very flavorful meat and carries the intense spices of anise and coriander, garlic, and ginger very well. Eric boned the squabs, so he had the bones to make a proper sauce. (You can ask the butcher to bone the birds, reserving the bones as well.) He made a mushroom stuffing, then wrapped each stuffed squab in caul fat for easy self-basting roasting. Braised endive accompanies the squab, along with a fennel puree that is light, almost ethereal. This special-occasion dish is a beautiful conception that sprang very much out of the Napa earth.

Soak the caul fat in a bowl of cold water for 10 minutes. Rinse under cold running water and reserve.

Cut off the wings and legs from the squabs; reserve. To bone the squabs, set a squab breast side down on a cutting board. Cut it open down the back. Keeping your knife against the bones, slide a small paring knife around the rib cage, being very careful not to puncture the skin, and work your way around the whole bird. Remove and reserve the bones. Continue with the remaining squab.

Preheat the oven to 400°F.

For the stuffing, heat 1 tablespoon of the canola oil in a large pan. Add the shiitake mushrooms and season with salt and pepper. Add the garlic, ginger, and shallots and sauté until the mushrooms are tender, about 4 minutes. Add the parsley and lemon zest. Transfer the mixture to a bowl and place in the freezer to cool quickly.

Once the stuffing is cool, add the egg, coriander, and star anise and stir to combine.

Cut the caul fat into 6 large sheets, approximately 10 by 17 inches. Lay one sheet on your work surface and place a squab skin side down in the center. Season the inside of the squab. Spread ¼ cup of the mushroom mixture over the flesh; don't overstuff the bird. The skin should easily cover the stuffing. Reshape the squab and wrap it in the caul fat, slightly overlapping the edges of the fat. Secure the caul fat with kitchen string, crossing it in the center. Repeat with the remaining squab, place on a platter or baking sheet, and refrigerate.

THE SAUCE

2 tablespoons canola oil

The reserved squab bones, wings, and legs

1 white onion, roughly chopped

½ head garlic, roughly chopped

2 oregano sprigs

1 teaspoon ground star anise

1 teaspoon ground coriander

1 teaspoon minced ginger

One 2-inch strip of lemon zest

THE GARNISH

8 tablespoons (1 stick) unsalted butter

2 tablespoons canola oil

6 endive heads, halved lengthwise

Fine sea salt and freshly ground white pepper

2½ cups chicken stock

3 fennel bulbs, roughly chopped (about 3 cups)

12 wild ramps (you can substitute baby leeks), trimmed

SPECIAL EQUIPMENT

Kitchen string

For the sauce, heat a large ovenproof saucepan over high heat and add the canola oil. Add the squab bones, legs, and wings and sear until golden brown on all sides, about 6 minutes. Add the onion, garlic, and oregano, place in the oven, and roast until the vegetables are soft and translucent and beginning to caramelize, about 20 minutes.

Remove the pan from the oven and place on the stovetop over medium heat (leave the oven on). Skim off the fat from the pan and add the ground star anise, coriander, ginger, and lemon zest. Cover with the chicken stock and bring to a boil, scraping up the browned bits in the bottom of the pan. Lower the heat and simmer for 30 minutes. Strain and reserve.

Meanwhile, for the garnish, heat an ovenproof sauté pan over high heat. Add 3 tablespoons of the butter and the canola oil. Add the endives cut side up and season with salt and pepper. Cook until golden brown on the first side, then turn the endives over and cook until browned on the other side. Add 1½ cups of the chicken stock, cover the pan with aluminum foil, and place in the oven. Cook until a knife is easily inserted in the center of the endive, about 20 minutes. Set aside. Leave the oven on.

While the endive halves cook, place the fennel in a saucepan with the remaining 1 cup chicken stock and 3 tablespoons of the butter. Cook until very soft, about 20 minutes. In batches, puree in a blender. Set aside.

In a sauté pan, melt the remaining 2 tablespoons butter in ½ cup water over medium heat. Add the ramps and season with salt and pepper. Cook until tender, adding more water as necessary. Set aside.

Heat a large ovenproof sauté pan over high heat and add the remaining 2 tablespoons canola oil. Add the squab and sear until golden brown on all sides, about 2 minutes per side. Transfer to the oven and roast for 10 to 12 minutes. To test for doneness, insert a metal skewer into the center of the stuffing: when it is removed, it should be warm to the touch. Transfer the squab to a platter and let rest for 10 minutes.

Meanwhile, gently reheat the fennel puree, endive, and ramps. Bring the sauce to a simmer.

To serve, spoon ⅓ cup of the fennel puree in the center of each plate. Remove the kitchen string from the squabs and slice them on the bias into ½-inch-thick slices. Place on top of the fennel puree in an overlapping circle. Place 2 endive halves on one side of each squab and 2 ramps on the opposite side. Spoon the sauce over each plate.

Lamb Shoulder and Portobello-Spinach Ravioli with Mushroom Jus

SERVES 6

THE PASTA DOUGH

**2 cups all-purpose flour,
   plus more for kneading**

1 teaspoon fine sea salt

5 large egg yolks

THE FILLING

4 portobello mushrooms

**Fine sea salt and freshly ground
   white pepper**

**6 garlic cloves, 5 coarsely chopped,
   1 minced**

3 rosemary sprigs

2 oregano sprigs

6 tablespoons extra virgin olive oil

1½ pounds spinach

2 tablespoons unsalted butter

2 tomatoes, cut into ½-inch-thick slices

PREP: 45 minutes, plus 30 minutes resting time — **COOK:** 1 hour

First we sear the lamb heavily, then we roast it beyond medium-rare until it is really medium. This is partly to make this toughter cut a little more tender, and partly because the flavor is better.

The portobello jus is what makes this dish very special, but you must take some care, or you will have only black water. Salt the mushrooms well to help extract their liquid for the jus, then roast them carefully and deglaze the pan with not too much water, or the jus will be diluted.

For the pasta dough, sift the flour and salt into a large mixing bowl and whisk to combine. Make a well in the center of the flour and add the eggs. Using a fork, slowly incorporate the eggs into the flour, until all the eggs have been absorbed. Transfer the dough to a counter that has been dusted with flour. Knead the dough, using the heel of your hand, for about 4 minutes: the dough is ready if when you press your finger into the dough, it bounces back into shape. Shape into a disk, wrap in plastic film, and place in the refrigerator to rest for at least 30 minutes.

Preheat the oven to 400°F.

For the filling, place the portobello mushrooms on a jelly-roll pan and season with salt and pepper. Sprinkle the chopped garlic over the mushrooms. Cut 2 rosemary sprigs and the oregano sprigs in half and place one of each on each mushroom. Drizzle ¼ cup of the olive oil over the mushrooms and roast for 10 minutes. Cover the mushrooms with 2 cups water and continue to roast for another 10 minutes. Remove the pan and cool on a rack.

When it is cool, strain the mushroom jus, pressing against the mushrooms to extract the maximum liquid. Set the jus aside. Cut the mushrooms into ¼-inch dice. Set aside.

Wash the spinach, spin-dry, and roughly chop. Melt the butter in a large sauté pan and add the minced garlic and spinach. Season with salt and pepper. Cook until the spinach has wilted and all the liquid has evaporated. Set aside.

THE LAMB

2 tablespoons canola oil

One 3-pound lamb shoulder,
boned and tied

Fine sea salt and freshly ground
white pepper

3 cups chicken stock

¼ pound Parmesan cheese, grated

Heat the remaining 2 tablespoons olive oil in a large sauté pan over medium-high heat. Season the tomato slices on both sides with salt and pepper. Add the tomato slices to the pan, along with the remaining rosemary sprig, and cook, turning once, until browned on both sides, about 1 minute per side. Chop into ¼-inch dice. Set aside.

Remove the pasta dough from the refrigerator and divide it into 4 pieces. Working with one-quarter of the dough at a time (keep the remaining dough covered to prevent it from drying out), roll it from the thickest setting to the thinnest setting on your pasta machine. Dust the dough with additional flour if it is sticky.

To make the ravioli, lay one pasta sheet on the work surface. Starting about 2 inches from one end of the sheet, place ½ teaspoon spinach topped with ½ teaspoon mushrooms and ½ teaspoon tomatoes at 4-inch intervals down the center of the pasta sheet. Brush water around the filling and top with another pasta sheet. Press to seal the edges, being careful not to trap air inside the ravioli. Cut out the ravioli with a 3-inch round cookie cutter and press on the edges to make the dough thinner. Place the finished ravioli on a parchment-lined baking sheet sprinkled with cornmeal, to prevent sticking. Repeat with the remaining dough and filling. You should get at least 18 ravioli. Cover the ravioli with a towel. Refrigerate until ready to cook.

For the lamb, preheat the oven to 400°F.

Heat the canola oil in a roasting pan on your stovetop over medium-high heat. Generously season the lamb with salt and pepper. Add the lamb and sear on all sides until golden brown, 5 to 7 minutes. Place in the oven and roast for 30 to 35 minutes for medium, or a little less if you prefer medium rare. Transfer to a platter and let rest for at least 10 minutes.

Shortly before serving, bring the chicken stock to a simmer in a large pot and season with salt to taste. Add the ravioli and cook until al dente, about 4 minutes.

Meanwhile, gently reheat the mushroom jus.

To serve, carve the lamb into thin slices. Place 3 or 4 slices on each plate. Place 3 ravioli on each plate and spoon the mushroom jus over all. Sprinkle the Parmesan cheese over the ravioli. Serve immediately.

I love ravioli. I love packages. I love the surprise
effect of food wrapped in something. You never
know what you will find.

So now I share with the world the secret of my genius as a master pâtissier: I hired Florian Bellanger to run the pastries and desserts at Le Bernardin.

I love sweets and desserts, and I like a meal to end with something sweet. As a boy, I devoured the fruit tarts my mother made. I need dessert in my life. But pâtisserie bores me to death. It has no suspense for me. I am not a pastry chef and have no desire to be. I have no instinct for it. At first, I enjoyed pâtisserie in school. But after learning puff pastry, I found I had no patience for all that measuring, for doughs and batters and egg whites and sugar. It's too scientific, too mathematic for me. There are a few chefs who have a true instinct for pastry, who can improvise

with flour and sugar and egg—chefs such as Michel Richard and François Payard—people who can play with the doughs and the pastry the way a chef saucier plays with the sauce. But until you reach that level of mastery, you must be very precise, and no matter how accomplished you are, you must follow recipes and measure everything.

I still make desserts and I still enjoy the challenge, but I do so as a cook, not as a pastry chef—a fundamental distinction. The following desserts, and most of those throughout this book, aren't four-star restaurant desserts— they're easy, at-home recipes, improvisations from the mind of a cook, relying on that same instinct for seasoning and invention that determines the flavor of my sauces or the seasonings of my stews. Many are simply compositions of items already at hand, such as the wine with berries and black pepper. There is no easier dessert, and with seasonal fruit, it's delicious and refreshing.

There are some great cooks out there who are dessert-challenged. I think it may be because they're trying to think like a pastry chef when they should instead remain cooks and use the same energy with which they approach the sauté and the roast to explore the realm of sugar and eggs and flour.

Tiramisù

SERVES 6

THE SAUCE
½ cup balsamic vinegar
½ cup port wine

THE LADYFINGERS
1 cup water
¼ cup sugar
½ cup raspberries
¼ cup framboise liqueur
12 ladyfingers (store-bought)

THE TOPPING
1½ pints raspberries
6 tablespoons sugar
1 pint strawberries, hulled and quartered
2 egg yolks
1 cup mascarpone cheese
1 teaspoon vanilla extract

PREP: 25 minutes, plus 30 minutes to macerate the fruit — **COOK:** 15 minutes

I love this dessert, though it's not a traditional tiramisù. Here, ladyfingers are marinated in framboise, served with a coulis of berries and marinated whole berries, topped with sweet mascarpone enriched with egg yolk, and garnished with a port and balsamic reduction.

For the sauce, combine the balsamic vinegar and port in a saucepan and bring to a boil, then lower the heat and simmer until reduced by half, about 10 minutes. Cool to room temperature.

For the ladyfingers, bring the water and sugar to a boil in a medium saucepan, stirring until the sugar has been dissolved. Remove from the heat.

Mash the raspberries, using a fork, and press through a fine-mesh sieve to remove the seeds. Add the raspberry puree and the framboise to the sugar syrup. Refrigerate until well chilled.

Place the ladyfingers on a platter and gradually brush the syrup evenly over them until you have used all the syrup. Allow the ladyfingers to sit for at least 10 minutes to absorb all of the liquid.

For the topping, puree ½ pint of the raspberries in a blender or food processor. Strain to remove the seeds. Place the puree in a bowl and add 3 tablespoons of the sugar. Add the strawberries and the remaining raspberries and macerate for 30 minutes.

Meanwhile, place the yolks and the remaining 3 tablespoons sugar in a medium bowl and whisk until pale yellow and very light, about 10 minutes. In a separate bowl, combine the mascarpone and vanilla and whisk until well blended and light. Add the yolk mixture and stir to incorporate.

To serve, place 2 ladyfingers in the center of each plate and top with the berries. Spoon the mascarpone over each. Drizzle the balsamic-port sauce around the plates. Serve immediately.

Chocolate, Ginger, and Coffee Pot de Crème with Anisette Cream

SERVES 6

2½ cups heavy cream

½ cup milk

**A 2-inch piece of ginger, peeled and
   thinly sliced**

1 tablespoon brewed espresso

1 vanilla bean, halved lengthwise

6 tablespoons sugar

8 large egg yolks

**¼ pound bittersweet chocolate,
   finely chopped**

**1 tablespoon Sambuca or other
   anise-flavored liqueur**

SPECIAL EQUIPMENT

Six 6-ounce ramekins

PREP: 10 minutes, plus 2 hours chilling time — COOK: 15 minutes

Another strategy for dessert is to return to a classic. The pot de crème is one of them, in the family of the crème brûlée and panna cotta. In this version, the hot custard is added to chocolate, almost like a ganache, and then chilled. The topping is simply Sambuca whipped into cream.

In a saucepan, combine 2 cups of the heavy cream, the milk, ginger, coffee, vanilla bean, and 2 tablespoons of the sugar and bring to a simmer. Simmer over low heat for 10 minutes to infuse the flavors into the cream. Strain and return to the pan

Combine the egg yolks and 2 tablespoons of the sugar in a medium bowl and whisk until pale yellow.

Pour a few tablespoons of the hot infused cream over the yolks and stir to combine. (This will temper the egg yolks, so they do not curdle.) Pour the yolk mixture into the remaining infused cream. Stir over medium heat until it thickens enough to coat the back of a spoon, about 5 minutes; be careful not to let the mixture boil, or the eggs will become scrambled. Remove from the heat.

Place the chocolate in a large bowl. Pour the hot cream mixture over it, and stir until the chocolate melts and the mixture is well blended. Pour into six 6-ounce ramekins and refrigerate until fully chilled, at least 2 hours.

To serve, place the remaining ½ cup cream, the remaining 2 tablespoons sugar, and the Sambuca in a bowl and whisk until it forms soft peaks. Spoon a quenelle of the cream over each pot de crème.

Pets de Nonne

1⅓ cups milk

1⅓ cups water

½ pound (2 sticks) unsalted butter

Pinch of salt

Grated zest of 1 orange

2 cups all-purpose flour

9 large eggs

4 cups vegetable oil

1 cup granulated sugar

PREP: 5 minutes — **COOK:** 40 minutes

These are delectable treats, sweet ethereal little clouds, thus their name: literally, nun's farts. In the doughnut or beignet family—deep-fried sweet dough—these are in fact very easy to make. The dough is like a basic pâte à choux: Flour is added to boiling liquid and stirred until the dough pulls away from the pan. The eggs are beaten in one at a time, then the dough is dropped into hot oil. Dusted with sugar and served warm, they are an unusual treat—you can't stop eating them, they're so good.

In a medium saucepan, bring the milk, water, butter, salt, and orange zest to a boil.

Sift the flour into a bowl, then add the flour to the boiling liquid all at once. Stir off the heat until the mixture comes together. Over the heat, stir vigorously until the dough pulls away from the sides of the pan and feels dry.

Place the dough in the bowl of a mixer fitted with the paddle attachment. Beating on low speed, begin adding the eggs one at a time. Do not add another egg until the previous one has been absorbed. When all eggs have been added, beat until the dough is cool to the touch. (This can also be done by hand, but be sure to beat the mixture until it has completely cooled.)

In a large deep saucepan, heat the oil to 350°F.

Place the dough in a piping bag fitted with a large round tip. Holding the piping bag over the oil, squeeze out a 3-inch rope of dough and cut it off with a sharp knife, dropping the dough into the oil. Repeat to make more pets, without crowding the pan. When the pets rise to the top, turn so they will cook evenly. Cook for 5 to 7 minutes, or until they are golden brown. Drain on paper towels. Repeat with the remaining dough.

Once they have cooled slightly, transfer the pets to a bowl filled with the sugar and turn to coat. Shake to remove excess sugar. They are best eaten warm, but can be served at room temperature.

Chocolate Ravioli in Bittersweet Chocolate Sauce

SERVES 6

PREP: 40 minutes, plus 2½ hours resting and chilling time — **COOK:** 25 minutes

THE PASTA DOUGH

1½ cups all-purpose flour

¼ cup cocoa powder, plus more for dusting

3 tablespoons sugar

Pinch of salt

3 large eggs

THE CHOCOLATE PASTRY CREAM FILLING

3 cups milk

1 vanilla bean, split lengthwise

½ cup sugar

5 egg yolks

⅓ cup cornstarch

2 tablespoons unsalted butter

½ pound hazelnut chocolate (gianduja),
   roughly chopped

This is the cook at work, switching a few ingredients from the pastry chef's *mise* to his own. Except for the sugar, chocolate, and pastry cream, this is just like cooking dinner. The sauce is simply an all-purpose ganache that can be used for all manner of desserts.

For the pasta dough, sift the flour, cocoa powder, sugar, and salt into a large mixing bowl and whisk to blend. Make a well in the center of the dry ingredients and place the eggs in the well. Using a fork, slowly incorporate the eggs into the flour, until all the eggs have been absorbed. Transfer the dough to a work surface and, using the palm of your hand, lightly knead the dough for 3 to 4 minutes. If the dough is sticky, sprinkle a little flour on the kneading surface. The dough is ready if, when you make an impression in it with the tip of your finger, the dough bounces back. Shape into a disk and tightly wrap in plastic film. Let the dough rest for at least 30 minutes in the refrigerator.

Meanwhile, make the pastry cream: In a medium saucepan, combine the milk and vanilla bean. Place over high heat and bring to a boil (be careful not to scorch the milk). Meanwhile, using a whisk, in a medium bowl, whip the sugar and egg yolks until pale yellow and frothy, about 2 minutes. Add the cornstarch and whisk to dissolve any lumps.

Remove the vanilla bean from the milk and discard. Temper the egg yolk mixture by pouring a little of the steaming milk into the yolks, whisking to incorporate. Whisk the yolks into the remaining milk in the pan, set the pan over medium heat, and whisk quickly and constantly until the mixture thickens and comes to a boil, then whisk for another minute. Add the butter and stir until incorporated. Transfer the pastry cream to a storage container and place plastic wrap directly against the cream to prevent a skin from forming on top. Refrigerate until fully chilled, about 2 hours.

Once the pastry cream has chilled, place the hazelnut chocolate in a microwave-safe container and microwave on high for 1 minute; or melt the chocolate in a double boiler over low heat. Remove the chocolate from the microwave and stir. Heat the chocolate for another minute, remove, and stir to melt the remaining chocolate. Add to the pastry cream and stir to incorporate. Return to the refrigerator and chill for at least 30 minutes.

Divide the pasta dough into 4 pieces. Using a pasta machine, one at a time, roll out each piece from the widest to the thinnest setting. Keep the remaining dough covered to prevent it from drying out.

THE SAUCE

½ cup heavy cream

½ cup milk

1 tablespoon sugar

5 ounces bittersweet chocolate,
   roughly chopped

1 tablespoon unsalted butter

THE POACHING LIQUID

8 cups water

2 cups sugar

To make the ravioli, dust a work surface with flour. Place one pasta sheet on the work surface. Starting about 2 inches from one end, place a teaspoon of filling every 4 inches down the pasta strip, ending about 2 inches from the other end of the strip. Brush the pasta dough with water, fold the dough over, and press to seal, being careful not to trap air inside the ravioli (or they will burst during cooking). Cut the ravioli into half-moons using a cookie cutter or pastry wheel. Press the edges together and squeeze to make the edges of the dough as thin as possible. Set the finished ravioli on a baking sheet lined with parchment and sprinkled with flour, to prevent sticking. Repeat with the remaining dough. You should get at least 24 ravioli. Refrigerate until ready to cook.

For the sauce, bring the heavy cream, milk, and sugar to a simmer in a small saucepan. Remove from the heat, add the chocolate, and stir until melted. Add the butter and stir to incorporate.

To cook the ravioli, bring the water and sugar to a boil in a large pot and boil until the sugar has dissolved. Add the ravioli to the pot and cook until al dente, about 5 minutes.

Meanwhile, gently reheat the chocolate sauce.

To serve, remove the ravioli with a slotted spoon, letting the excess liquid drain, and arrange 4 ravioli on each plate. Drizzle the sauce over each plate. Serve immediately.

Goat Cheese Marinated in Oil and Rosemary

SERVES 6

6 fresh goat cheese buttons
   (you can substitute an 11-ounce
   goat cheese log, cut into 6 slices)
2 cups extra virgin olive oil
4 rosemary branches
1 garlic clove, halved

PREP: 5 minutes, plus at least 2 days marinating time

For the seriously dessert-impaired or the uninterested, there's always the cheese course, followed by a port. This is an easy way to enhance goat cheese to make it worthy of its own course. Serve with good wine and crusty bread.

Place all the ingredients in a bowl or on a platter. Cover and marinate in the refrigerator for at least 2 days, or up to a week.

To serve, bring to room temperature. Serve with sliced French bread.

Strawberries Floating in Red Wine

SERVES 6

3 cups merlot
⅓ cup granulated sugar
¼ teaspoon crushed black pepper
3 cups strawberries, hulled and quartered
1 tablespoon dark brown sugar

PREP: 10 minutes, plus 30 minutes chilling time

In spring, when strawberries are abundant and in their prime, this is an amazing last-minute dessert. Mix sugar, wine, berries, and pepper together, and a half hour later it's a dish. This wouldn't be a good choice after a long wine-rich dinner, but after a light meal, it is tasty and refreshing. Note the effect of the pepper with the fruit—pepper is a great seasoning for most fruits.

Place the red wine, granulated sugar, and black pepper in a medium bowl and stir to combine. Add the strawberries and place in the refrigerator for at least 30 minutes.

To serve, divide the berries and wine among six wineglasses. Top each with ½ teaspoon brown sugar. Serve immediately.

AND THE ARTIST'S PASSION It's the sleepy wedge of an afternoon, three o'clock, when you give in to eyes that want to close, let the blood leave the head for the stomach, and restore yourself for the evening's work. The house is quiet. But Eric, taking no break, has returned to the kitchen. He has tied a crisp apron around his waist and hefted the huge rib cage of a baby lamb onto a board, bones far more plentiful than meat. He steels a flexible boning knife. Then he runs his hand heavily over the saddle.

He pauses, then, one hand holding the knife, the other hand leading it, he draws the blade between muscle and bone until, toward the end of the chest-length cut, he stops. "If I remember, there's a little bone here that you have to skip," he says. He doesn't so much look at what he's doing as feel his way—left index finger pressing into the meat, the knife blade zigzags once. And the first line of boning the saddle is done.

"I haven't worked with lamb for a long time," he says, "but the hands remember."

The hands remember. It seems almost literally true. The subject has jumped out at me repeatedly in conversation with Valentino and with Eric. When we first arrived, Valentino had said he'd brought his hands, the most important thing. It would seem so obvious as to not need mentioning, and yet it's a critical piece of both Eric's cooking and Valentino's draftsmanship.

Stuffed Lamb Saddle with Lamb Jus and Spring Vegetables, page 238

Valentino's method is simple: He draws with a pencil or sometimes a razor-point black pen. He then follows the lines of the sketch with a brush dipped in black ink. When this is dry, he paints the objects in various hues of brown ink. Then he paints over them in white. When this is finished, he begins layering in the color, rubbing deep reds and blues and golds into the paper. He mixes his own colors, expensive powders he buys in London and Paris. They come in small bottles, and he combines them with turpentine, or with pressed linseed oil, to find the colors he wants. The mixing of these paints is part of the art, part of the process he loves. The more layers of paint, the deeper the colors become—not unlike Eric's work as he repeatedly seasons a Moroccan stew or develops a sauce. Tammar, hearing a discussion along these lines, says, "For us, lighting is the flavor." It's all process to Valentino. To him, just staring out is painting.

But the most fundamental component is hands. "If you think, it goes away," he says, describing the process of a sketch. "There must be no calculation. It is a way of life. My hand is my brain. My hand is my memory."

Eric reiterates this as he works over the saddle of lamb, discussing the bone his hands remembered to skip over. "Instinct is something you develop over the years. You have a sensitivity—that's part of what instinct is. In your hands, you can feel more than someone else feels. Like some people can touch your shoulder and know exactly where the muscle hurts. I try to develop that in my hands. I'm a very intuitive person, but with my hands.

It's more than a touch. My hands give me important information."

A moment later, Eric says, "I'm struggling." He rarely says this. He has finished the first critical phase of the saddle, removing it from the bone with as little waste as possible and with no unnecessary holes. He knows he's going to stuff this saddle, and good boning is the fundamental first step. His hands have told him what to do.

As he's working, he's thinking. He wants to do something like a porcetta, baby pig stuffed with spinach and pine nuts and garlic and cooked on a rotisserie, a preparation Eric has seen in the region of Genoa, Italy. He slides the bones into a hot oven—all these bones will make a perfect jus, a sauce made in the roasting pan.

A friend who lives nearby shows up. She has worked with one of Eric's mentors, Jean-Louis. It's appropriate that she is here, I think, because she had noted a similar fact about Jean-Louis and hands: No one, she had told me, touched food the way Jean-Louis touched food.

Eric now knows what he'll do with this saddle. "This is my homage to Jean-Louis." Palladin was all about powerful flavors, robust dishes. And so Eric will put all his skills to work to honor him. The stuffing will be uncomplicated and robust, packed with liver and sausage, spinach, and aromatics. He sautés the liver, saying, "There's nothing worse than getting a bite of raw liver." He blanches the spinach, chops pepper and onion and cooked liver. He mixes the ingredients together with egg, seasons the mixture forcefully, tastes, and then seasons some more.

The bones roasting in the oven are now a golden brown. He deglazes the pan with white wine and adds chicken stock, garlic, and rosemary.

Next he stuffs the saddle, paying careful attention not to overstuff it, or the expanding mixture will squeeze out like Play-Doh. He wraps the bundle in caul fat to help keep the saddle together and coat it with fat as it melts. Eric ties the roast in the manner he learned from Jean-Louis, using just two knots, firmly bound but not strangled.

And then he begins the final critical part of the dish: roasting it. You never really know how you've done until you serve it: It's a mystery. Eric uses a long needle to gauge the temperature of the interior, inserting it into the center of the roast, removing it and holding the needle to his skin to guage the internal temperature. He squeezes the roast, he smells it, he looks at it. "Okay, I think it is done." For the half hour the saddle rests, he finishes the vegetables, strains and finishes the sauce. When he begins to slice, he sees that it's not just nicely done—it's perfect. We'll eat outside, where stars fill the sky.

Even Eric is pleased. This is perfection. And he seems to acknowledge this, not out of pride but rather because it didn't come from him. He has honored his past with this one dish and the six busy hours he spent in its conception and preparation. "Until now," he says, "I never knew how important Jean-Louis was to me." And then he repeats, "This dish is an homage to Jean-Louis Palladin."

Stuffed Lamb Saddle with Lamb Jus and Spring Vegetables pictured on page 236

Serves 6

THE STUFFED SADDLE

1 pound caul fat

1 bone-in lamb saddle (see Note)

1½ pounds spinach

3 tablespoons canola oil

3 ounces lamb's liver (you can substitute
   chicken livers)

2 tablespoons chopped red bell pepper

2 tablespoons minced onion

2 teaspoons chopped oregano

1 tablespoon chopped flat-leaf parsley

2 links sweet pork sausage or merguez
   (spicy lamb sausage) (about 2 ounces),
   casing removed

¼ cup freshly grated Parmesan cheese

2 large eggs

Fine sea salt and freshly ground
   white pepper

THE JUS

Reserved lamb bones, roughly chopped
   (see Note)

2 tablespoons canola oil

½ cup diced onion

1 head garlic, halved

1 tomato, cut into large dice

2 rosemary sprigs

1 cup dry white wine

4 cups chicken stock (or lamb stock)

Fine sea salt and freshly ground
   white pepper

PREP: 45 minutes — **COOK:** 1 hour and 45 minutes

Soak the caul fat in a bowl of cold water for 10 minutes. Rinse under cold running water and reserve.

Put the saddle meat side down on your cutting board (see the first photograph on page 239). To remove the bones, place your knife at a 45-degree angle against the bones and, keeping your knife at this angle, carefully carve the meat away from the bones, making sure you do not cut a hole through the saddle. Reserve the bones for the sauce. Remove any excess fat from the skin side of the saddle. Cover the saddle with plastic wrap and refrigerate.

For the jus, roughly chop the lamb bones with a cleaver. Heat the canola oil in a large heavy-bottomed pot over medium-high heat. Add the bones and sear for about 4 minutes, turning occasionally. Lower the heat and add the onion, garlic, tomato, and rosemary. Cook until the bones are nicely caramelized and the vegetables are softened, 10 to 15 minutes. Deglaze with the white wine, scraping up the browned bits in the bottom of the pan, and simmer until the wine has almost evaporated. Add the chicken stock and simmer for another 30 minutes. Season to taste with salt and pepper. Strain through a fine-mesh strainer and set aside.

Meanwhile, for the stuffing, remove the stems from the spinach and wash thoroughly in a large basin filled with water. Bring a large pot of water to a boil and salt generously. Blanch the spinach until wilted, about 30 seconds. Drain and plunge the spinach into an ice water bath to stop the cooking. Drain and squeeze out as much water as possible. Finely chop the spinach. Set aside.

Place a nonstick skillet over medium-high heat and add 1 tablespoon of the canola oil. Season the liver, add to the pan, and sear for 1 to 2 minutes per side. The liver should still be slightly rare in the center. Finely chop.

Preheat the oven to 450°F.

In a medium bowl, combine the spinach, liver, red pepper, onion, oregano, parsley, sausage, Parmesan cheese, and eggs and stir to mix the ingredients. Place the stuffing on your cutting board and chop all the ingredients together to combine. Season with salt and pepper.

Lay out the saddle skin side down on your work surface and season with salt and pepper (see the second photograph on page 239). Place the stuffing down the center of the saddle. Enclose the stuffing by bringing both flaps over the stuffing, then closing the saddle book style. Wrap the saddle in the caul fat, making sure to reinforce it at each end. Tie the saddle with 5 or 6 lengths of kitchen string to secure it.

To cook the saddle, heat the remaining 2 tablespoons canola oil in a large ovenproof sauté pan over medium-high heat. Season the outside of the saddle with salt and pepper. Add to the pan and sear until golden brown on all sides, about 2 minutes per side. Place in the oven and roast for 20 to 25 minutes. Test for doneness by inserting a thermometer into the stuffing; it should register 130°F (it will continue cooking while resting).

THE VEGETABLES

1 lemon, halved

¼ cup extra virgin olive oil

Fine sea salt

6 baby artichokes

2 round zucchini, cut into 6 wedges each

Freshly ground white pepper

2 cups baby arugula

¼ cup Vinaigrette (page 205)

2 ripe yellow tomatoes,
    cut into 6 wedges each

SPECIAL EQUIPMENT

Kitchen string

While the saddle is roasting, prepare the vegetables: Bring a large pot of water to a boil. Squeeze the juice from the lemon into the pot and add 2 tablespoons of the olive oil and 2 tablespoons salt. Meanwhile, prepare the artichokes by removing the outer tough green flesh from the stems and cutting away all the tough outer green leaves. Add the artichokes to the boiling water and cook until tender, 5 to 7 minutes. Drain and, when cool enough to handle, cut in half.

When the lamb is done, transfer the saddle to a platter and let rest for at least 10 minutes.

Remove all but 1 tablespoon of the fat from the sauté pan and place over medium heat. Deglaze the pan with the sauce. Bring to a boil, then lower the heat to a simmer until the sauce has thickened slightly (you should have at least 1½ cups sauce). Season to taste with salt and pepper.

Place a large sauté pan over medium-high heat and add the remaining 2 tablespoons extra virgin olive oil. Add the zucchini cut side down and season with salt and pepper. Cook until golden brown on the first side, then turn over and cook until golden on the second side and cooked through.

Meanwhile, reheat the lamb jus over low heat.

Place the arugula in a mixing bowl and season with salt and pepper. Add enough of the vinaigrette to coat the arugula and toss. Divide the arugula evenly among the plates, mounding it at the 11 o'clock position on each plate. Place 2 wedges each of zucchini at 12 o'clock. Place 2 tomato wedges each at 1 o'clock. Place 2 artichoke pieces at 3 o'clock. Cut the saddle into 1-inch slices and place one slice in the center of each plate. Spoon about ¼ cup of the sauce over each lamb slice. Serve immediately.

NOTE: You can bone the saddle yourself, as described in the recipe, or have the butcher do this. Ask him to roughly chop the bones for you.

{ **autumn** }

Vermont—The Source of Heat

Eric had brought us to Cavendish, a small rural town on the southern edge of Vermont, in mid-October. The foliage blazed brightly, the days were warm and the nights cold—the time of year when winter's approach is in the air, encouraging cravings for rich fall foods and rustic cooking. Eric looked forward to squab and pheasant, duck and goose, root vegetables. He would use only American fish, he would braise tough common cuts of meat until they were meltingly tender. What he hadn't planned on, though, the surprise that excited him most, was the fireplace and a barn full of wood.

THE RETURN OF THE CHEF

The first thing Eric did was drag in a load of wood from the barn. With the maples all gone to vibrant yellows and pink-oranges, the oaks to brown, the air still fragrant with fallen pine needles, and a dark front approaching from the west, we all wanted a fire on this, the first night of our final outing. The fireplace opening was nearly five feet wide and three and a half feet high at the arch, with a hearth a foot off the ground that made it inviting. By the time beets, potatoes, and apples had been peeled and wrapped in foil with some olive oil, salt, and pepper, enough coals had fallen from the flaming logs to create a small hot heap of ash and ember to roast the packages in.

"We're going to be using this a lot," Eric said, throwing another log on top of the fire, more cooking embers falling through the grate. He glanced across the long room toward the open kitchen of our temporary home. The old range, its electric burners black against foil-covered burner pans, didn't inspire him. He'd known from the moment he set foot in this otherwise lovely country house where the true source of heat was.

And then, we all did what we'd been doing since we'd arrived in Sag Harbor more than a year before—we readied our tools and began to work. Shimon and Tammar scouted vantages and set up their equipment throughout the house. Valentino rearranged furniture in his room to create a small studio to ink his drawings and add some watercolor. Andrea, who'd arrived a day earlier to set up, conferred with Eric on the list of goods readied for this fall cooking trip:

- Produce: Yukon, russet, chef, and red potatoes; beets; parsnips; eggplant; corn; yellow squash, spaghetti squash, and acorn and butternut squash; pumpkin; cabbage; red, yellow, and green peppers, jalapeños, and Scotch bonnets; onions, leeks, shallots, and garlic; tomatoes; lemons and limes; herbs; apples; figs; chanterelle, black trumpet, portobello, and oyster mushrooms
- Meat: two pheasants, wild pigeons, ducks, duck gizzard confit, capon, ten pounds of oxtails, a dozen veal cheeks, bacon, a few pounds of diced pork shoulder, caul fat, dried sausages, foie gras terrine
- Dry goods: lentils, black beans, and navy beans; porcini; risotto, polenta, and pasta; assorted staples—sugar, rock salt, fine Balene sea salt, flour; Vermont honey, maple syrup, and canned black truffles
- Seafood: six pounds of live crayfish (writhing and pinching in the big Le Bernardin cooler); abundant smoked shellfish—mussels, scallops, shrimp—and smoked trout, smoked salmon, and salt cod

And, oh yes, a 125-gram tin of the world's best caviar and two white truffles each the size of a demented egg and weighing about three ounces.

Eric is easy and confident now. In Sag Harbor, he was manic, not knowing what might happen—that was the point. "Otherwise, why go anywhere?" he asked. "We could do this all in a studio in New York." But now he seems all instinct and focus. He has changed on these trips, matured even, and on this first night something he says underscores it. As he watches us cleaning and prepping and peeling, he grins and says, "Everybody works and I don't. *Ha!* I am a chef again!"

For dinner, we are going to do something very crazy—cook the risotto only in truffle juice, the juice produced by a truffle's first cooking. It's over the top, but that's what the truffle is all about. And since we're going all out on this first dish, a celebration of our last week together, I start the shallots in a little foie gras fat I can scrape off the terrine.

For white truffle, you want to do almost nothing other than serve it on top of a rich starch. Pasta is a good idea, but risotto— another customary white truffle backdrop— is more elegant. With the pasta still in my

thoughts and bacon in the refrigerator, I thought of carbonara—bacon, egg yolk, cream, Parmesan, some parsley. Why not use that carbonara idea with risotto? Voilà: I do a bacon cream sauce to finish the risotto, and we top each with a raw yolk, and smother the plate with shaved white truffle.

We eat only a couple of dishes tonight; for the rest of the trip, we will feed ourselves as if we are the geese raised for foie gras. Risotto followed by a "salad" using the beets, apples, and potatoes roasting in the fire, Vermont goat cheese, and arugula, then figs for dessert.

Risotto Carbonara with White and Black Truffles

SERVES 6

1 tablespoon foie gras fat
   (you can substitute unsalted butter)

¼ cup minced shallots
   (about 3 large shallots)

1½ cups Vialone Nano rice
   (you can substitute Arborio)

Two 14-ounce cans truffle juice
   (we recommend Pébeyre brand;
   see Sources, page 320)

Fine sea salt and freshly ground
   white pepper

2 bacon slices, cut crosswise into julienne

One 8-ounce container crème fraîche

4 tablespoons unsalted butter

2 ounces Parmesan cheese, grated
   (about ¼ cup)

6 large egg yolks (don't separate the eggs
   until just before serving)

Gray sea salt for garnish

One 2-ounce white truffle, cleaned with
   water and a clean toothbrush (optional)

PREP: 10 minutes — COOK: 30 minutes

Eric adapted a traditional pasta dish for risotto, a lesson in the flexibility of good ideas. Carbonara might work with just about any starch, but it transfers to risotto especially well. Eric was proud to have created a dish using both black and white truffles—a rarity given that each has a different season, only barely overlapping. White truffles are extraordinary used this way, but as far as I'm concerned, the carbonara is just as good without.

Melt the foie gras fat in a large heavy-bottomed pot over medium heat. Add the shallots and sweat until softened but not colored, about 3 minutes. Add the rice and stir to coat with the fat.

Begin adding the truffle juice slowly, while stirring the rice. As each addition of truffle juice is absorbed into the rice, add about ⅓ cup more, constantly stirring. Season with salt and pepper to taste.

Meanwhile, sauté the bacon in a medium pan until it has rendered its fat and is crispy. Drain off the rendered bacon fat, add half of the crème fraîche to the pan, and stir to combine.

Once all the truffle juice has been absorbed into the rice—this should take 20 to 25 minutes—add the butter, the remaining crème fraîche, and the Parmesan and stir to incorporate.

To serve, get all your dinner guests involved. The risotto should be plated quickly, to keep it hot from pan to table. Divide the risotto among six warmed plates, making an indentation in the middle of each to accommodate an egg yolk. Place an egg yolk in the center of each plate. Season the yolks with gray salt. Spoon the bacon–crème fraîche sauce over the risotto, shave the white truffle over the top, and serve immediately.

THE BLACK TRUFFLE

Black truffles are beautiful and fascinating. The flavor so delicate, and at the same time, so powerful—a concentration of the flavors of the earth. I love the white truffle too; you shave it on something rich and fatty that conveys its power. But if you cook it, you destroy it.

Black truffles, on the other hand, have infinite uses. Because of their cost and rarity, and also because their flavor is so volatile, disappearing into the air if you're not careful, fresh black truffles must be handled with sensitivity and sound technique. You can't use them everywhere, but you can use them raw, warmed, or cooked, with meat, in a broth, in a risotto, or in mashed potatoes. When you cook a a black truffle, you have to pair it with a fatty or starchy item to capture the flavor. You can chop a black truffle with butter—chop the exterior and save the heart to slice—and add it to bean stews. Or you can simply shave it on toast, or over a salad. Pork may be the best meat to cook with truffles—cut the truffle into sticks and insert them into the center of the meat so that they only get warm. They explode with flavor that way.

Robuchon was a black truffle fanatic. He created what I think is the best dish you can do, a black truffle tartlet: young onions cooked with some bacon, spread on crispy phyllo, crowned abundantly with sliced black truffles, and just warmed in the oven (too much heat and you lose the flavor), and finished with good rock salt. I've yet to encounter a more powerful use of the truffle.

Buy carefully—truffles grown outside France or Italy are sometimes marketed fraudulently. No truffles are as good as those from the Périgord region in France. If you are buying truffles for the first time, I recommend going with someone who can teach you how to evaluate them. You don't want to spend four hundred dollars a pound for a truffle that's ten days old or has been handled or stored improperly. (If you are on your own, buy only a truffle that is very fragrant—you'll know it when you smell it. It should always be hard, not spongy; the interior should be gray with white veins.) Store truffles in plastic wrap or an airtight container—not in rice, which will steal their flavor—and use them soon after you buy them.

If they're the right kind, canned truffles are perfectly acceptable for soups or stews. I rely on those from the Pébeyre family.

Fire-Roasted Vegetable and Goat Cheese "Parfait"

Serves 6

THE PARFAIT

3 large beets (about 1½ pounds)

3 large russet (baking) potatoes
  (about 1½ pounds)

6 lady apples (you can substitute
  3 Cortland apples)

Fine sea salt and freshly ground
  white pepper

3 tablespoons olive oil

10 ounces fresh goat cheese,
  preferably from Vermont

¾ cup sour cream

1 small shallot, minced
  (about 1 tablespoon)

1 tablespoon thinly sliced chives

THE SAUCE

About 4 ounces reserved beet scraps
  (from above)

3 tablespoons sherry vinegar

2 tablespoons walnut oil

THE SALAD

1 large bunch arugula

About ⅓ cup Vinaigrette (page 205)

1 tablespoon thinly sliced chives

SPECIAL EQUIPMENT

Six 2-inch by 3-inch-high ring molds

PREP: 30 minutes — **COOK:** 45 minutes

Though a traditional parfait usually includes ice cream, Eric calls this a parfait because it's tall and has a creamy texture. Chunks of roasted beet, potato, and apple are set up in a ring mold and held together with goat cheese whipped with some sour cream. The trick in this packaging is temperature: The vegetables must be room temperature—too hot, and they'll melt the cheese; too cold, and they won't have the best flavor. The sharp arugula, the beet–walnut oil sauce elevate the idea above a run-of-the-mill beet-and-goat-cheese salad. It's got a beautiful balance.

Start a large fire in your fireplace. You will need a good amount of glowing embers for the cooking.

Individually wrap the beets, potatoes, and apples in aluminum foil, seasoning with salt and pepper and adding 1 tablespoon of the olive oil to each package. Place the packages under the grate of your fire, next to and under burning embers. Keep a close watch on the vegetables, turning as necessary to evenly cook. The apples should be tender in 15 to 20 minutes (longer if using Cortland apples), the beets and potatoes will need 35 to 40 minutes. Remove them to a platter as they finish. *(The vegetables can be roasted in a 400°F oven. The cooking time will be slightly shorter.)*

When the vegetables are cool enough to handle, peel and cut them into ½-inch cubes: you will need 60 cubes each from the potatoes and apples, and 96 beet cubes. Reserve the beet scraps, and set all the vegetables aside separately at room temperature.

Meanwhile, combine the goat cheese and sour cream in a bowl and stir to blend. Add the shallot and chives and stir to combine. Season to taste with salt and pepper. *(If making ahead, cover and refrigerate. Bring to room temperature before serving.)*

For the sauce, place the beet scraps in a blender with the sherry vinegar and puree to a smooth consistency. Transfer the beet puree to a bowl and mix in the walnut oil; do not emulsify—this should be a broken vinaigrette. Set aside.

Place a ring mold in the center of each plate and spread 1 tablespoon of the goat cheese mixture in the bottom. Top the goat cheese in each mold with 10 cubes of potato, another dollop of goat cheese, 10 cubes of apple, another dollop of goat cheese, and 10 cubes of beet. Finish with a layer of goat cheese.

Toss the arugula with enough vinaigrette to coat. Top each parfait with a bit of the arugula salad, and remove the molds. Drizzle the beet sauce around the plates. Sprinkle the remaining beet cubes and the chives around the parfaits. Serve immediately.

On the first morning of the first full day of cooking, the day is clear and cool, the color of the leaves seems to have deepened overnight. Eric is up early, has made coffee, and is stoking a fire from last night's ashes. This fireplace has flooded him with memories of Georges Desbouges's farm in the heart of southern France.

The main house had a fireplace, but it wasn't used much for cooking. Right next to the main house was a small one-room house, maybe forty by fifteen feet, where the cooking was done for the farm workers. They cooked everything in the fireplace, starting with the morning coffee. They cooked fries in duck fat over the fire—not exactly safe, but it's how they did it, and they were like nothing else. It was a real cooking fireplace and ran nearly the length of the house—you could put two chairs in it and sit down while there was a fire going. The grandmother would stew a hare in one corner of it. It would never reach a boil. She'd cook it for two days, and when she was done, you could eat it with a spoon. The ceiling was hung with hams and saucisson, collecting the smoke. In the hot summer, these preserved meats would be moved into the cellar dug below the house, where all the confit was kept.

Eric had finished three years at Jamin with Joël Robuchon, and Robuchon had agreed to find him a job in the United States, where Eric had always wanted to go. But it would take Eric's new boss, Jean-Louis Palladin, some time to get the proper papers in order for Eric to work at Palladin in the Watergate Hotel. Eric spent the interim with his girlfriend's family on Georges's farm in Moissac, near Cahors, not far from where Eric had been stationed during his military service. He had gotten to know the family well then. On this visit, he cooked for them, but mainly he hung out with Uncle Georges, following him to the markets, watching him run the farm. Jean-Louis was not a great bureaucrat and seemed unable to arrange for Eric to work in the States. Eric stayed not just a few weeks, as planned, but half a year, fully engaging in the life of a fruit and vegetable farm.

Eric put the first pan on the fire instinctively. He'd covered some black and white beans with water to soak overnight and now dumped them into a large enameled cast-iron pot with some vegetables. He cut a thick slab of Parma ham and threw that in the pot, along with some pork sausage, a pepperoni sausage, and chorizo. He carried the pot to the hearth. With a shovel, he made a bed of hot coals below one of two grates; the other grate held the blazing logs. He set the pot on the grate over the coals, partially covering it with a lid. "That's the real thing," he said again. Lunch was begun.

White and Black Bean Ragout with a Variety of Sausages, page 258

White and Black Bean Ragout with a Variety of Sausages pictured on page 257

SERVES 6

2 cups white beans (preferably navy
   beans), soaked overnight in water
   to cover generously

2 cups black beans, soaked overnight
   in water to cover generously

10 cups chicken stock

1 link smoked pepperoni (about 8 ounces)

2 links chorizo (about 5 ounces)

3 links fresh pork sausage
   (about 6 ounces)

5 ounces smoked bacon ends
   (available at specialty butchers)

A 14-ounce chunk of prosciutto
   (from the shank end)

9 garlic cloves, peeled

3 large carrots, peeled and cut into thirds

1 large onion, halved

Fine sea salt and freshly ground
   white pepper

2 tablespoons chopped flat-leaf parsley

Pinch of Espelette pepper powder
   (you can substitute cayenne)

2 tablespoons balsamic vinegar (optional)

PREP: 20 minutes — COOK: 2½ hours

Start a large fire in your fireplace. You will need a good amount of glowing embers for the cooking. Arrange the logs on one side of the grate and leave enough room on the other side of the grate to accommodate a large pot. You will need to let the a fire burn for about an hour before you can begin cooking, and the dish will need a constant supply of orange embers from a long-burning fire.

Using a shovel, make a bed of orange embers, collected from under the burning logs, under the part of the grate that will accommodate your bean pot.

Drain the beans. Combine all the ingredients except the parsley, Espelette powder, and balsamic vinegar in a large heavy-bottomed pot and set on the grate. Cover with the lid slightly ajar and let the beans come to a simmer. They should remain cooking at a steady simmer; don't let them boil. To keep the heat steady under your pot, you will need to monitor the fire closely, adding logs and moving embers under the pot as necessary. Cook until the beans are tender, about 2 hours. Season with salt and pepper about an hour into the cooking. *(The cooking can be done on your stovetop; the cooking time will be slightly less.)*

To serve, divide the beans among six warmed bowls. Cut up the meats and divide evenly among the bowls. Cut the carrot pieces in half and the onion into six wedges, and divide the vegetables evenly among the bowls. Sprinkle the parsley and pepper powder over the beans, drizzle the balsamic vinegar, if using, into the bowls, and serve immediately.

Eric has discovered a special kind of spicy ground chile pepper called *piment d'Espelette*, from the town of that name in the Basque region of France. It looks and tastes very much like cayenne, but its heat is gentler, its flavor sweeter and fruitier. He would use it here as he used Tabasco on Long Island, and cayenne in Napa. (It can be found at some specialty stores, see Sources, page 320.) It's almost always superior to cayenne.

Georges was a wise man. I loved to follow him. He could put his hand into the down of a goose, feel its belly, and tell you the quality of the foie gras. We would buy ducks and geese and he would take the foie gras out while it was still warm, then use the rest of the bird. The breasts of these birds were especially plump and juicy, but we'd eat the feet as well. This was how you lived.

The women did the confit. Everything had to be very, very clean. If you left even a crumb of bread on the table, you were banished from the kitchen, because one crumb could make an entire batch of confit moldy. The confit would sit for months in earthenware, and sometimes it would get so warm that the duck lard on top would become loose and translucent. But the duck legs stayed well preserved.

In the winter they also killed the pigs—*"Demain on tue le cochon,"* they would say with a grin. It's rough. I almost passed out. They just cut the pig's throat, and the women rushed in to gather all the gushing blood. They used chains to lift the pig and dunk it in boiling water to remove its hair. The pig turned a ghostly white, but blood was still coming out and streaking it.

Then the pig was taken apart, incredibly fast. The women began grinding meat into sausage; in two hours, the pig was pâté. They preserved most of the animal—hams, bacon, smoked sausage. The intestines were used for the sausage, the stomach went into the blood sausage, the liver into the pâté. The head and neck were cooked that day to make a stew; the blood sausage was eaten immediately as well.

They would confit the pork loin, which was amazing. It would keep unrefrigerated until deep summer, when everyone was so busy on the farm that no one had time to make lunch. Then they would slice it like cold cuts and eat it all summer.

They used everything, absolutely everything. Even when they cooked duck, they roasted the bones until they were brittle and then munched on them, pretending it was a delicacy.

I grew up in a rustic village, but it was sophisticated—like Aspen. I had never had any contact with such people, with farm life, with rural living. They were amazingly efficient in how they used what little land they owned, what food they got. They were and are great, great people. In a way, they prepared me for my next stage of cooking—cooking for Jean-Louis. He was from that country, that's what his cooking was about—the powerful flavors of meat and innards and fat. I'd just come from the most refined kitchen in the world. If I hadn't had those months on the farm, I would never have understood Jean-Louis.

This fireplace brings this all back. I never realized how powerful memories are, how they're stored in me—the hams hanging, the grandma stewing hare, fries in duck fat, the morning coffee. It was a very happy time in my life. I learned so much from these people.

It's a gloomy morning, with the wind whipping leaves off the trees, covering the road with slick color. The routine has begun—Eric has got the fire going and made coffee, and we all sit in front of the fire waiting for the sleep to lift. Tammar appears, her waist-length red hair wet from a shower, and then Shimon, and they sit at the table and talk and eat a muffin with their coffee. Valentino won't be up for hours, having stayed up late in the silent house working on his paintings. I've put on Bach's *Goldberg Variations* because their quiet intensity is perfect for this moody Saturday. There will be time for taking notes later. Now I enjoy the morning. It's like a vacation. . . .

Braised Oxtails in Cabbage Leaves, page 262

Eric marinated the oxtails in wine with mirepoix all night and now has separated the three components. He spreads out coals on the hearth next to the logs he keeps blazing. He puts a pan on the coals and sears the oxtails. When they are browned, he transfers them to the large enameled cast-iron pot he used for yesterday's bean pot. He then caramelizes the mirepoix from the marinade—onions, celery, and carrot. But this time he shoves the pan beneath the grate of flaming logs so it's getting great heat from both top and bottom, hot ash and coal beneath and flaming logs above. He adds the fire-roasted mirepoix to the cast-iron pot.

Next he brings the marinade to a boil on the stove and skims it. He adds this to the pot, along with plenty of chicken stock, then sets this on the grate and shovels more burning coals beneath it.

The fire is roaring. Eric stands, red in the face and sweating from working so close to the fire. "Oh, wow," he says, "that's an adventure."

Within an hour, the pot is bubbling and the whole house is filled with the smell of the stew. The wind blows leaves and rain against the windows of the old stone house. I wish for a moment that all of life could feel this essential, this elemental. I want to find a way to cook for people exactly this way. Tammar and Shimon, mesmerized by the pot on the grate, are photographing it. Andrea is running through the morning prep list. The house is alive, and I know where this deep sense of well-being and life comes from—from the fire and the pot.

This is the first time I've used a fireplace so intensively, and I find it amazing. The reason to do it is flavor. It smokes the food, communicates the smoke and the wood to the food—just like it smokes your clothes. Also, it's not as intense as a professional gas burner. The slower cooking allows the food to give up its flavors more fully to the whole dish. Every ingredient has time to interact with the others, bringing out the best of each other.

The fireplace offers three kinds of heat: in decreasing order of intensity, there are the burning-hot coals, the direct heat of the flame, and the hot ash.

The challenge and the beauty are that you use your whole body in the cooking. You're entirely involved, always tending the fire, regulating the heat. This isn't just turning knobs on a stove—you're in the heat with the food. You're shoveling coals around, and you gauge the heat by how it feels on your hand and arm—is it just hot, or so hot you have to wrap a towel around your hand? Are you squinting in the heat, do you feel it on your face? There's no "medium-high" on a knob, no oven temperature to read. It's a very sensual, exciting way of cooking. You're playing sorcerer. It gives you both humility—feeling the force of the fire—and a sense of power in controlling it, domesticating it.

I love this way of cooking. It's fun, but it's no piece of cake. You have to take your time, the fire gives you time. Because you have to be so engaged, it's a way of cooking that encourages reflection. And this too is one of the great advantages of cooking in the fireplace. It's at once a powerfully physical and a deeply meditative process.

Braised Oxtails in Cabbage Leaves pictured on page 260

pictured on page 260

SERVES 6

10 pounds meaty oxtails

4 bottles red wine

½ cup Cognac

3 medium carrots, chopped

1 large onion, chopped

2 ribs celery, chopped

1 head garlic (about 12 cloves),
  separated into cloves, peeled,
  and halved

Pinch of Espelette pepper powder
  (you can substitute cayenne)

About 6 tablespoons duck fat
  (you can substitute canola oil)

Fine sea salt and freshly ground
  white pepper

⅓ cup all-purpose flour

1 cup Armagnac

8 cups chicken stock

1 head green cabbage, cored and
  separated into leaves

1 head red cabbage, cored and
  separated into leaves

2 tablespoons unsalted butter

Gray sea salt for garnish

SPECIAL EQUIPMENT

Chinese bamboo steamer
  (or colander with feet)

Wok (or pot large enough to
  accommodate colander)

PREP: 1 hour, plus 24 hours marinating time — COOK: 3 hours

This classical braise technique works in the oven or the fireplace. When the meat is falling off the bone, it's done. Eric decided to shred the meat and wrap it in cabbage leaves; these packages, wrapped in plastic, can be done well in advance of serving the dish and simply steamed to reheat. The sauce is the strained cooking liquid, reduced. It's super-intense from all the wine and stock and bones and vegetables, but Eric added some extra butter at the end to round it out and make it velvet on the palate. This meat would work equally well wrapped in lasagna noodles.

Place the oxtails, red wine, Cognac, carrots, onion, celery, garlic, and Espelette powder in a large bowl or other container and marinate in the refrigerator overnight.

Start a large fire in your fireplace. You will need a good amount of glowing embers for the cooking. Arrange the logs on one side of the grate and leave enough room on the other side of the grate to accommodate a large pot. You will need to let the fire burn for about an hour before you can begin cooking, and the dish will need a constant supply of orange embers from a long-burning fire.

Drain the oxtails, reserving the liquid, and set the oxtails and vegetables aside. Strain the liquid into a pot and bring to a boil on the stovetop, skimming any foam that rises to the top. Reduce the liquid by a third. Set aside.

Meanwhile, separate the oxtails and vegetables. Using a shovel, make a bed of glowing embers, collected from under the burning logs, under the empty part of the grate, and place a large heavy pot on the grate. Add 2 tablespoons of the duck fat to the pot. Season the oxtails on both sides with salt and pepper. When the fat is hot, add only enough of the oxtails as will fit in a single layer and sear, turning once, until golden brown on both sides. Transfer the oxtails to a platter and continue searing the remaining oxtails, adding more duck fat as necessary. As the embers die out, replace them with more from under the burning fire, replenishing the fire as necessary.

Add 2 more tablespoons of duck fat to the pot. When it is warm, add the vegetables from the marinade and set the pot under the fire to cook. Once the vegetables are nicely caramelized, pull the pot out and sprinkle the flour over them. Continue to cook over the bed of orange embers, stirring, until the flour is toasted, another 3 minutes. Pour the Armagnac over the vegetables, light with a match, and flambé. After the flames subside, stir the bottom of the pot to release any browned bits.

Return the oxtails to the pot and cover with the reduced marinade and the stock. Let it come to a simmer and simmer, replacing the logs for your fire and the glowing embers under the cooking grate as necesary, until the oxtails begin to fall off the bone, about 2 hours. *(This can also be done on the stovetop; the cooking time will be slightly less.)*

Drain the oxtails in a colander, reserving the liquid. Strain the liquid through a fine-mesh sieve and reserve. Separate the meat and vegetables, placing them in two bowls. Debone the oxtails, discarding the bones and fat. Set aside.

Meanwhile, bring two large pots of salted water to a boil. Blanch the green and purple cabbage leaves separately until tender, about 5 minutes for the green leaves and 10 minutes for the purple. Plunge into an ice water bath to stop the cooking process; drain. Remove the tough, thick central core from the leaves.

To prepare the stuffed cabbage, lightly brush your cutting board with canola oil and place a 12-inch square of plastic wrap on top. Place a large cabbage leaf in the center (use more than one leaf if they are small) and place 2 tablespoons of the meat and 1 tablespoon of the vegetables in the center. Season with salt and pepper. Pull up the corners of the plastic wrap and twist tightly to close—make sure there is no space between the film and the cabbage, or the package will not hold its round shape. Cut off the excess plastic and set aside. Continue until you have 12 green parcels and 6 purple parcels.

To finish, place the parcels in one layer in your bamboo steamer (or in the colander); use two steamer baskets if necessary. Place a wok (or large pot) filled with 2 inches of water over high heat and bring to a boil. Place the steamer over the wok (or pot), making sure the water does not touch the bottom, cover, and steam until the centers of the parcels are warm, about 10 minutes.

Meanwhile, bring the sauce to a simmer. Whisk in the butter.

To serve, place 2 green cabbage parcels and 1 purple cabbage parcel in the center of each warmed plate. Spoon the sauce over the parcels. Season each parcel with a pinch of gray salt. Serve immediately.

Grilled Magrets with Arugula and Cranberry

Serves 6

THE GARNISH

1 tablespoon duck fat

½ cup chopped onions

1 tablespoon minced ginger

½ pound cranberries (about 2 cups)

1 cup water

3 tablespoons sugar

1 teaspoon minced Lemon Confit
   (page 21)

Pinch of Espelette pepper powder
   (you can substitute cayenne)

4 Cortland apples

2 tablespoons foie gras fat or duck fat

Fine sea salt and freshly ground
   white pepper

12 fresh figs, halved

PREP: 20 minutes — **COOK:** 20 minutes

To grill in the fireplace, you need an actual grill or device for holding the meat, and a good bed of hot coals. Eric found a handheld contraption that folded over the meat, but any kind of movable grate, with a couple of stones or other supports to hold it above the coals, will work. Plan ahead, build a good fire, and give it time to create coals. Then shovel those coals between your stones, and you have your heat source. Anything you'd cook on a barbecue grill you can cook this way—fish, chicken, beef, vegetables—but Eric chose the special duck breasts called magrets, the breasts from foie gras–producing ducks. The breasts are beautifully plump and, cooked medium-rare, they taste as rich as a strip steak. In a separate pan in the same fire, Eric pan-roasted the cranberries, adding some sugar to make a very tart chutney. Sautéed apples and figs and peppery arugula finish off the rich dish.

Start a large fire in your fireplace. You will need a good amount of glowing embers for the cooking. Arrange the logs at one side of the grate and leave enough room on the other side of the grate to accommodate a large sauté pan. You will need to let the fire burn for about an hour before you can begin cooking, and the dish will need a constant supply of orange embers from a long-burning fire.

Shovel hot embers from the fire under the empty part of the grate. Place a small pot on the grate and add the duck fat. When the duck fat is warm, add the onions and ginger and cook until translucent, about 3 minutes. Add the cranberries, water, sugar, lemon confit, and Espelette powder and simmer until the cranberries begin to pop. Maintain the heat under the pan by replacing the embers as they begin to die out. Set aside near the fire to keep warm. (The cooking can be done on your stovetop; the cooking time will be slightly less.)

Peel and core the apples and cut into ½-inch-thick slices; you need a total of 12 slices. Place a sauté pan on the grate, piling on more embers to make the heat a bit stronger. Melt the foie gras fat. Add only as many apples as will fit in a single layer and cook, turning occasionally and seasoning with salt and pepper, until nicely browned on both sides. Transfer the apples to a platter and continue in this manner until all the apples are cooked. Keep the heat steady by replacing the embers as they die out. Cook the figs in the same way, using more fat if necessary. Transfer the figs to the platter with the apples and loosely tent with foil to keep warm.

THE DUCK

3 magrets (see Sources, page 320)

Fine sea salt and freshly ground
white pepper

THE SALAD

2 bunches arugula

6 duck gizzard confits
(see Sources, page 320),
thinly sliced (optional)

12 slices Duck Ham (page 269)

Fine sea salt and freshly ground
white pepper

¼ cup Vinaigrette (page 205)

SPECIAL EQUIPMENT

Grill rack or basket large enough to
accommodate the magrets

For the duck breasts, make a bed of embers on your hearth and place two large stones that rise about 4 inches above the heat on either side of the embers. Prepare the duck breasts by trimming the fat to ½ inch thick. Score a crosshatch pattern in the skin to prevent it from curling while cooking. Season generously with salt and pepper. Place the breasts in a grilling basket or on a grate set over the fire. Grill over the hot embers skin side down until medium-rare, 5 to 7 minutes. Keep the intensity of the heat steady by adding more glowing embers as necessary. *(The cooking can be done on your stovetop in a hot sauté pan. Cook the breasts on the skin side only to make the skin very crispy. The cooking time may vary slightly.)* Transfer the magrets to a platter and let rest for 5 minutes.

For the salad, combine the arugula, confit if using, and duck ham in a bowl. Season with salt and pepper and toss with enough vinaigrette to coat.

To serve, slice the duck crosswise into thin slices. Arrange 5 or so slices of duck at the bottom of each plate, fanning them out. Spoon a bit of the cranberry sauce over each. Place 2 apple slices and 4 fig halves at the 10 o'clock position on each plate. Mound the salad at 2 o'clock on each plate. Serve immediately.

Fire-Roasted Pheasant à la Ficelle with Truffled Lentils

THE PHEASANT

Two 3-pound pheasants

Fine sea salt and freshly ground
   white pepper

6 thyme sprigs

½ cup duck fat, melted

Two 2-inch squares day-old French bread

THE LENTILS

2 slices bacon, cut crosswise into julienne

½ cup diced (¼-inch) carrots

½ cup diced (¼-inch) onions

1¾ cups French green lentils
   (lentilles de Puy)

4 cups chicken stock

2 cups water

Fine sea salt and freshly ground
   white pepper

4 tablespoons unsalted butter,
   at room temperature

3 ounces fresh duck foie gras
   (you can substitute foie gras terrine)

1 ounce black truffle, roughly chopped

SPECIAL EQUIPMENT

Kitchen string

PREP: 25 minutes — **COOK:** 1½ hours

À la ficelle means on a string, a common way of roasting in front of the fire. Leg of lamb is often cooked *à la ficelle* in France, but we did it with pheasant, because we could, and because they looked so good there. Game birds hanging in front of a blazing fire are more work to tend, and you have to be careful not to overcook them or they'll be tasteless, but cooking this way gives an extra punch of flavor to the very neutral meat some even consider bland. In France, they use a technique called *faisanter*—hanging the bird, whole and still feathered, for a few days to develop some flavor. The bones don't make a good jus, so you have to get flavor from other sources, such as the fire and basting it with duck fat or butter. Eric served the pheasant, which was juicy and delicate, on top of a strong stew of lentils enriched with foie gras–truffle butter. (Again, truffles are great, but in this dish not the main point and should be considered optional.)

Start a large fire in your fireplace. You will need a very hot fire for the cooking. You will need to let the fire burn for about an hour before you begin cooking, and the dish will need a constant supply of orange embers from a long-burning fire.

Rinse the birds and pat dry. Season the cavities with salt and pepper and stuff each with 3 sprigs of thyme. Pour ½ cup of the duck fat into each opening and plug with a square of bread. Season the outsides of the birds with salt and pepper.

Tie the legs of each bird together using a long piece of kitchen string. Tie the ends of the kitchen string to the fire-irons rack. Put the rack inside a large roasting pan to catch the drippings and set the rack 18 inches from the fire. Cook in front of the hot fire for 1 hour, rotating the birds every 10 minutes, or until the birds are tender and the juices run clear. Baste the birds with the duck fat as it drips into the roasting pan. Transfer the birds to a platter and let rest for 10 minutes. *(You can roast the birds in a roasting pan in a 350°F oven for about an hour, being sure to baste them every 10 minutes.)*

Meanwhile, sauté the bacon in a medium pot over medium heat until it renders its fat, 2 to 3 minutes. Add the carrots and onions and sweat until limp, about 3 minutes. Add the lentils, cover with the chicken stock and water and bring to a simmer. Cook for 35 minutes, or until the lentils are tender. Season with salt and pepper halfway through the cooking time. Set aside.

While the lentils are cooking, place the butter and foie gras in the container of a food processor and pulse until smooth. Add the chopped truffles and pulse until combined. Cover with plastic wrap and refrigerate.

Just before serving, bring the lentils to a boil. Cut the foie gras–truffle butter into small chunks and whisk into the boiling lentils until fully combined.

To serve, carve the pheasant and slice the breast and leg meat. Spoon the lentils onto six warmed plates. Divide the sliced leg and breast meat among the plates, arranging the breast meat on one side of each plate and the leg meat on the other. Serve immediately.

Duck Ham

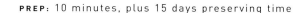

MAKES 2 "HAMS"

2 duck magrets

3 cups gray sea salt
   (you can substitute rock salt)

1 cup red wine vinegar

2 teaspoons freshly ground black pepper

SPECIAL EQUIPMENT

2 pieces cheesecloth measuring
   36 inches by 12 inches

Kitchen string

PREP: 10 minutes, plus 15 days preserving time

This is an easy preparation to do at home, and a delicious product to have on hand. Use it as you would prosciutto. Always sliced thin, it's delicious on salads, or on toasted slices of baguette. It also gives a very nice flavor to stews or stewed beans. You can use any duck breast for this, but magrets will give you the biggest, most flavorful ham.

Trim the duck breast fat to ½ inch thick.

Place 1½ cups of the gray salt in a nonreactive casserole or a baking dish. Place the duck breasts on top of the salt skin side up. Cover with the remaining 1½ cups salt. Cover the casserole with plastic wrap and refrigerate for 24 hours.

Remove the magrets from the salt and rinse under cold running water. Pour the vinegar over the magrets for a final rinse. Pat dry with paper towels. Sprinkle the pepper over the flesh side only.

Lay out a piece of cheesecloth and place a breast at the top in the center. Fold each side over the breast and roll up to close. Secure the cheesecloth with kitchen string, tying it once lengthwise, then three times crosswise. Repeat with the second breast. Tie a long string to each bundle and hang in a cold place, like your basement, or garage in the winter. The duck is ready to eat after 2 weeks of aging.

PRESERVATION TECHNIQUES

One of the main forms of cooking on a farm, especially before refrigeration, was preservative cooking. Some seasons produce more food (such as duck, fruit, or pork, for instance) than you would want to eat but that might feed you throughout the year if you knew how to treat it. Preservation of meat typically involves removing the water from the product. Bacteria are what cause food to rot—if you remove the oxygen-carrying water, they cannot survive and the food will be preserved.

The primary way to remove water is with salt. Food to be preserved is almost always salted first. Salt draws water out like a magnet (and the salt jumps in—so it's easy to oversalt). After salting, a meat is sometimes poached in an oxygenless, waterless environment (fat), killing any bacteria that might eventually cause rot, and stored submerged in the fat, which prevents any air from reaching the meat. This is the confit technique, used for many products, but most often associated with duck legs.

A second method of preventing bacterial growth is to dry the meat. This is how the leg of a pig becomes cured ham. The salted meat is wrapped in cloth and hung to dry. The resulting meat and fat become very dense and flavorful (especially if this ham comes from Parma, Italy, which makes extraordinary cured ham, sold sliced thinly as prosciutto). The happy fact is that you don't have to have a whole leg of pig hanging around to enjoy home-cured meat, or to purchase an entire belly to make your own bacon. Duck breast works beautifully. Some restaurant chefs call it duck prosciutto, and I know one who cures it with tons of pepper and bills it as duck pastrami, but it's all really duck ham, easy to make, and really delicious.

Eric fills a stack of notebooks and loose sheets of paper with lists of ingredients, combinations of ingredients, whole dishes. Sometimes after a while they don't mean anything, even to him. "Look at this," he says as I examine one of his pages. "Fresh bay leaves and butter. I have no idea what I was thinking!"

But there's a method to these notes. They begin very rough, sometimes a series of near-senseless ideas. I found the following in a notebook in Napa.

bouillabaisse des legumes au fennel

poulet aux olives

riz truffé

arugula pesto

riz crème

oxtail broth

rognons gyromitre d'herbes aux papillotes

string beans, porc, ail

baked ham

eggplant pizza

borscht

Baked ham? Well, okay.

His next step is to refine his many lists. He rereads a list and writes down the items that are still meaningful to him. From what he calls "stupid ideas" comes a little more cogent list. This list is edited from "stupid ideas" he'd been working on for Vermont—I've starred the ones that ultimately came to something on the trip.

borscht

pumpkin soup*

garlic soup*

codfish vegetable bouillabaisse

lobster consommé with ravioli*

foie gras terrine with quince*

scallops with truffle butter

leeks and chix livers velouté

endive salad with celeriac and
*   goat cheese dressing*

foie cooked in terrine with green salad*

potatoes and goat cheese

meat ceviche ("I was thinking you sear
*   the meat, very rare, and marinate")*
*   and pine nuts*

carpaccio of bone marrow

mushrooms, watercress salad with
*   mustard vinaigrette*

fillet of beef with a garnish of tartare

smoked fish with apples, watercress,
*   and walnuts*

fish on top of beef carpaccio with
*   horseradish cream*

salt cod with eggplant, with peppers

porcini, crayfish ravioli*

oxtails and ravioli

vegetables gratin*

potato cake with goat cheese with sabayon

olives, tomato compote

veal loin stuffed with sausage

duck with lime

oxtail shepherd's pie

poached goose with poached foie gras
*   consommé with vegetables**

poulet stuffed with chestnuts

venison with sauce royale

raw apples with cheese and fish

I began this list making when I was with Jean-Louis. I saw his fluency and creativity and it appealed to me and seemed so satisfying. Until then I had been a technician, and now I could begin to think creatively. I began to take notes, just writing ideas down. Pages and pages of stupid ideas, some good ones. I'd narrow them down—twenty pages would become five, would become one. Then I'd see that some items at the bottom of the page went with some at the top, and I'd write that down.

I did this for three years. And then one day I got stuck. I couldn't write a single idea down. I was very nervous and very insecure, but I threw it all out. Hundreds and hundreds of pages of notes, in the garbage.

What Eric found was that fresh new ideas came. First a couple and then more and more, and he realized that the act of sitting down could itself generate ideas, and a few ideas generated more ideas. It was infinite, and he never worried again. He knew the ideas would always come as long as he remembered to throw away all the notes every now and then. And some of the meals that emerge have never seen life as written words until after they are eaten; these meals begin as one thing and change in midair. Such as the crayfish recipe on page 272.

Eric had dumped the live crayfish, in batches of fifty, into the hot sauté pan, and he'd asked Andrea to clean them, reserving the heads to make a sauce. But a little later, as he sautéed the heads, he scrutinized the pan and knew he had too much fatty gray matter in the shells, that it was all steamy and muddy and wouldn't produce a clean, flavorful sauce. So he moved to a butter sauce—a great fallback, butter—added flavoring, and voilà, instant sauce! It's particularly fine if your flavoring happens to be chopped truffle.

Or the garnish for the wild squab, cabbage cooked in duck fat—that idea was around for about thirty seconds before the cabbage was actually stewing in the fireplace.

This is what cooking is, a combination of routine, calculation, personal history, basic knowledge of how food works, imagination, and inspiration.

Palombe (Wild Squab) with Cabbage Confit and Porcini, page 274, before being sauced

Crayfish Ravioli with Mushrooms and Truffle Butter Sauce

SERVES 6

THE DOUGH

2 cups all-purpose flour,
  plus more for kneading

1 teaspoon fine sea salt,
  plus more to taste

5 large egg yolks

THE FILLING

2 cups dry white wine

6 pounds live crayfish
  (see Sources, page 320)

1 tablespoon foie gras fat
  (you can substitute canola oil)

6 ounces large chanterelles,
  plus 3 ounces small chanterelles
  (if small ones aren't available,
  use large ones, halved)

3 ounces black trumpet mushrooms

Fine sea salt and freshly ground
  white pepper

1½ tablespoons minced shallots

¼ teaspoon thyme leaves

6 tablespoons unsalted butter,
  at room temperature

1 ounce black truffles, finely chopped

PREP: 50 minutes — **COOK:** 45 minutes

For the pasta dough, sift the flour and salt into a large mixing bowl and whisk to combine. Make a well in the center of the flour and add the egg yolks. Using a fork, slowly incorporate the yolks into the flour, until all the yolks have been absorbed. Transfer the dough to a counter that has been dusted with flour. Knead the dough, using the heel of your hand, for about 4 minutes: The dough is ready if when you press your finger into the dough, it bounces back into shape. Shape it into a disk, wrap in plastic, and place in the refrigerator to rest for at least 30 minutes.

For the filling, bring ½ cup of the wine to a boil in a large heavy-bottomed pan. Add one-quarter of the crayfish, cover, and steam for 3 minutes, or until bright red and cooked through. Transfer to a platter to cool. Continue cooking the crayfish one-quarter at a time, replacing the wine for each batch.

Once the crayfish are cool enough to handle, pull off the tails and crack them to remove the meat. Devein the tails by running a small knife down the back of each one; remove the vein and discard. Reserve the crayfish in the refrigerator.

Heat the foie gras fat in a large sauté pan over high heat. Add the large chanterelles and the black trumpets and sauté until tender, 5 to 7 minutes. Season with salt and pepper. Add 1 teaspoon of the shallots and half the thyme and cook until all the liquid has evaporated. Remove from the heat and allow the mushrooms to cool to room temperature. Finely chop and set aside.

Melt 1 tablespoon of the butter in the same sauté pan and sauté the small chanterelles, seasoning with salt and pepper, until tender and all the liquid has evaporated, 5 to 7 minutes. Add the remaining 1 tablespoon shallots and remaining thyme and cook for 2 more minutes. Set aside.

Make a truffle butter by combining the remaining 5 tablespoons butter and the finely chopped truffles. Refrigerate.

Remove the pasta dough from the refrigerator and divide it into 4 pieces. Working with one quarter of the dough at a time, roll it from the thickest setting to the thinnest setting on your pasta machine. Use additional flour if the dough is sticky. Keep the remaining dough covered while rolling to prevent it from drying out.

THE SAUCE

4 tablespoons unsalted butter,
   at room temperature

3 ounces fresh duck foie gras
   (you can substitute foie gras terrine)

2 ounces black truffles, chopped

1 cup truffle juice (we recommend
   Pébeyre brand; see Sources, page 320)

For the ravioli, starting about 2 inches from one end, place 1 teaspoon of the mushroom mixture, topped with ½ teaspoon truffle butter and 2 crayfish tails, at 4-inch intervals down one pasta sheet. Brush water around the filling and top with another pasta sheet. Seal the edges, being careful not to trap air inside the ravioli. Cut out the ravioli with a 3-inch cookie cutter, and press the edges to make the dough thinner. Place the finished ravioli on a parchment-lined baking sheet. You will need 30 ravioli for this dish; you may have a few extra. Cover with a towel and refrigerate until ready to cook.

For the sauce, make a foie gras butter by placing the butter and foie gras in the container of a food processor and pulsing until smooth. Add half of the chopped truffles and pulse until combined. Cover with plastic wrap and refrigerate until cold.

Shortly before serving, bring the truffle juice and the remaining chopped truffles to a boil in a small saucepan. Lower the heat to a steady simmer. Whisking constantly, add the foie gras butter bit by bit until all the butter has been incorporated. Set aside.

Bring a large pot (we used a roasting pan) of salted water to a simmer. Add the ravioli and cook until al dente, about 7 minutes.

Meanwhile, gently reheat the sauce; do not bring to a boil, or the sauce will break. Gently reheat the chanterelles.

To serve, place 5 ravioli on each plate, scatter the chanterelles around, and spoon the sauce over the top. Serve immediately.

Eric had ordered crayfish because they are such an American shellfish. There is a moment of drama and tension as you dump the batches of live crustaceans into a hot sauté pan, but they are quickly stilled once the cover is on.

Some time is required for this ravioli, but the actual preparation is easy. The truffle butter added to the mushroom-crayfish filling is a great touch. The sauce is a simple, though expensive, one that will work for virtually any pasta; here the truffles and foie gras connect beautifully with the mushrooms.

Palombe (Wild Squab) with Cabbage Confit and Porcini pictured on page 271

pictured on page 271

SERVES 6

THE CABBAGE

1 large head green cabbage,
  cored and leaves separated

⅓ cup duck fat

¼ teaspoon coarsely ground
  juniper berries

Fine sea salt and freshly ground
  white pepper

THE PALOMBES

¼ cup duck fat

6 palombes or other wild squabs,
  about 1½ pounds each
  (see Note; see Sources, page 320)

Fine sea salt and freshly ground
  white pepper

4 tablespoons unsalted butter,
  at room temperature

1 ounce black truffles, chopped

½ pound porcini, quartered lengthwise

1 slice bacon, cut crosswise into julienne

½ cup sliced shallots

5 garlic cloves, thinly sliced

½ teaspoon thyme leaves

Pinch of Espelette pepper powder
  (you can substitute cayenne)

½ teaspoon all-purpose flour

¾ cup Armagnac

1¾ cups chicken stock

PREP: 30 minutes — **COOK:** 40 minutes

This is a beautiful, rustic dish: The squabs are roasted, then the rib cages and backbones are removed to fortify the sauce, to which truffle butter and porcini mushrooms are added. The cabbage is slow-cooked in duck fat, tamed into sweetness.

For the cabbage, bring a large pot of salted water to a boil. Stack the cabbage leaves and cut into 2-inch squares. Add the cabbage to the boiling water and cook until bright green, about 2 minutes. Drain and set aside.

Melt the duck fat in a large pot over low heat. Add the juniper berries and stir to combine. Add the cabbage and season with salt and pepper. Cook over low heat, stirring occasionally, until the cabbage is tender, about 1 hour. Set aside.

Preheat the oven to 350°F.

For the squabs, melt 2 tablespoons of the duck fat in each of two large ovenproof sauté pans over medium heat. Season the squabs with salt and pepper. When the oil is hot, add 3 birds to each pan and sear on both sides, about 5 minutes per side. Place in the oven and cook until the internal temperature of the thigh is 150°F, about 20 minutes.

Meanwhile, combine the butter and truffles in a small bowl, blending well. Cover and refrigerate.

Transfer the squabs to a platter. Add the porcini mushrooms to one of the sauté pans and sauté until softened, about 5 minutes. Add the bacon and cook until it begins to render its fat, about 3 minutes. Add the shallots, garlic, thyme, and Espelette powder and cook until the shallots are translucent, about 2 minutes. With a slotted spoon, transfer the porcini mixture to a platter, leaving the duck fat in the pan, and set aside. Set the pan aside.

Meanwhile, when the birds are cool enough to handle, remove the bones: Using a paring knife, cut each one down the center of the back, then follow the rib cage closely with the knife to remove the ribs and backbone. (Leave the leg bones in the bird.) Reserve the bones. Return the birds to the platter, cover with foil, and keep in a warm spot in the kitchen.

Set the sauté pan you used to cook the birds and mushrooms over medium-high heat and add the reserved bones. Sear until nicely browned, 5 to 7 minutes. Sprinkle the flour over the bones and cook until the flour is toasted, about 5 minutes. Add the Armagnac and carefully ignite to flambé. Cook until the flames subside. Add the chicken stock, bring to a boil, and cook for 5 minutes. Strain the sauce into a small saucepan.

Just before serving, gently reheat the cabbage. Bring the sauce to a boil and add the truffle butter in small chunks, whisking to incorporate. Add the porcini mixture to the sauce and keep warm.

To serve, divide the cabbage among six warmed plates, placing it in the center of each plate. Cut each bird in half and arrange on top of the cabbage mounds. Spoon the sauce over each plate, evenly distributing the porcini mushrooms. Serve immediately.

NOTE: Palombes are wild squabs from Scotland. They're a deep red, nearly purple, and often taste of what they fed on—if you're lucky, one that raised itself on juniper berries.

Pear Tart à la Mode

THE DOUGH

2¼ cups (8 ounces) all-purpose flour

⅓ cup sugar

1 teaspoon fine sea salt

12 tablespoons unsalted butter
   (1½ sticks), cut into small cubes
   and chilled

1 large egg yolk

⅓ cup ice water, or as needed

THE FILLING

10 small pears (about 2½ pounds)

4 tablespoons unsalted butter

⅓ cup sugar

3 vanilla beans, split

⅓ cup Armagnac

1½ cups good-quality store-bought
   vanilla ice cream

3 tablespoons Vermont maple syrup

SPECIAL EQUIPMENT

Six 3-inch by 2½-inch-high ring molds

PREP: 30 minutes, plus 1 hour chilling time — **COOK:** 30 minutes

This is the kind of tart Eric grew up on, but polished in its presentation. Eric uses a ring mold to form it and then to form an identical disk of ice cream on which the tart sits.

For the dough, place the flour, sugar, and salt in a bowl and whisk to combine. Add the butter cubes and, using a pastry blender or two knives scissors-style, incorporate the butter until the mixture resembles very coarse sand. Add the yolk and all the water and mix to combine. The dough should just barely hold together; if it doesn't, add more cold water a little at a time. Transfer the dough to a lightly floured surface and knead for about 1 minute, until it comes together. Shape into a disk and wrap in plastic film. Refrigerate until well chilled, at least 1 hour.

Preheat the oven to 350°F. Chill a baking sheet in the freezer and six plates in the refrigerator.

For the filling, peel the pears and thinly slice them. Melt the butter in a large ovenproof nonstick sauté pan and add the sugar and vanilla beans. Cook until the sugar has melted and is lightly golden. Add the pears and cook over medium heat until the fruit gives up its liquid and it has evaporated, about 5 minutes. Add the Armagnac and cook until the fruit is softened and lightly golden, another 10 minutes or so. Place in the oven to caramelize, about 10 minutes.

Meanwhile, roll out the dough to less than ⅛ inch thick. Using a ring mold, cut out 6 circles of dough. Place on a parchment–lined baking sheet and bake for 12 to 15 minutes, or until crisp and golden brown. Cool on a rack.

To serve the dessert, you must work quickly; it is best if someone helps you, as the ice cream will melt quickly. Place the tart shells on a baking sheet and place a ring mold on top of each. Fill each ring mold about halfway with the pear mixture and flatten the top with a spoon. Remove the molds and clean them.

Place the ring molds on the chilled baking sheet and fill each about halfway with ice cream. Using a large spatula, transfer the ice cream, in the molds, to the six chilled plates. Remove the ring molds and top with the pear tarts, pressing down to connect the tart crusts and ice cream. Drizzle the maple syrup evenly over each dessert. Serve immediately.

Foie Gras Pot-au-Feu with Truffle Juice and Goose Broth, page 278

Roasted Goose with Sautéed Potatoes and Dandelion Salad, page 279

Here are two recipes that ought to be cooked together, as they make an amazing first and main course. The foie gras pot-au-feu is essentially a very light broth, made from poaching the goose, served with lightly poached foie gras and winter vegetables. The lean broth and vegetables come to life when contrasted with the rich foie gras.

The goose is poached for a couple of hours (Eric did this the day before we ate it) in water or stock, and it is a great way of cooking a goose, which is a tough bird and requires a long, slow cooking. Once the goose is poached, with most of the fat having rendered out of the skin, it's roasted until golden brown. The high fat content of the bird allows it to remain moist and juicy. Eric served it with dandelion salad, using the smallest, most tender dandelion leaves we could find in the grass around the house, to add a light bitter component to counter balance the rich bird.

Foie Gras Pot-au-Feu with Truffle Juice and Goose Broth pictured on page 276

pictured on page 276

SERVES 6

2 quarts goose-infused chicken stock
   (see page 279 or you can substitute
   chicken stock)

Six 3-inch pieces celery

3 medium turnips, peeled and halved

2 large carrots, peeled

3 medium leeks, white part only

1 Grade A duck foie gras, the large
   lobe only (reserve the remaining
   small lobe for another use)

Fine sea salt and freshly ground
   white pepper

1 cup truffle juice
   (we recommend Pébeyre brand;
   see Sources, page 320)

THE GARNISH

½ teaspoon gray sea salt

1 tablespoon thinly sliced chives

¼ teaspoon pepper mignonnette
   (lightly crushed black peppercorns)

6 tablespoons red wine

PREP: 25 minutes — COOK: 20 minutes

In a large pot, bring the stock to a simmer. Add the vegetables and cook until tender, about 15 minutes. Remove the vegetables and set the broth aside. Cut the carrots into 6 pieces measuring 3 inches by ½ inch (reserve the remaining carrots for another use). Cut the leeks into 6 pieces measuring 3 inches by ½ inch (reserve the remaining leeks for another use). Set the vegetables aside.

Fill a pitcher full of hot water and place it to the side of your cutting board. With a very sharp knife, cut the foie gras crosswise into six ¾-inch slices, dipping your knife in the hot water in between each slice. Remove the large veins and discard. Place the foie gras slices in a casserole large enough to accommodate them in a single layer. *(If preparing ahead, cover the foie gras with plastic wrap placed directly against the surface. Refrigerate; bring to room temperature before serving.)*

Season the foie gras on both sides with salt and pepper. Bring 6 cups of the broth to a boil and add the truffle juice. Cover the foie gras with the boiling broth and set aside to poach in the hot liquid for 2 to 3 minutes; it should still be rare.

To serve, place a carrot, leek, turnip, and celery piece in each of six warmed bowls. Cover with the hot truffled broth. Divide the foie gras among the bowls. Garnish each portion of foie gras with a pinch of gray salt, some chives, and a pinch of pepper mignonnette. At the table, pass a small carafe of the red wine so your guests can pour 1 tablespoon each into their bowls.

Roasted Goose with Sautéed Potatoes and Dandelion Salad pictured on page 277

SERVES 6

THE GOOSE
One 8-pound goose
2 gallons chicken stock
   (you can substitute water)
Fine sea salt and freshly ground
   white pepper

THE POTATOES
6 large Yukon Gold potatoes
   (about 2 pounds)
3 tablespoons duck fat
   (you can substitute vegetable oil)
Fine sea salt and freshly ground
   white pepper
4 tablespoons unsalted butter
2 tablespoons chopped flat-leaf parsley
1 teaspoon chopped garlic

THE SALAD
3 tablespoons olive oil
1½ cups bread cubes (about ½-inch;
   use any firm white bread,
   such as a French baguette)
2 teaspoons chopped garlic
Fine sea salt and freshly ground
   white pepper
2 teaspoons Dijon mustard
2 tablespoons sherry vinegar
2 tablespoons minced onion
¼ cup canola oil
¼ pound dandelion greens, washed
   thoroughly to remove sand
   (you can substitute frisée)

Dijon mustard for serving

PREP: 25 minutes — **COOK:** 3½ hours

Place the goose in a large pot and cover with the chicken stock. Bring to a boil, skimming the foam as it rises to the top, then lower the heat to a simmer. Season the broth with salt and pepper to taste. Poach the goose until tender, about 2 hours. Transfer the goose to a platter. Reserve the cooking liquid for another use (such as the foie gras pot-au-feu on page 278).

Preheat the oven to 375°F.

Place the goose on a rack in a large roasting pan. Roast the goose until the skin is crispy, about 1 hour. If necessary, turn on your broiler to crisp the skin for 1 to 2 minutes. Remove the goose from the oven and let rest for at least 10 minutes.

Meanwhile, peel and halve the potatoes. Cut each half into 6 wedges. Melt the duck fat in a large nonstick sauté pan over medium heat and add the potatoes. Season with salt and pepper to taste. Cook, stirring occasionally, until the potatoes are crisp on the outside and tender inside. Set the pan aside.

For the salad, heat 1 tablespoon olive oil in a large sauté pan over medium heat. Add the bread cubes and toast them lightly. Add 1 teaspoon of the chopped garlic and toss to combine. Drain on paper towels and season with salt and pepper.

In a small bowl, combine the Dijon, sherry vinegar, and onion and whisk to combine. Season with salt and pepper. Whisking constantly, slowly drizzle in the remaining 2 tablespoons olive oil, then the canola oil. Set aside.

When ready to serve, reheat the potatoes over medium heat, tossing until crisp. Add the butter, parsley, and garlic and toss to combine. Adjust the salt and pepper. Toss the dandelion greens, croutons, and the remaining 1 teaspoon garlic in a bowl. Drizzle enough vinaigrette over the salad to coat and toss to combine. Adjust the seasoning.

Carve the goose and slice the breast meat and leg meat. Place 3 slices of breast meat and 2 slices of leg meat at the bottom of each plate (you may have some left over). Mound the salad at the 10 o'clock position on each plate and place the potatoes at 2 o'clock. Serve immediately. Pass the Dijon mustard at the table, for the goose.

After our civilized lunch of pot-au-feu and roasted goose, followed by an Armagnac in the brilliant fall sun, we move to a new house, a sprawling country mansion that's both rustic and aristocratic.

Most of the nine bedrooms have fireplaces. The main fireplace in the grand central living room is the one we'll keep lighted—but not to cook in; this house doesn't really lend itself to that. We've said good-bye to the old fireplace, the main character of our short stay at the previous house. Here inspiration comes from the whole house, and Eric's cooking alters accordingly.

He's spread his notes out on the generous granite island in the kitchen. This is the best one we've had, a spacious country kitchen with a six-burner professional range against a white tile wall, hardwood floor, and a ceiling that must be twelve feet high.

The first thing Eric does is to put the pot of chicken stock on. He refers to this as a family member, or as liquid gold. The stock simmers very gently all day. At night it is left on the stove. It's important that air circulate below the pot when it cools or the stock might become sour. Finally, he strains and refrigerates it, but

we cooked that thing for days, adding every available good poultry item and every scrap of sweet vegetable.

"We lost the rhythm," Eric says, looking up from his notes. "It's a big house."

"Where's Valentino?"

"Asleep. I think I killed him with the walk." Eric and Valentino walked the three miles to this new house. "Veal cheeks. I know we're going to do that for sure. They're a very gelatinous cut of meat. Maybe I'll do it with Uncle Ben's Instant Rice—I like that one." Eric is fascinated by this product, which he found in a cupboard; rice that requires only a one-to-one ratio of water to rice and five minutes of cooking. "We're going to make it nice. And a squash soup, but not with a lot of spices and junk in it. You want to taste the squash."

Pork and Liver Pâté en Croûte

SERVES 6

1 tablespoon canola oil

¾ pound boneless pork shoulder
(it should be fatty), cut into
1-inch cubes

Fine sea salt and freshly ground
white pepper

Espelette pepper powder
(you can substitute cayenne)

¼ pound chicken livers

¼ cup minced shallots

1 tablespoon minced garlic

¼ cup Cognac

¼ cup chicken stock

1 tablespoon chopped flat-leaf parsley

One 17¼-ounce package (2 sheets)
frozen puff pastry, thawed

1 large egg

SPECIAL EQUIPMENT

One 3-inch round cookie cutter

One 4-inch round cookie cutter

PREP: 35 minutes, plus 30 minutes chilling time — COOK: 20 minutes

This is a fancy version of the English meat pasty (in French, *pâté en croûte*). Ground pork is powerfully seasoned and then baked in puff pastry—here as individual pâtés. It's very easy to do; the pâté can be mixed in advance and refrigerated. These could also be made smaller and served as canapés.

Heat the canola oil in a large sauté pan over medium heat and add the pork cubes. Season with salt, white pepper, and Espelette powder and sear the meat until nicely golden, about 7 minutes. Transfer to a platter and add the chicken livers to the pan. Season with salt, pepper, and Espelette powder and sear on all sides, 5 to 7 minutes; they should still be slightly rare in the center. Transfer to a platter.

Add the shallots and garlic to the pan and cook until tender and translucent, 2 to 3 minutes. Deglaze the pan with the Cognac, scraping up the browned bits from the bottom of the pan. Bring to a boil. Add the chicken stock and bring to a boil. Set aside.

Place the pork and livers in a food processor and pulse four times to roughly chop. Transfer to a bowl and cover with the shallot–chicken stock mixture. Add the parsley and stir to combine. Adjust the seasoning with salt, pepper, and Espelette powder. Cover with plastic wrap and refrigerate until well chilled.

Meanwhile, dust your countertop lightly with flour and lay a puff pastry sheet on it. Using a rolling pin, roll the puff pastry out to a thickness of ⅛ inch. Cut out six circles using a 3-inch round cookie cutter. Place on a parchment-lined baking sheet and refrigerate. Roll out the remaining puff pastry sheet in the same manner and cut out 6 circles using a 4-inch round cutter. Place on another parchment-lined baking sheet and refrigerate until well chilled, at least 30 minutes.

Preheat the oven to 450°F.

To make the pâtés, top each 3-inch circle with 3 tablespoons of the chilled pork-liver mixture, leaving a ½-inch border all around. Cover with the 4-inch circles and crimp the edges, using the tines of a fork. Whisk the egg with 1 tablespoon water and brush the pastries with the egg wash.

Bake for 20 minutes, or until golden brown. Serve hot from the oven.

Braised Veal Cheeks with Wild Mushrooms and Potato Puree

Serves 6

THE VEAL

3 pounds veal cheeks

Fine sea salt and freshly ground
   white pepper

3 tablespoons duck fat
   (you can substitute canola oil)

½ cup thinly sliced shallots
   (about 3 large shallots)

¼ cup thinly sliced garlic

½ cup halved and thinly sliced carrots

¼ cup thinly sliced celery

1 large tomato, peeled, seeded,
   and chopped

1½ tablespoons all-purpose flour

½ cup Armagnac

8 cups light veal stock
   (you can substitute chicken stock)

4 Lemon Confit quarters (page 21),
   cut into julienne

THE MUSHROOMS

2 tablespoons duck fat
   (you can substitute canola oil)

3 ounces chanterelles

3 ounces oyster mushrooms

3 ounces porcini

2 ounces black trumpet mushrooms

Fine sea salt and freshly ground
   white pepper

1 bacon slice, cut crosswise into julienne

½ teaspoon thyme leaves

THE POTATOES

2 pounds Yukon Gold potatoes

1 pound unsalted butter,
   at room temperature

¾ cup milk, warmed

SPECIAL EQUIPMENT

Food mill

PREP: 35 minutes — **COOK:** 2 hours and 15 minutes

Clean the veal cheeks by removing the silverskin (membranes) and excess fat. Season with salt and pepper.

Melt 2 tablespoons of the duck fat in a large heavy-bottomed pot over high heat. Add the veal cheeks to the pot, in batches, and sear until nicely browned on both sides, 5 to 7 minutes. Transfer to a platter.

Add the remaining 1 tablespoon duck fat to the pot, add the shallots and garlic, and cook until translucent, about 2 minutes. Add the carrots and celery and cook until tender, another 3 minutes. Add the tomato and cook until softened, 1 to 2 minutes. Sprinkle the flour over the vegetables and cook until toasted, about 2 minutes. Deglaze the pot with the Armagnac, scraping up the browned bits in the bottom of the pot.

Return the meat to the pot, along with any juices that have collected on the platter. Cover with the veal stock and bring to a simmer. Simmer for 2 hours.

Meanwhile, for the mushrooms, melt the duck fat in a large sauté pan. Add all the mushrooms, season with salt and pepper, and cook until softened, about 5 minutes. Add the bacon and cook until it renders its fat. Add the thyme and cook for 2 minutes. Using a slotted spoon, transfer the mushrooms and bacon to a platter, leaving the fat behind in the pan. Set aside.

Thirty minutes before the veal is ready, peel the potatoes and place in a pot of cold salted water. Bring to a boil and cook the potatoes until tender, about 20 minutes. Drain and pass the potatoes through a food mill, then through a fine-mesh strainer or drum sieve (tamis).Transfer to a pot and gradually add most of the butter, stirring with a rubber spatula to incorporate. Place the pot over low heat and add the remaining butter. Add the milk and stir to incorporate. The potato puree will be very thin. Keep warm over low heat.

Just before the veal is done, add the mushrooms and cook for 5 minutes to incorporate the flavors.

To serve, stir the lemon confit into the veal. Spoon some of the potato puree into the center of each warmed plate, forming a circle. Spoon the veal over the potatoes. Serve immediately.

Veal cheeks are plump, tough muscles, loaded with collagen, and therefore perfect morsels to braise for hours in a rich stock. They're an unusual item but shouldn't be too difficult or expensive to special-order from your butcher— and are every bit as delicious as osso buco or short ribs, maybe more so given their rarity in the home cook's repertoire. There may be no more comforting fall or winter dish on earth than veal cheeks served with these potatoes.

A word about the potatoes. They're mashed and mixed with butter, but mashed potatoes they aren't. Eric's conception of mashed potatoes was formed under Robuchon, who made his potatoes with an equal ratio of potatoes to butter—a pound of butter whipped into a pound of potatoes. This isn't easy to do. Mashed potatoes can become gluey if overworked. You have to whip the butter vigorously into the potatoes with a wooden spoon or a rubber spatula, creating, in effect, an emulsion of butter in potato. Add the last of the butter over heat— this is critical to maintaining the emulsion. Eric loves the shininess the potatoes take on, the smooth, creamy, starchless feel on the palate. "It's a great way to eat butter," he says.

Buttermilk is Eric's great new find—he loves it. True, it's not exactly uncommon, but he has never worked with it before, and it amazes him. Traditionally, buttermilk was the liquid left from churning cream into butter; today buttermilk is skim milk to which a bacterial strain has been added. A lean, slightly sour product—like sour cream or crème fraîche without the fat—it's perfect for desserts. Panna cotta is generally one of the easiest desserts there is to make, and also one of the most versatile and satisfying.

Buttermilk Panna Cotta with Grapefruit, page 286

Snails in a Spicy Tomato Sauce, page 287

Buttermilk Panna Cotta with Grapefruit picture on page 284

SERVES 6

1¼ cups heavy cream

¾ cup sugar

3 gelatin sheets

1¾ cups buttermilk

Vegetable oil cooking spray

4 large pink grapefruit

1 vanilla bean, split and scraped

2 tablespoons Vermont honey

SPECIAL EQUIPMENT

Six 6-ounce ramekins

PREP: 15 minutes, plus 4 hours chilling time — **COOK:** 35 minutes

Bring the cream and sugar to a boil in a medium saucepan, stirring until the sugar has dissolved. Remove from the heat and let cool slightly. Add the gelatin sheets and stir to melt. Let cool, then add the buttermilk.

Spray six 6-ounce ramekins with vegetable spray. Divide the buttermilk-cream mixture among the ramekins and cover with plastic wrap. Chill until set, at least 4 hours or overnight.

Meanwhile, cut off the top and bottom of each grapefruit. Using the tip of your knife, cut the peel and pith from the grapefruit. Holding the grapefruit over a bowl to catch the juice, cut the segments of pulp out of the membranes, transferring them to another bowl. Squeeze the membranes over the bowl of juice to release all the juice. Refrigerate the grapefruit segments.

Place the grapefruit juice (you should have at least 1½ cups) in a small pot and add the vanilla bean and scraped seeds. Bring to a boil and reduce by half, about 30 minutes. Set aside.

To serve, dip the ramekins in hot water for 3 seconds. Run a thin knife around the edge of each ramekin and invert the panna cotta onto the center of a plate. Arrange the grapefruit segments around the panna cotta in a spiral fashion. Spoon the sauce over the grapefruit and drizzle the honey over the sauce. Serve immediately.

Both meals we prepared here in the new house are superb to serve to groups. For each, much of the work should be done well ahead of time and in single batches—the rustic pâté and the panna cotta made early and refrigerated, the veal cheeks done as much as a day or two in advance. This leaves time for the potato puree, which is as refined as a sauce (but simple mashed potatoes would work well too).

The meal that follows also features what can be considered a pâté, one that is perhaps easier to make, but is on the opposite side of the spectrum from the pâté en croute. How simple is a baked potato? Be sure to cook your potatoes in a hot oven so the skins are very crisp and have their accompaniments ready. (If you are lucky enough to have a fireplace to cook them in, by all means do so.)

Eating in groups is often the best way to eat, but cooking for groups can be hard. These meals are good examples of how that task can be made easier with thoughtful preparation.

SERVES 6

THE SNAILS

5 pounds fresh or frozen snails

½ cup gray sea salt
   (you can substitute rock salt)

½ cup white vinegar

2 slices bacon, cut crosswise into julienne

1 cup thinly sliced shallots

½ cup thinly sliced garlic,
   plus ½ teaspoon minced garlic

Fine sea salt and freshly ground
   white pepper

½ teaspoon Espelette pepper powder
   (you can substitute cayenne)

3 tomatoes, peeled

2 tablespoons tomato paste

¼ teaspoon saffron threads

3 cups chicken stock

5 sage leaves

1 star anise

6 tablespoons unsalted butter

2 tablespoons chopped flat-leaf parsley

THE GARNISH

1 loaf French bread, halved horizontally
   and cut into twelve 3-inch pieces

2 tablespoons olive oil

Espelette pepper powder
   (you can substitute cayenne)

12 rosemary sprigs
   (about 2 inches long)

12 thin slices prosciutto

PREP: 20 minutes — COOK: 1 hour and 45 minutes

The snails are excellent served with cocktails before dinner—an exotic and unusual snack. Snails have little flavor, so this dish is all about the spicy sauce. When the sauce is good, snails are really fun to eat. If you have any aïoli on hand, finish the sauce with it just before serving.

Place the snails in a colander and spinkle the gray salt over all. After a minute or two, pour the vinegar over the snails to rinse off the salt. Set aside.

Heat a large heavy-bottomed pot over medium heat. Add the bacon and cook until the fat is rendered and the bacon is almost crisp. Remove the bacon with a slotted spoon and set aside. Add the shallots and sliced garlic to the pot and cook until softened and translucent, about 3 minutes. Season with salt, pepper, and Espelette powder.

Halve the tomatoes and scoop the seeds into a strainer set over a bowl to catch the juices; discard the seeds. Roughly chop the tomatoes.

Add the tomatoes to the pot along with their juices. Return the bacon to the pot and add the tomato paste and saffron. Cook until the tomato paste is slightly darkened, about 5 minutes. Cover with the chicken stock, stir, and bring to a simmer. Add the sage, star anise, and the snails and simmer for 1½ hours.

Meanwhile, preheat the oven to 375°F.

Just before serving, place the bread on a baking sheet. Drizzle the olive oil over the bread and sprinkle with Espelette powder. Top each piece with a rosemary sprig and toast in the oven.

Whisk the butter into the snails. Add the minced garlic and the parsley and stir to incorporate.

To serve, divide the snails among six warmed plates. Remove the rosemary from the toasts and top each with a slice of prosciutto. Serve immediately, passing the toasts at the table.

Foie Gras–Quince Terrine with Raisin English Muffins pictured on page 290

Serves 6

1 Grade A 1½- to-2-pound duck foie gras

Fine sea salt and freshly ground
white pepper

½ cup thinly sliced shallots

3 quinces, peeled, halved, cored,
and cut into ¼-inch slices

Coarse sea salt and coarsely ground
black pepper

3 raisin-studded Thomas's English muffins

Special equipment

7-inch by 2½-inch by 3-inch high
terrine mold

Prep: 25 minutes, plus at least 24 hours refrigeration time — cook: 25 minutes

This terrine of alternating layers of sliced foie gras and quince is an all-but-foolproof technique because the foie gras is cooked—sautéed with sliced shallots—before it's sliced. The terrine is weighted down and the fat sets, holding it all together. The next day, it's ready to slice and serve. I like foie gras cooked through, just past medium-rare; that is how they like it in southwestern France, where it's produced—they don't eat it rare in cold preparations.

Heat a large sauté pan over high heat. Season the foie gras generously with salt and pepper and add to the pan. Sear until golden on all sides, about 5 minutes per side. Lower the heat to medium. Add the shallots and cook until softened and translucent, about 7 minutes. Transfer the foie gras to a platter.

Add the quince slices to the pan and season with salt and pepper. Cook until golden and nicely softened, 5 to 7 minutes. Transfer the quince slices to a platter. Strain the foie gras fat, discarding the solids, and reserve the fat for another use.

Slice the foie gras lengthwise into ½-inch slices and remove all visible veins (slicing the foie gras this way makes it easier to devein).

Layer the foie gras and quince in the terrine mold, starting and ending with foie gras (you should have 4 layers of foie gras and 3 of quince); season each layer with the coarse salt and pepper. Cover with plastic wrap and top with a plastic-wrapped piece of cardboard cut to fit inside the mold. Place a heavy weight (I use two 28-ounce cans) on top of the cardboard and refrigerate for at least 24 hours to marry the flavors and compact the terrine. *(The terrine can be refrigerated for up to a week.)*

To serve, remove the weight, cardboard, and plastic wrap. Slide a thin knife around the sides of the terrine and invert onto a platter. Using a long thin-bladed knife, slice the terrine into ½-inch slices; for clean slices, dip your knife in a pitcher of hot water after each slice.

Place 2 slices of terrine in the center of each plate and sprinkle with a pinch of coarse sea salt and coarsely ground black pepper. Toast the English muffins and serve on the side.

Ash-Baked Potatoes with Smoked Salmon and Caviar pictured on page 290

Serves 6

6 russet (baking) potatoes

2 tablespoons unsalted butter

2 tablespoons sliced scallions

2 tablespoons thinly sliced chives

½ cup sour cream

5 ounces osetra caviar

4 ounces salmon eggs (roe)

4 ounces smoked salmon,
   cut into ½-inch by 3-inch strips

SPECIAL EQUIPMENT

½ cup ashes from your fireplace (optional)

PREP: 10 minutes — COOK: 1 hour and 5 minutes

I love taking something basic and rough and making it elegant. A baked potato cooked in the ashes of a fire couldn't be more "peasant," or smoked salmon and caviar more *"aristocrate."* Combine the two, with some sour cream and butter, and you'll have the best baked potato of your life.

Start a large fire in your fireplace. You will need a good amount of glowing embers for baking the potatoes. *(Alternatively, preheat the oven to 400°F.)*

If you want a smokier flavor, wet each potato slightly and roll in ashes. Wrap each potato in aluminum foil, place in your fireplace, and bake until tender, about 40 minutes. *(Alternatively, bake in the oven until tender, about 1 hour.)* Remove and let cool slightly.

Preheat the oven to 350°F *(or reduce the oven temperature to 350°F).*

When they are cool enough to handle, cut off the top third of each potato and scoop out the inside of each potato into a bowl, leaving a ¼-inch shell. *(The potatoes can be prepared ahead to this point.)*

To serve, combine the potato pulp and butter in an ovenproof bowl and gently reheat in the oven, about 5 minutes. Meanwhile, place the potato skins on a baking sheet and reheat in the oven.

When the pulp is warmed through, add the scallion, chives, and sour cream and mix to combine. Add 2 ounces of the osetra caviar, the salmon eggs, and smoked salmon and gently stir to combine. Be very careful not to break the caviar or salmon eggs. Divide the mixture evenly among the warmed potato skins and top each with a dollop of the remaining caviar. Serve immediately.

FOIE GRAS

Foie gras, the enlarged liver of specially raised ducks and geese, is one of the most rarefied of all foods. Duck foie gras is now produced in the United States by two companies; the product is excellent but very expensive—a Grade A foie can cost more than a hundred dollars when the required overnight shipping is included. The cost has likely prevented more home cooks from using it, and thus enhanced its mystery and made it an intimidating item to work with. But the fact is, it's one of the easiest things to cook because it's composed almost entirely of fat, and, because there are only two U.S. producers, every cook and chef gets relatively the same quality.

Many people still think of foie gras only as pâté, but with more restaurants serving it hot, it is increasingly popular that way. It sautés nicely, developing a crisp sweet crust while the rich interior is molten on the palate. It can be poached, as in Eric's pot-au-feu (page 278), it can be roasted, or it can be molded and baked in a water bath for a terrine or pâté.

WHAT "RUSTIC COOKING" MEANS

We use the term *rustic* a lot without really pinpointing the qualities that define the term. We think of one-pot meals—stews and such. We think of peasant-style cooking—inexpensive ingredients cooked for a long time. But "rustic" is really a more sophisticated idea than that.

Rustic cooking means cooking ingredients of the season and of the location—you don't import raspberries from Chile in October. The ingredients are inexpensive and abundant—cauliflower, cabbage, potatoes; meats such as shank, innards including stomach and liver and kidney. Most important, they are handled with a minimum of preparation, with very little fuss or manipulation. "Rustic" or "peasant" doesn't mean less technique or precision. Rustic food and highly refined food both require technique and care. It's not casual versus fancy. Each is a philosophy. In Napa we made a squab dish with a fennel puree—the components were very worked over and the presentation was very pretty. Here (see page 274) we do a squab with cabbage cooked in duck fat in the fire and served simply. One is the debutante, the other the country girl. Both require equal thought on the part of the cook.

Opposite: Foie Gras–Quince Terrine with Raisin English Muffins, page 288. Above: Ash-Baked Potatoes with Smoked Salmon and Caviar, page 289.

Walnut and Armagnac Frozen Parfait with Wine–Poached Prunes

SERVES 6

THE PRUNES

3 cups dry red wine

1 tablespoon sugar

1 whole nutmeg, cracked

1 teaspoon ground cinnamon

1 star anise

3 cloves

½ pound pitted prunes

THE PARFAIT

1 cup sugar

¾ cup walnuts, toasted

2 large eggs, separated

3 large egg yolks

1½ cups heavy cream

¼ cup Armagnac

SPECIAL EQUIPMENT

Six 4-ounce ramekins

PREP: 25 minutes, plus 3 hours freezing time

For the prunes, place the red wine, sugar, nutmeg, cinnamon, star anise, and cloves in a pot and bring to a boil. Cook, stirring, until the sugar has dissolved. Remove the wine from the heat and add the prunes. Cover and refrigerate overnight.

For the parfait, melt ½ cup of the sugar in a nonstick sauté pan over high heat and cook until the sugar is light gold in color. Add the walnuts and stir to coat. Pour onto a sheet of parchment paper or a baking sheet that has been sprayed with vegetable spray. Let cool. Roughly chop the caramelized nuts. Set the remaining nuts aside, reserving 3 tablespoons for the garnish.

In a large bowl, whip the egg yolks with ¼ cup of the sugar until thick and pale. In a separate bowl, whip the egg whites until soft peaks are formed. Slowly add the remaining ¼ cup sugar and continue to whip the whites until stiff peaks are formed. Be careful not to overwhip, or they will become dry. Fold the whites into the yolks.

Whip the heavy cream in a large bowl until stiff peaks are formed, whisking in the Armagnac at the last minute. Fold the whipped cream into the whipped egg mixture. Fold in the reserved caramelized walnuts. Fill the ramekins with the mixture to the top. Cover with plastic wrap and freeze for at least 3 hours.

To serve, dip each mold in warm water for about 30 seconds, and invert the parfait onto a dessert plate. Spoon the sauce and prunes around and garnish with the remaining walnuts. Serve immediately.

venison

Venison is a great fall meat, rich and flavorful but not overly gamy. Eric does two preparations. The first is a pseudo-carpaccio—the loin is seasoned and seared quickly, left to cool, and then sliced very thin and served with a salad of apple, beet, endive, watercress, and walnut. The salad and the almost buttery tenderloin, finished with rock salt and lemon juice, make a great dish.

For the second preparation, a venison loin, Eric had been thinking a sauce royale, which is in essence a stock mounted with foie gras. The initial task was to make the venison stock— marinating the bones in red wine and mirepoix first (much like the oxtails; see page 262). He eventually used the stock to make a classic red wine sauce stock spiked with pepper, and served the loin with cranberries, lightly cooked with sugar so that they served as a kind of chutney. The root vegetable puree is a light but rich balance for the dish.

Juniper-Crusted Venison "Carpaccio" pictured on page 298

SERVES 6

THE VENISON

One 1¼-pound venison loin

**1 tablespoon coarsely ground
   black pepper**

**1 tablespoon coarsely ground
   juniper berries**

1 teaspoon fine sea salt

1 tablespoon canola oil

THE SALAD

1 large beet

**Fine sea salt and freshly ground
   white pepper**

½ cup Cortland apple julienne

**1 large endive head, cut into 3-inch by
   ¼-inch bâtonnets**

½ cup small watercress sprigs

Pinch of ground juniper berries

1 tablespoon fresh lemon juice

2 tablespoons canola oil

1 tablespoon walnut oil

THE GARNISH

2 tablespoons walnut oil

2 tablespoons canola oil

1 teaspoon rock salt

2 tablespoons thinly sliced chives

1 lemon, halved

SPECIAL EQUIPMENT

Kitchen string

PREP: 30 minutes, plus 2 hours chilling time — **COOK:** 30 minutes

Preheat the oven to 350°F.

For the venison, tie the loin with kitchen string: once lengthwise, and every inch crosswise. Season the loin with the black pepper, juniper, and salt.

Heat the canola oil in a large sauté pan over high heat. When the oil is hot, add the venison and sear until golden on all sides, 1 to 2 minutes per side; it should still be mostly raw inside. Refrigerate until well chilled, at least 2 hours.

Meanwhile, season the beet with salt and pepper and wrap in aluminum foil. Roast until tender, about 30 minutes. Remove, and when cool enough to handle, peel and cut into 3-inch by ¼-inch bâtonnets. Cover and refrigerate.

Remove the venison from the refrigerator and slice as thin as possible. Arrange the carpaccio rounds on six chilled plates in a circular fashion, covering the entire plate but not overlapping the slices. *(The venison can be prepared several hours in advance. Cover each plate with plastic film placed directly against the venison. Reserve in the refrigerator.)*

To serve, place the beets, apple, endive, and watercress in a large bowl. Sprinkle the juniper over the salad and season with salt and pepper. Drizzle the lemon juice, canola oil, and walnut oil over the salad and toss to combine.

Whisk together the 2 tablespoons each walnut oil and canola oil. Brush the venison generously with the oil. Mound the salad in the center of each plate. Sprinkle the rock salt and chives over the plates. Squeeze the lemon juice over the venison and serve immediately.

Venison Loin with Parsnip-Celeriac Puree and Cranberries pictured on page 298

SERVES 6

THE SAUCE

4 pounds venison bones (see Note)

2 bottles dry red wine

½ cup Armagnac

¼ cup olive oil

2 celery ribs, roughly chopped

1 carrot, peeled and roughly chopped

1 onion, roughly chopped

10 garlic cloves, roughly chopped

1½ teaspoons juniper berries

1 teaspoon black peppercorns

2 tablespoons canola oil

6 cups chicken stock

1 tablespoon all-purpose flour

**4 ounces (8 tablespoons) truffle butter
(you can substitute unsalted
plain butter)**

¼ teaspoon ground juniper berries

THE PUREE

1½ pounds parsnips

2 tablespoons salt

1 celeriac knob

**6 tablespoons unsalted butter,
at room temperature**

¼ cup heavy cream

PREP: 25 minutes, plus 24 hours marinating time — **COOK:** 2 hours and 15 minutes

For the sauce, chop the bones and place in a large bowl. Cover with the wine, Armagnac, and olive oil. Add the celery, carrot, onion, garlic, juniper berries, and peppercorns and marinate in the refrigerator for 24 hours.

Drain the bones and vegetables in a colander, reserving the liquid. Strain the liquid through a fine-mesh sieve, pour it into a pot, and bring to a boil. Lower the heat and simmer to reduce for 30 minutes, skimming any foam that rises to the top. Set aside.

Preheat the oven to 400°F.

Separate the bones and vegetables. Heat a roasting pan over medium heat and add the canola oil. Add the bones to the roasting pan and sear until nicely browned, about 5 minutes. Add the vegetables, place in the preheated oven, and roast until the bones and vegetables are nicely caramelized, about 30 minutes.

Meanwhile, bring the chicken stock to a boil in a large saucepan and boil gently until reduced to 3 cups. Set aside.

Place the roasting pan over medium heat on the stovetop. Sprinkle the flour over the bones and cook until the flour is toasted, about 3 minutes. Cover with the reserved marinating liquid and the reduced chicken stock. Simmer for 1 hour, skimming as necessary. Strain through a fine-mesh sieve into a saucepan and set aside.

For the puree, peel the parsnips and roughly chop them. Place in a pot, cover with water, add 1 tablespoon salt, and bring to a boil. Cook until the parsnips are soft, about 25 minutes. Drain, reserving the cooking liquid. Puree the parsnips in a blender, adding some of the reserved cooking liquid as necessary.

Bring 2 quarts water to a boil in a medium pot and add 1 tablespoon salt. Peel and roughly chop the celeriac knob. Add the celeriac to the boiling water and cook until soft, about 25 minutes. Drain, reserving the cooking liquid. Puree the celeriac in a blender, adding some of the cooking liquid as necessary. Combine the celeriac puree and parsnip puree (you should have a total of 2 cups).

THE CRANBERRIES

1 cup cranberries

¼ cup water

2 tablespoons maple syrup

1 tablespoon sugar

Fine sea salt and freshly ground
white pepper

THE VENISON

Two 1¼-pound venison loins

1½ tablespoons fine sea salt

2 tablespoons coarsely ground
black pepper

3 tablespoons ground juniper berries

2 tablespoons canola oil

For the cranberries, place in a saucepan, add the water, maple syrup, and sugar and bring to a simmer over medium heat. Cook until the cranberries begin to pop and split, about 7 minutes. Season with salt and pepper and set aside.

Season the venison with the salt, pepper, and juniper berries. Heat two large sauté pans over medium-high heat and add 1 tablespoon of the canola oil to each. Add a venison loin to each pan and sear until nicely browned on all sides but still quite rare in the center, 5 to 7 minutes. Set aside to rest for 5 minutes.

Meanwhile, bring the sauce to a boil and gradually whisk in the truffle butter. Add the ground juniper. Gently reheat the parsnip-celeriac puree, and stir in the butter and heavy cream. Gently reheat the cranberries.

To serve, slice the venison into ½-inch-thick slices. Spoon the celeriac puree down the center of six warmed plates. Lay 4 slices each of venison over the puree. Spoon the cranberries over the venison. Spoon the sauce around. Serve immediately.

NOTE: Venison is available from specialty butchers and through mail order; ask the source you use for the venison bones as well.

Cabbage and Apple Salad

SERVES 6

2 cups shredded purple cabbage

2 cups shredded green cabbage

2 Cortland apples, peeled, cored,
and cut into julienne

¼ cup canola oil

¼ cup cider vinegar

2 teaspoons ground juniper berries

Fine sea salt and freshly ground
white pepper

PREP: 15 minutes, plus 1 hour chilling time

In a large bowl, combine the shredded cabbage and apples. Toss with the oil and vinegar. Sprinkle the juniper over and toss to combine. Season to taste with salt and pepper. Cover and refrigerate until chilled, or for up to 3 hours.

Left and center: Preparing Juniper-Crusted Venison "Carpaccio," page 295. Right: Venison Loin with Parsnip-Celeriac Puree and Cranberries, page 296.

soup-sauce meditation

Sauce has more prestige than soup in a professional kitchen, but the differences are in fact subtle. It's about body. Body is what gives soup its flavor. You make a carrot soup, the carrot becomes the body and flavor; potato-leek soup, flavor and body come from the vegetables themselves. With a carrot sauce, you don't use the carrot for the consistency, you're catching its essence. Same with a truffle sauce. The essence is much more volatile, and a sauce is lighter than a soup, so it requires tuning like a fine instrument or an engine.

Soup is thicker, you can touch it, the flavors are durable. To make a sauce, you're like a painter trying to catch the colors on your canvas. Painter, alchemist, mechanic—elements of each go into a sauce.

There are two ways to do a soup. One is to throw a vegetable in a pot, boil, salt and pepper, puree, and serve. The other is to stay close to the pot, to take care of it, to taste and connect with what's cooking. Like a sauce, soup changes continuously during its cooking, so you must always be tasting and reacting to the taste.

You talk to two cooks in a kitchen. One says "saucier," and immediately he has an aura. The other simply says, "I make the soup." Soups are perceived as lacking technique, lacking polish, but it's possible to make great soup by treating it as if it were a sauce, by giving it great care.

Roasted Garlic Soup *pictured on page 302*

pictured on page 302

SERVES 6

8 garlic heads

3 tablespoons extra virgin olive oil

3 cups chicken stock

1½ cups heavy cream

Fine sea salt and freshly ground

   black pepper

THE GARNISH

6 slices French bread

2 tablespoons extra virgin olive oil

3 thyme sprigs, halved

1 garlic clove, peeled

1 small tomato, halved and seeded

2 ounces black truffles, chopped (optional)

1 tablespoon thinly sliced scallion

Pinch of Espelette pepper powder

   (you can substitute cayenne)

1 ounce white truffle (optional)

PREP: 20 minutes — **COOK:** 40 minutes

This may be the best garlic soup you've ever had, and it's just roasted garlic, chicken stock, and cream. The critical points are to have the right amount of garlic and to roast it perfectly so that it's thoroughly cooked but not overcooked.

Start a large fire in your fireplace. You will need a good amount of glowing embers for the cooking.

Place the heads of garlic on a large piece of aluminum foil. Drizzle the olive oil over them, and tightly close the foil to seal. Roast the garlic in the hot embers of your fire until the cloves are softened, about 30 minutes. *(The garlic can be cooked in a 375°F oven; the cooking time may be slightly less.)* Remove from the heat and let cool slightly.

When the garlic is cool enough to handle, peel the cloves and place in the jar of a blender. Add 1 cup of the chicken stock and blend until satiny smooth. Pass through a fine-mesh sieve into a medium heavy-bottomed saucepan. Add the remaining 2 cups chicken stock and the heavy cream and bring to a boil, then lower the heat to a simmer and cook for 5 minutes. Season with salt and pepper to taste.

For the garnish, place the bread in a grilling basket and drizzle with the olive oil. Place ½ sprig of thyme on each slice. Close the basket and grill over the open fire until nicely toasted. *(Alternatively, you can toast the bread in a hot oven on a baking sheet.)* Remove from the heat and rub the garlic clove, then the tomato over each toast.

To serve, place a garlic toast in the center of each warmed soup bowl. Sprinkle the black truffles, if using, around the croutons. Ladle the soup into each bowl. Sprinkle the scallions over each bowl. Sprinkle a dash of the pepper powder over each and shave the white truffle, if using, around the toasts. Serve immediately.

We learned an amazing lesson from two soups, both garlic infused but utterly different in character, a lesson that might apply to many soups. The first was a seemingly simple cream of garlic—eight heads roasted in the fire until they were cooked and sweet, then pureed with chicken stock and finished with cream, salt, and pepper. The garlic was powerful without being overpowering, sweet and smooth.

But the revelation came after a few days of stuffing ourselves like foie gras ducks. Eric recalled his grandfather, who, three days each week, drank a broth made simply from garlic, sage, water, and olive oil, to purify his blood. Eric used this idea to purify us, infusing a developing chicken broth with sage, garlic, and lemon confit. The confit was immediately good. But as the soup continued to gently cook, Eric, always tasting, shook his head and furrowed his brow. The lemon was disappearing, simply vanishing. And the garlic—where was it? He couldn't even taste it. He'd already strained the broth, and bowls were being warmed to serve—but what was happening? This was a different soup. No lemon, no garlic.

Quickly, Eric cut a dozen garlic cloves in half, not bothering to remove the skin or the germ, wrapped them in cheesecloth, and steeped them in the broth, raising the heat to speed the process. Meanwhile, he minced more lemon confit. The confit had proved to be so volatile in the fatless broth that he put some in each bowl along with some sliced scallion. He then added alphabet pasta to the soup (he'd loved this as a kid), and finished it with Espelette pepper.

Eric had elevated the soup with the extra garlic, and the lemon confit was almost as powerful as lime, but as we ate, the lemon became less and less distinct. The soup was changing as we ate—like a sauce.

Roasted Garlic Soup, page 301

Garlic-Sage Broth with Alphabet Pasta

SERVES 6

7 cups chicken stock

Fine sea salt and freshly ground
white pepper

8 garlic cloves, halved

15 sage leaves

1 cup alphabet pasta

1 tablespoon diced Lemon Confit
(page 21)

1 tablespoon sliced scallions

Pinch of Espelette pepper powder
(you can substitute cayenne)

PREP: 10 minutes — **COOK:** 20 minutes

One must think like a saucier with this dish. It's low-fat, and the flavors are volatile, so it becomes a drama at the end, tasting and adjusting all the way up until it's in the bowl, always reacting to it. For this recipe, you have to have instinct, have to have taste, have to have feeling.

Bring the stock to a boil in a large saucepan, then lower the heat to a simmer and season to taste with salt and pepper. Add the garlic cloves and sage and let infuse for 4 to 5 minutes.

Strain the broth and return to the pan. Bring to a boil, add the pasta, and cook until al dente, about 5 minutes.

Meanwhile, sprinkle ½ teaspoon lemon confit and ½ teaspoon scallions into each of six warmed soup bowls.

To serve, ladle the soup into the bowls. Sprinkle a pinch of the pepper powder over each bowl and serve immediately.

Pumpkin, Acorn, and Butternut Squash Soup with Nutmeg and Walnut Oil

SERVES 6

6 tablespoons unsalted butter

1 cup sliced onions

2 cups peeled and diced sugar pumpkin
(about ½ a small pumpkin)

2 cups peeled and diced acorn squash
(about 1 medium squash)

2 cups peeled and diced butternut squash
(about 1 small squash)

Fine sea salt and freshly ground
white pepper

5 cups chicken stock

1 cup heavy cream

3 thyme sprigs

3 ounces sharp cheddar cheese,
preferably Vermont cheddar

1 tablespoon walnut oil

1 whole nutmeg, for grating

SPECIAL EQUIPMENT

Cheesecloth

Kitchen string

PREP: 20 minutes — COOK: 50 minutes

Eric almost didn't make this soup because he's so put off by overspiced squash soups. While he does add some gratings of fresh nutmeg at the end, the fresh thyme and the walnut oil are the primary seasonings, and the soup retains the flavors of the squash.

Melt 2 tablespoons of the butter in a large pot over medium heat. Add the onions and cook until translucent, about 3 minutes. Add the pumpkin and acorn squash dice and sauté until softened, about 10 minutes. Season with salt and pepper to taste.

Cover with the chicken stock and bring to a simmer. Cook until the squash is tender, about 30 minutes.

Puree the soup in batches in a blender until satiny-smooth. Pass through a fine-mesh sieve to remove any remaining lumps, and return the soup to the pot. Add the cream and the remaining 4 tablespoons butter. Bring to a simmer.

Wrap the thyme sprigs in a square of cheesecloth and tie with kitchen string. Add to the simmering soup and let infuse for 10 minutes. Remove the thyme bundle and adjust the seasoning.

To serve, divide the soup among six warmed soup bowls. Shave the cheese over each bowl and drizzle the walnut oil over the cheese. Grate nutmeg over each bowl to taste and serve immediately.

Cauliflower Soup with Smoked Scallops

Serves 6

1 large cauliflower

2½ cups chicken stock

2½ cups water

Fine sea salt and freshly ground
    white pepper

8 tablespoons (1 stick) unsalted butter,
    cut into ½-inch chunks

2 cups heavy cream

½ pound smoked scallops (see Sources,
    page 320), cut into ½-inch dice

1 teaspoon finely chopped Lemon Confit
    (page 21)

12 small dill sprigs (tips only)

PREP: 15 minutes — **COOK:** 35 minutes

This is a creamy comforting soup, and the smoked fish adds an intriguing complexity without making the preparation more difficult. Eric liked it so much he decided to put it on the Le Bernardin menu (the only difference is that his brigade will smoke their own scallops, first seasoning them and tossing them with ginger oil, then smoking them over oak chips for one minute).

Prepare the cauliflower by removing the green leaves and the inner core. Roughly chop the florets and place in a heavy-bottomed pot. Cover with the chicken stock and water and bring to a simmer. Season to taste with salt and pepper. Cook until tender, about 30 minutes.

Preheat the oven to 350°F.

Puree the soup in a blender in batches, blending it to a satiny-smooth consistency. Pour the soup into a clean pot and bring to a simmer. Whisk in the butter and heavy cream. Adjust the seasoning to taste.

Meanwhile, divide the scallops among six soup bowls. Place on a baking sheet in the oven until the scallops are warmed through, 1 to 2 minutes.

To serve, add the lemon confit and dill to the soup and stir to incorporate. Ladle the soup into the bowls and serve immediately.

Lobster and Capon Soup with Potatoes and Leeks

SERVES 6

One 2-pound lobster

Fine sea salt and freshly ground
 white pepper

Pinch of Espelette pepper powder
 (you can substitute cayenne)

3 tablespoons unsalted butter

2 cups sliced leeks (halved and cut into
 ¼-inch by ½-inch slices)

⅓ cup diced fennel

1 tablespoon minced ginger

½ teaspoon minced Scotch bonnet pepper

6 cups chicken stock

1 cup diced (½-inch dice) potatoes

¼ teaspoon ground star anise

1 teaspoon minced Lemon Confit
 (page 21)

1 cup shredded cooked capon leg meat
 (you can substitute chicken)

1 teaspoon thinly sliced tarragon

1 lime, halved

PREP: 45 minutes — COOK: 30 minutes

Eric created this all-purpose soup to use leftovers, another great reason for soups—they give leftovers new life. Lobster makes a worthy addition, but not a critical one. The capon can instead be leftover chicken. The leeks import great flavor to the soup, but the most important factor here is a very good homemade or store-bought chicken stock.

Preheat the oven to 375°F.

Kill the lobster by plunging a knife through its head just above the eyes, making sure the knife goes all the way through the head, and then pulling your knife in a downward motion through the eyes. Twist off the claws where they join the body and reserve. Twist the tail away from the head. (Clean and reserve the head for another use, such as lobster stock, if desired. Freeze for up to a month.) Place the tail on your cutting board, press to flatten, and split the tail from end to end, using a sharp knife. Remove the vein that runs down the center of the tail.

To cook the lobster tail, place it on a large piece of aluminum foil and season with salt, pepper, and the Espelette powder. Cut 1 tablespoon of the butter into small chunks and scatter over the tail. Wrap the lobster in the foil and cook in the oven just until the meat is slightly opaque, 5 to 7 minutes. Be careful not to overcook the lobster meat, or it will become chewy. When cool enough to handle, separate the tail meat from the shell and cut into ½-inch slices. Place the meat on a plate, cover, and refrigerate.

Meanwhile, for the claws, bring a large pot of salted water to a boil. Add the claws to the pot and cook for 5 minutes. Remove the claws and set aside until cool enough to handle.

Separate the knuckles from the claws. Using a pair of kitchen scissors, cut through the knuckles and remove the meat. Crack the claws with the heel (back end of the blade) of your chef's knife and twist to open. Extract the claw meat and cut it into ½-inch slices. Add the knuckle and claw meat to the platter with the tail meat.

For the soup, melt the remaining 2 tablespoons butter in a large pot over medium heat. Add the leeks, fennel, ginger, and Scotch bonnet pepper and cook until translucent, about 3 minutes. Season with salt and pepper. Cover with the chicken stock and bring to a simmer. Add the potatoes and cook until tender, about 10 minutes. Adjust the seasoning.

Add the star anise and lemon confit to the soup and simmer for 5 minutes. Add the lobster and capon meat and simmer until warmed.

To serve, ladle the soup into six warmed bowls and garnish with the tarragon. Squeeze the lime juice over each. Serve immediately.

a perfect meal

There's no such thing as the perfect last meal, because we don't want perfect meals to end. The perfect meal is one that keeps going, an endless movable feast. Eric had brought us on a journey to explore the art and craft of what he did away from the pressures of the restaurant. The journey had been rich with changes and discoveries and certainly the pleasure that is bound up in the work of cooking and eating. The end of such a journey, the last meal, must be the best, the essence of cooking and eating.

In Puerto Rico, I'd asked Eric about lobster stock, and he said that the process of making it was very special. It's one of the few things a home cook makes that requires him or her to kill a living creature. "Lobster stock," he said, "is a meditation." In Vermont, Eric, always a teacher, decided to take it one step further. "We'll clarify it with the coral, to make a consommé," he said. Lobster stock, elevated to its finest, purest form.

Consommé makes an extraordinary beginning to a main course of roasted capon and cauliflower gratin. As it's a hallmark of craftsmanship in cooking, it lends the more elemental fare that follows it a perfect counterpoint.

Capon is a castrated rooster, a big bird. Eric diced some bread, chopped up the liver, stirred it all together with some egg and salt and pepper, and stuffed the bird. Then he roasted it. He scarcely thought about what he was doing, but when he pulled the bird from the oven, he deemed it well cooked, and as he let it rest on the counter in its pan, he admired its beauty. It was *perfect*.

We ate simply: chicken, a spoonful of stuffing, and a perfect green salad Andrea had made, one whose vinaigrette heightened the flavor of the jus in an almost melodic way. And I began to understand what *perfect* can do to a group that eats together.

Later, long after the meal was over, Eric said that this meal was, for him, the highlight of Vermont, perhaps of all the meals we'd shared. "The capon," he said, "is the sum of all my knowledge."

What an extraordinary comment.

Lobster Stock and Consommé, page 312

Roasted Capon with Bread Stuffing, page 314

LOBSTER STOCK

It's not easy—nor should it be—to kill a lobster, and the most humane way to do it may also be the most viscerally difficult—again, as it should be. If it were easy, you might take it lightly.

There are many ways to kill a lobster. I guess the most common way is to throw it into a pot of boiling water. But the quickest, and therefore most humane way, is to push a big strong knife through the head. This isn't like peeling an onion. It requires fortitude, certainty, and acceptance. You can turn away from a lobster in a pot or cover it with a lid. With a knife, you must face it. By resting the point of a chef's knife at the back joint of the head, pushing down so that the point is in the cutting board, and pressing the knife quickly down 90 degrees through the head, you can quickly kill the lobster though it will continue to jerk. This is spooky; it reminds you of what you've done. But you can now, with a clear conscience, break it down. Twist off the claws. Twist the tail from the body. (We used three for this preparation, and after I'd done all this, one bodyless tail clenched around my index finger and hung on.)

If you are making lobster stock and then consommé, reserve the tails, the most prized part of the lobster, to be used not more than a day after. If you have female lobsters, remove all the coral (the gelatinous green goo) place it in a clean bowl, and refrigerate immediately. Cook the claws in boiling water for five or six minutes. Shell and reserve the claw meat. Split or cut the knuckles, remove the meat, and reserve.

Pull the heads from the bodies and scrape the gelatinous film from the inside of the shells. Cut the shells into pieces. Scrape or cut the feather-like lungs from the bodies, remove all the other organs, and discard. Chop all the shells into small pieces.

Heat a good heavy pot that will encourage caramelization. Eric used an enameled cast-iron pot—a better pot I have not encountered. Add a film of oil and when it is hot, add the lobster shells. This first caramelization is critical. The shells must sear. You should hear a good hiss and crackle, and the shells should stick lightly to the bottom of the pan. If they steam, you are on the wrong path. The idea is to toast the shells—just so, and no more.

Once they are toasted, add the aromatic vegetables: sliced shallots, fennel stalk, celery, and saffron. (If you add the vegetables too early, the pot will become too humid and the shells will steam.) Sweat the vegetables well.

Eric tends his pot closely, doing only this. He is watching and gently scraping the flavorful golden *fond*, or crust, off the bottom of the pot as it develops. He adds the tomato paste last, because it will immediately stick to the pan. He cooks this too, then stirs. Maybe a minute. Depending.

Next he deglazes the pan with Cognac, pushing the flat wooden spoon over the bottom to scrape up the *fond*. "This will give it amazing gold color," Eric explains. "It's not really for flavor." Then he says, "Now, if we only had some lobster stock, that would be really helpful." He adds water instead, just enough to cover. As the water comes to a simmer, he seasons it lightly. A little pepper. A little salt (not much, because lobster is salty to begin with). One star anise and a stem of tarragon. Eric stirs gently, tastes, then tastes again. After a few minutes he removes the star anise—the anise flavor is becoming too strong.

As the stock cooks, he continually skims the foam and fat. It takes time as he maneuvers the skimming spoon around the floating islands of shells, picking up patches of impurities here and there. When you sense that it is done (the taste and color of a spoonful will tell you), raise the heat to ensure it's at a vigorous simmer and then immediately remove it from the heat to let it rest.

"That's how we did it at Robuchon," Eric explains.

He was referring more to the attention he gave it, the concentration involved, than to any particular technique. "You don't just put star anise in and forget about it. You're like a mechanic, always tuning the engine."

After it has rested for twenty minutes or so, he strains it through a perforated metal strainer or a colander and crushes the shells to extract as much liquid as possible. Then he strains it the again through cheesecloth.

The lobster stock is superlative.

LOBSTER CONSOMMÉ

Eric doesn't make meat consommés, because clarifying them removes too much flavor, and this doesn't seem logical to him from the standpoint of food costs and common sense. He does make lobster consommé, on the other hand, because the clarifying agent, the lobster's coral, is itself a flavoring agent and comes with the female.

Eric reheats the lobster stock, skimming, skimming, skimming away foam and fat. He passes the chilled coral through a fine-mesh sieve. The consistency is like that of egg white, the clarifying agent for consommés. He adds a big handful of crushed ice to the coral to make it very cold and pours it into the stock. (Unless it is very cold, the coral will coagulate too quickly and not form the raft properly.)

He drags a wooden spoon along the bottom of the pan to prevent the coral from sticking, then continues to move the spoon slowly forward and back through the stock. Eric is nervous; he doesn't know if the gods are with him. Slowly the stock comes up to heat and the coral, changing from forest green to deep pink, rises to the surface. When the consommé has come to a simmer, Eric lowers the heat to prevent it from boiling, as boiling will break up the raft and cause the consommé to be cloudy. He lifts a spoonful and examines it for clarity. He nods and grins. It is perfectly clear. Magic: the essence of lobster.

Lobster Stock and Consommé pictured on page 308

Three 2-pound female lobsters

1 tablespoon canola oil

¼ cup sliced shallots

¼ cup sliced fennel

3 tablespoons sliced celery

15 saffron threads

1 tablespoon tomato paste

½ cup Cognac

7 cups water

Fine sea salt and freshly ground
white pepper

1 tarragon sprig

1 star anise

½ cup crushed ice

Espelette pepper powder
(you can substitute cayenne)

SPECIAL EQUIPMENT

Cheesecloth

PREP: 25 minutes — **COOK:** 1 hour

Kill each lobster by plunging a knife through its head just above the eyes, making sure the knife goes all the way through the head, then pulling your knife in a downward motion between the eyes. Twist off the claws where they join the body and refrigerate. Twist the tails away from the heads. Refrigerate and reserve the tails for another use (such as Lobster and Capon Soup with Potatoes and Leeks, page 307).

To clean the shells, remove the bright green coral from each lobster. Transfer to a bowl and refrigerate until ready to use. Separate the bodies from the heads. Scrape out and discard the intestines and the lungs from the body. Scrape the head clean. Cut the shells and legs into 1-inch pieces. Set aside.

Bring a large pot of salted water to a boil. Add the lobster claws and cook for 5 minutes. Drain.

When they are cool enough to handle, crack open the claws and knuckles and retrieve the meat. Leave the claw meat whole; cut the knuckles into ½-inch pieces. Cover and refrigerate.

Heat the canola oil in a large pot over medium heat. When the oil is hot, add the reserved shells and legs and sear until bright red, about 10 minutes. Add the shallots, fennel, celery, and saffron and cook until tender and translucent, about 5 minutes. Add the tomato paste and cook until toasted, about 3 minutes.

Deglaze the pot with the Cognac, scraping up any browned bits with a wooden spoon. Carefully ignite the Cognac with a match and cook until the flames subside. Cover with the water and add a pinch each of salt and pepper. Simmer for 10 minutes, skimming any foam that rises to the top. Add the tarragon and star anise and simmer for an additional 20 minutes.

Strain the lobster stock through a colander or sturdy strainer, pushing on the shells to extract the maximum amount of liquid. Strain the stock again through the fine-mesh strainer lined with a double layer of slightly dampened cheesecloth. After all the stock has passed through the strainer, pour ½ cup water over the cheesecloth to extract the maximum flavor from the residual stock. Squeeze the cheesecloth to extract all the liquid.

Place the lobster stock in a medium pan over high heat and bring to a boil.

Meanwhile, using a plastic spatula, pass the reserved coral through a fine-mesh strainer. Place the roe and crushed ice in a bowl and stir to combine.

When the stock is boiling, add the coral mixture. Stir the pot slowly around the perimeter and bottom, so the coral does not stick to the bottom. Soon a "raft" of coral will begin to form in the center. Lower the heat to a simmer and continue simmering until the stock is clear. The raft will collect the impurities from the stock and leave it clear. This process should take about 10 minutes.

Meanwhile, remove the lobster meat from the refrigerator to come to room temperature.

Place a coffee filter in a fine-mesh strainer and pour the stock through it, being careful not to break up the raft too much. Pour the consommé into a pan and bring to a simmer.

To serve, divide the lobster meat among six warmed bowls and cover with the lobster consommé. Sprinkle a pinch of Espelette powder over each bowl. Serve immediately.

Roasted Capon with Bread Stuffing pictured on page 309

pictured on page 309

SERVES 6

One 6-pound capon

1 cup ½-inch cubes fresh bread

⅓ cup milk

1 large egg, lightly beaten

¼ pound chicken livers, chopped

3 ounces prosciutto, diced

2 small fresh pork sausage links
    (about 3 ounces), casings removed

1½ tablespoons minced garlic

2 tablespoons diced shallots

2 tablespoons chopped flat-leaf parsley

½ teaspoon thyme leaves

1 tablespoon duck fat, melted
    (you can substitute unsalted butter)

Fine sea salt and freshly ground
    white pepper

2 cups chicken stock

SPECIAL EQUIPMENT

Trussing needle and kitchen string

PREP: 20 minutes — **COOK:** 1 hour and 40 minutes

You almost can't give a recipe for this. You have to have a really good capon (or chicken) and some experience and some instinct for choosing and roasting a bird and for making a simple jus. Perhaps most important, you have to have at some moment in your life eaten a beautifully roasted bird and appreciated it. The stuffing is easy. The garlic and shallots give it a nice flavor; the liver, while mild, makes it intensely savory. You want a tasty stuffing whose steam gives good flavor to the meat. You want a crispy skin, moist flesh, and a flavorful jus. Every step is easy, and every step is critical. You need only to pay close attention.

Preheat the oven to 400°F.

Rinse the capon and pat dry. Cut off the wings and reserve.

Soak the bread in the milk, then squeeze out the excess milk and place the bread in a large bowl. Add the egg, chicken livers, prosciutto, sausage, garlic, shallots, parsley, thyme, and duck fat. Season with ½ teaspoon salt and ¼ teaspoon pepper.

Season the cavity of the capon with salt and pepper and fill with the stuffing. Thread a trussing needle with a piece of kitchen string at least 18 inches long. Sew the opening in the chicken closed using a crisscross pattern: Pierce the skin of the bird just above the breast and cross down through the opposite leg, pulling the string tight, then repeat on the other side of the bird. Finally, pierce the top of the breast and pass the needle through the bottom of the bird. The opening should be completely closed at this point. Tie the legs together with string. Season the bird with salt and pepper.

Place the wings in a roasting pan and place the capon on top of the wings. Roast for 1½ hours, or until the juices run clear when the leg is pierced and the stuffing reaches 150°F. Transfer the capon to a platter and let it rest for at least 10 minutes.

Meanwhile, place the roasting pan over high heat and add the chicken stock to deglaze the pan, stirring up the browned bits in the bottom of the pan. Bring to a boil, then remove from the heat. Strain into a pan or bowl and season to taste with salt and pepper, then transfer to a sauceboat.

To serve, carve the capon and slice the breast meat and leg meat. Place 2 slices of each and a spoonful of the stuffing on each warmed plate. Spoon the sauce over the plates and serve immediately. Pass the extra sauce at the table.

Green Salad

Serves 6

1 head green leaf lettuce

1 bunch watercress

2 endive heads

½ cup basil leaves

½ cup flat-leaf parsley leaves

**Fine sea salt and freshly ground
white pepper**

¼ cup Vinaigrette (page 205)

PREP: 10 minutes

Thoroughly wash and dry the lettuce and watercress. Tear the lettuce into "bite-size" pieces, no larger than 2 square inches. Trim the thick, tough ends from the watercress and discard. Cut the endive heads into 1-inch pieces. Combine all the greens, including the herbs, in a large bowl and set aside in the refrigerator.

To serve, season the greens with salt and pepper to taste. Toss the greens with enough vinaigrette to lightly coat. Serve immediately.

Buttermilk Custard Tart with Mixed Berries

Serves 6

THE DOUGH

2½ cups all-purpose flour (8 ounces)

2 tablespoons sugar

Pinch of salt

**8 tablespoons (1 stick) cold unsalted
butter, cut into small dice**

1 large egg yolk

¼ cup ice water, or more as needed

**1 tablespoon unsalted butter,
at room temperature**

1 large egg

THE FILLING

2 cups buttermilk

3 large eggs

3 large egg yolks

⅔ cup maple syrup

1 vanilla bean, split lengthwise

Pinch of salt

**½ cup fresh blueberries, or ½ cup dried
blueberries, plumped in warm water
and drained**

¼ cup raspberries

PREP: 15 minutes, plus 1 hour chilling time — **COOK:** 50 minutes

Buttermilk is a great base for a custard-style dessert because of its rich texture and light acidity. This is a straightforward tart that has an almost cheesecake-like texture and taste. Fresh blueberries are nowadays available almost year-round, but "reconstituted" dried berries are acceptable here for an autumn dish.

For the dough, place the flour, sugar, and salt in a bowl and whisk to combine. Add the cold butter to the flour and using a pastry blender or two knives scissors-style, cut the butter into the flour until the mixture resembles coarse sand. Add the yolk and ice water and mix together. Add a little more water if necessary to hold the dough together. Transfer the dough to a lightly floured surface and knead briefly to combine. Shape the dough into a disk and wrap in plastic film. Place in the refrigerator until well chilled, at least an hour.

Preheat the oven to 400°F.

Rub a 9-inch tart pan with the 1 tablespoon butter and coat with flour; tap the sides to remove excess flour. On a lightly floured surface, roll the dough out to a thickness of ⅛ inch. Fold the dough in half and place in the tart pan. Unfold the dough and fit it into the tart pan, running your rolling pin over the top to cut off the excess. Flute the edge of the dough by using two fingers of one hand and one finger of the other hand, pressing the dough between your fingers. Whisk the egg and brush over the edges of the dough.

Bake the pastry shell for 20 minutes, or until golden. Set aside until cool. Leave the oven on.

For the filling, whisk together the buttermilk, eggs, yolks, and maple syrup in a bowl. Scrape the seeds from the vanilla bean and whisk into the filling. Whisk in the salt. Pour the mixture into the prepared tart shell and scatter the berries over the top. Place the tart on a baking sheet and bake for 30 minutes, or until the custard is almost set. Serve warm or at room temperature.

Eric was eager from the beginning to make a couple of gratins, the hot rich concoctions that evoke fall and winter for him. In these seasons, his mother often made gratins—of turnips, macaroni, potato—and he still adores the crunchy top of the browned cheese, the melting vegetables and cream inside, and the way the aroma of their baking fills the house.

American kitchens today may overlook the gratin because of the cream and the cheese, but the following gratins are simple luxuries that make excellent side dishes for roast chicken or any roasted meat. (Eric was so pleased by the cauliflower gratin that he would pair it with the lobster consommé for the restaurant.)

Rutabaga Gratin

SERVES 6

PREP: 15 minutes — COOK: 30 minutes

6 tablespoons unsalted butter

1 rutabaga (about 1½ pounds)

6 garlic cloves, 2 thinly sliced,
   4 peeled and left whole

Fine sea salt and freshly ground
   white pepper

¼ teaspoon freshly grated nutmeg

1½ cups heavy cream

½ cup milk

¾ cup grated sharp white cheddar cheese,
   preferably Vermont cheddar

Preheat your oven to 375°F. Butter a 9-inch round gratin dish with 1 tablespoon of the butter.

Peel the rutabaga, cut in half, and thinly slice on a mandoline or with a very sharp knife. Cut the remaining 5 tablespoons butter into small chunks. Layer the rutabaga, sliced garlic, and butter chunks in the gratin dish, seasoning each layer with salt, pepper, and nutmeg. Pour the heavy cream and milk over the vegetables. Tuck the remaining 4 garlic cloves into the gratin. Sprinkle the cheddar over the top. *(The gratin can be assembled ahead and refrigerated until ready to bake; remove from the refrigerator while you preheat the oven.)*

Place the gratin dish on a baking sheet to catch any spills. Bake for 30 minutes, or until the gratin is nicely browned on top and the sauce is bubbling.

Cauliflower Gratin

SERVES 6

PREP: 15 minutes — COOK: 30 minutes

1 large head cauliflower

4 tablespoons unsalted butter

¼ cup all-purpose flour

3 cups cold milk

1 cup grated sharp white cheddar cheese,
   preferably Vermont cheddar

½ nutmeg

Fine sea salt and freshly ground
   white pepper

Bring a large pot of salted water to a boil. Meanwhile, remove the green leaves and the core from the cauliflower. Separate the cauliflower into florets. Blanch the cauliflower until crisp-tender, 3 to 4 minutes. Plunge into an ice water bath to stop the cooking. Drain thoroughly. Set aside.

Preheat the oven to 375°F.

Melt the butter in a large saucepan over medium heat. Add the flour and cook, stirring frequently, until the flour is nicely toasted and bubbling, about 3 minutes. Slowly add the cold milk, whisking to incorporate. Lower the heat and gradually add the cheese, stirring until melted and combined. Grate the nutmeg into the sauce and stir to combine. Season to taste with salt and pepper.

Add the cauliflower to the sauce, then spread in a gratin dish large enough to accommodate all the florets in a single layer. *(The gratin can be assembled ahead and refrigerated until ready to bake; remove from the refrigerator while you preheat the oven.)*

Place the gratin dish on a baking sheet to catch any spills. Bake for 20 minutes, or until the gratin is bubbling and nicely browned on top.

George Davis's Pancakes

SERVES 6

2 cups all-purpose flour

2 teaspoons baking powder

1 teaspoon baking soda

1 teaspoon salt

2 cups milk

3 large eggs

¼ cup canola oil

2 tablespoons white vinegar

3 tablespoons bacon fat

Maple syrup, preferably from Vermont

PREP: 5 minutes — **COOK:** 10 minutes

Place the dry ingredients in a large bowl and whisk to mix.

Whisk together the milk, eggs, and canola oil in a medium bowl. Add the vinegar and whisk to combine. Add the wet ingredients to the dry and whisk until the batter is just combined. The batter should still be lumpy.

Heat a large heavy-bottomed skillet (George uses a cast-iron pan) over medium heat. Melt 2 teaspoons of the bacon fat in the skillet. Using a 2-ounce ladle (or a ¼-cup measure) for each one, pour the batter for four pancakes into your skillet. When bubbles start to form on the tops of the pancakes and the edges look set, flip the pancakes. Cook until golden brown on the second side. Transfer to a plate or plates, and continue with the remaining batter.

The pancakes are best served hot, as they are made to retain their crisp edges, although you can hold briefly on a baking sheet in a warm oven. Pass Vermont maple syrup at the table.

George Davis, whose house we stayed in, was formerly an attorney in Boston. He joined us that last night for dinner in front of the fire, a spiritual counterpart to Uncle Georges who had been on Eric's mind so much here. The next morning, he insisted on making us all pancakes that were so good that we offer the recipe here. The bacon fat gives the exterior a very light crunch while the interior remains soft and light. If you're going to indulge in pancakes, don't skimp on the fat!

WHEN COOKING ACHIEVES THE LEVEL OF ART

Five years ago, looking to improve the food at Le Bernardin, I began going to art museums. I had always sensed that food and art were related and I thought I could raise the level of the food by studying art. I would go to MOMA in Manhattan, for instance, and study the Matisse with the red fish, *Les Poissons Rouges*. I would then return to Le Bernardin and play with composition. But this was wrong. A chef's primary focus shouldn't be on presentation. Presentation must be in the service of flavor.

Where, then, is the art in cooking? We tend to forget that for most of history, art had a religious motive. An artist before the Renaissance had a mission to pay homage to God. No matter what form God took— whether a human face or a spirit—art was a message.

When I talk about art in cooking, I mean that pre-Renaissance conception. As a cook and a chef, I'm attempting to convey a message that food is sacred. I'm paying homage to God, to our mother earth, to the life force of this world. To realize this in food, I believe, is when cooking becomes art.

When you have a perfect truffle, you have to be a craftsman to ensure that its superlative flavor pleases the senses of those who eat it. But at the same time, if you're artistic, you can somehow convey that this is divine, a gift.

When you make lobster stock, you have a live animal before you and you must pay respect. You don't sacrifice the life of that animal and spoil it. You have before you something that's sacred because it's alive. And with it we're thanking the gods.

It would be absurd and unnatural to try to bring out the best of the ingredients and the best of myself if the food isn't to be shared and enjoyed. And those moments of sharing are a kind of religious experience for me, an actual communion. They connect us, and encourage us to learn, to express ourselves, nourish ourselves spiritually from the same source of energy that is created at the table. Artists are craftsmen with a spiritual message. And cooks may convey spiritual messages as well.

SOURCES

Fish, Crayfish, Periwinkles, Pibales, Salmon Eggs, and Caviar: **Browne Trading Company** 207-766-2402

Caviar: **Paramount Caviar** 800-992-2842

Smoked Salmon: **Perona Farms** 800-750-6190

Lamb: **Jamison Farm** 800-237-5262

Game and Gizzard Confit: **D'Artagnan, Inc.** 973-344-0565

Foie Gras, Duck Fat, and Magret: **Hudson Valley Foie Gras** 845-292-2500

Truffles and Truffle Juice (Pébeyre): **Aquipro** 571-278-4776

Crème Fraîche and Butter: **Vermont Butter and Cheese Company** 800-884-6287

Espelette Pepper Powder: **Williams-Sonoma** 800-541-2233

Valentino Cortazar's paintings are available online at: **valentinocortazar.com**

ACKNOWLEDGMENTS

A Return to Cooking was a fantasy. It became reality thanks to the tremendous help and commitment of friends, partners, sponsors, and sympathizers who envied us our adventure.

Valentino Cortazar, Michael Ruhlman, Shimon and Tammar Rothstein, and Andrea Glick worked nonstop with so much passion and love that I would like to thank them first for being so inspiring.

Susan Lescher, my agent, and Ann Bramson, my publisher, not only worked very hard with us on producing this book, but also trusted me when I needed it most and gave me total freedom to accomplish my goals.

The book would not be as beautiful as it is if it were not for Cliff Morgan and David Hughes of Level, who visited us in Napa in order to better understand and connect with us on this project and who ultimately designed the book. Thanks also for the talent and hard work of Judith Sutton, and thanks to Deborah Weiss Geline, Nancy Murray, Rachel Godfrey, and Barbara Peragine at Artisan, whose attention to detail was invaluable.

The Puerto Rico chapter wouldn't exist without the great friendship and help from Alfredo Ayala, "The Organizer." We were guests in the fantastic house of my friends Dolly and Juan Colon and in Arnold Benus's Copamarina Beach Resort. Thanks also to Richard Carrion from Banco Popular for his generosity.

During our trips, we drank great wines, for creativity, of course. For their contributions, thank you to Schneider and Gristina Vineyards on Long Island. In Puerto Rico, Carlos Alvarez, from Mendez and Company. In California, Iron Horse Vineyards. Palmer Vineyards and Deutz Champagne in Vermont. In all locations we cooked with Le Creuset and All-Clad pots and pans and ate our lunches and dinners on the beautiful china from Bernardeau and, in Puerto Rico, Alfredo Ayala's private collection.

Many friends in the food industry also supplied us with products and help: Rod Mitchell from Browne Trading, Joe Guerra and Bryan Young from Citarella, The Vermont Butter and Cheese Company, Debragga and Spitler, Hudson Valley Foie Gras, Roberta Quick, George Davis, and my special friend Laurent Manrique.

I became a cook because of the support of my mother, Monique, who, with my family, inspired me to become a culinary student. And then, not one but three mentors educated me: Joël Robuchon, Jean-Louis Palladin, and Gilbert Le Coze. Thank you so much!

During my absences to work on this book, everything was on "cruise control" at Le Bernardin thanks to the great jobs done by our team; special thank-yous to my dear friend and partner Maguy Le Coze, to Chris Muller in the kitchen, and to Florian Bellanger, who gave me many tips on pastry. Also, thank you to my wife, Sandra, for her unconditional love, patience, and support.

It sounds odd, but during our journey, we all felt the divine protection from spirits, angels, or maybe simply the great architect of the universe. How can we pay homage to them? I guess by giving the best of ourselves: love, passion, and humility.

Merlot, in strawberries floating in red wine, 235
mesclun greens:
    in lobster salad with mango and foie gras, 174
    in salade Monique, 6
mille-feuille, banana, with gingered chocolate sauce, 136
mint:
    in flash-marinated fluke with lemon confit, 60
    in grilled rack of lamb and cucumber salad, 35
    pesto, pan-roasted monkfish with lemon carrots and, 59
    in spicy tomato consommé, 42
mixed grill, marinated, 76
monkfish, 149
    pan-roasted, with lemon carrots and mint pesto, 59
    sautéed, with "sofrito" in dende oil, 147
Montauk periwinkles with basil aïoli, 51
monter au beurre, 124
morels:
    in barely cooked salmon with Parmesan polenta and mushroom consommé, 178
    veal chops with herb butter sauce and, 167
Mueller, Eberhard, 83
mushroom(s):
    consommé, barely cooked salmon with Parmesan polenta and, 178
    crayfish ravioli with truffle butter sauce and, 272–73
    wild, braised veal cheeks with potato puree and, 282
    see also specific mushrooms
mussels:
    in shellfish and chorizo in broth, 141
    in shellfish ragout, 29
    with spicy Italian sausage, 54

N

nage, 100
    tarragon, poached spiny lobster with, 123
ñame, in Sancocho, 140
nonne, pets de, 231

nutmeg, pumpkin, acorn, and butternut squash soup with walnut oil and, 305

O

oil:
    dende, sautéed monkfish with "sofrito" in, 147
    ginger, see ginger oil
    goat cheese marinated in rosemary and, 235
    pepper, see pepper oil
    walnut, pumpkin, acorn, and butternut squash soup with nutmeg and, 305
okra, sautéed mahi mahi with citrus vinaigrette and, 153
olive(s):
    Kalamata, in goat cheese and ricotta terrine, 69
    Niçoise, in caramelized onion tart, 71
    oil-cured, in tapas still life, 63
    and pesto pasta salad, 70
onion(s):
    glazed, sautéed grouper with bacon-butter sauce and, 135
    tart, caramelized, 71
orange(s):
    blood, in mango, passion fruit, and tarragon salad, 101
    juice, in citrus gelatin with guanabana sauce, 109
    -soy vinaigrette, curried Napa cabbage bundles with, 126, 129
    in tropical fruit en papillote, 125
oxtails, braised, in cabbage leaves, 262–63
oyster mushrooms, in braised veal cheeks with wild mushrooms and potato puree, 282

P

paella, 144
Palladin (restaurant), 56, 83
Palladin, Jean-Louis, 26, 83, 237, 257, 271
palombe (wild squab) with cabbage confit and porcini, 274
pancakes, George Davis's, 318

panna cotta, 173
    buttermilk, with grapefruit, 286
    fennel-scented, with wild strawberries, 175
pan-roasted monkfish with lemon carrots and mint pesto, 59
pan-seared:
    Muscovy duck breast with cherries and rhubarb purée, 200–201
    skirt steak with herbed-butter frites and bitter greens, 199
paprika-spiked beef tenderloin and eggplant, 138, 141
parfait:
    fire-roasted vegetable and goat cheese, 253
    walnut and Armagnac frozen, with wine-poached prunes, 293
Parmesan:
    in cold cucumber soup, 45
    in lamb shoulder and portobello-spinach ravioli with mushroom jus, 226–27
    polenta and mushroom consommé, barely cooked salmon with, 178
    in risotto carbonara with white and black truffles, 251
    in roasted chicken with poached egg, asparagus, and truffle jus, 216
    in stuffed lamb saddle with lamb jus and spring vegetables, 238–39
Parmesan-cucumber sauce, 44
    steamed littlenecks with, 45
parsley:
    in green salad, 315
    sauce, frogs' legs with sautéed frisée and, 186
    in veal chops with morels and herb butter sauce, 167
parsnip-celeriac puree, venison loin with cranberries and, 296–97
passion fruit, mango, and tarragon salad, 101
pasta:
    alphabet, garlic-sage broth with, 303
    salad, olive and pesto, 70
    see also specific pasta

pâté en croûte, pork and liver, 281
Payard, François, 228
peach:
    and apricot crumble with rhubarb puree, 193
    and basil salad, grappa-marinated, 37
    and plum tart, 7
peanuts, in curried Napa cabbage bundles with soy-orange vinaigrette, 129
pear:
    poached, with Poire William caramel sauce, 31
    tart à la mode, 275
    tomato, see tomatoes
peas, in roasted whole turbot with spring vegetables and truffle sauce, 217
peekytoe crab, curried, and Granny Smith apple napoleon, 212
pepper oil:
    sautéed baby calamari with garlic and, 58
    sautéed pibales with, 185
pepperoni, in white and black bean ragout with a variety of sausages, 258
peppers, banana:
    in grilled rack of lamb and cucumber salad, 35
    in rare-seared tuna with ratatouille, 152
    in salade Monique, 6
    in Sancocho, 140
    in sautéed monkfish with "sofrito" in dende oil, 147
peppers, bell:
    in chicken and lamb tagine with Mediterranean spices, 20–21
    in paella, 144
    in rare-seared tuna with ratatouille, 152
    in Sancocho, 140
    in sautéed baby calamari with pepper oil and garlic, 58
    in sautéed monkfish with "sofrito" in dende oil, 147
    in sautéed summer vegetables with garlic and herbs, 76
    in seared tuna paillard with spring vegetables, 205

tuna, 150
  tartare with endive, 206
tuna, seared:
  with escabeche of pear
    tomatoes, 113
  paillard with spring vegetables,
    205
  rare-, with ratatouille, 152
turbot, 219
  roasted whole, with spring
    vegetables and truffle sauce,
    217, 219
  sautéed, with creamy jasmine
    rice and coriander broth,
    198
turnips:
  in seared tuna paillard with
    spring vegetables, 205
  in spring vegetable salad with
    poached egg and herb
    vinaigrette, 166

V

veal:
  and beef shank, poached,
    with herbed vinaigrette
    and celeriac salad,
    182–83
  chops, with morels and herb
    butter sauce, 167
veal cheeks, 283
  braised, with wild mushrooms
    and potato puree, 282
vegetable(s):
  fire-roasted, and goat cheese
    "parfait," 253
  sautéed summer, with garlic
    and herbs, 76

tropical root, escabeche of,
  bacalao and, 111, 114
  see also specific vegetables
vegetable(s), spring:
  roasted whole turbot with
    truffle sauce and, 217, 219
  seared tuna paillard with, 205
  stuffed lamb saddle with lamb
    jus and, 238–39
venison:
  "carpaccio," juniper-crusted,
    295
  loin with parsnip-celeriac puree
    and cranberries, 296–97
verbena-tomato water, striped
  bass with, 43
vermicelli, ginger-cilantro,
  chicken pot-au-feu with, 119
vichyssoise, arugula, 191
vinaigrettes, 32–33, 205
  barigoule, warm artichoke
    salad with, 19
  citrus, sautéed mahi mahi with
    okra and, 153
  herb, spring vegetable salad
    with poached egg and, 166
  herbed, poached beef and veal
    shank with celeriac salad
    and, 182–83
  soy-orange, curried Napa
    cabbage bundles with, 126,
    129

W

walnut:
  and Armagnac frozen parfait
    with wine-poached prunes,
    293

oil, pumpkin, acorn, and
  butternut squash soup with
  nutmeg and, 305
warm artichoke salad with
  barigoule vinaigrette, 19
warmed snapper with ginger oil,
  148
watercress:
  in green salad, 315
  in juniper-crusted venison
    "carpaccio," 295
  in pan-seared skirt steak with
    herbed-butter frites and
    bitter greens, 199
  in poached beef and veal shank
    with herbed vinaigrette and
    celeriac salad, 182–83
  in warm artichoke salad with
    barigoule vinaigrette, 19
watermelon, yellow, in tapas
  still life, 63
white wine:
  in citrus gelatin with
    guanabana sauce, 109
  in crayfish ravioli with
    mushrooms and truffle butter
    sauce, 272–73
  in mussels with spicy Italian
    sausage, 54
  in paprika-spiked beef
    tenderloin and eggplant,
    141
  in roasted leg of lamb and
    garlic with goat cheese
    mashed potatoes, 222–23
  in salmon, crab, and scallop
    chowder, 180
  in sautéed sepia with chorizo
    broth and spaghetti, 187

in stuffed lamb saddle with
  lamb jus and spring
  vegetables, 238–39
in warm artichoke salad with
  barigoule vinaigrette, 19
wine, see port wine; red wine;
  white wine

Y

yautia:
  in bacalao and tropical root
    vegetable escabeche, 114
  in Sancocho, 140
yogurt, goat's milk, dressing,
  arugula salad with, 73
yuca:
  in bacalao and tropical root
    vegetable escabeche, 114
  and blood sausage shepherd's
    pie, 138, 142

Z

zucchini:
  in chicken and lamb tagine
    with Mediterranean spices,
    20–21
  in rare-seared tuna with
    ratatouille, 152
  in roasted leg of lamb and
    garlic with goat cheese
    mashed potatoes,
    222–23
  in sautéed summer vegetables
    with garlic and herbs, 76
  in stuffed lamb saddle with
    lamb jus and spring
    vegetables, 238–39